PRAISE FOR

HOW TO HAVE AN ORGASM. . . AS OFTEN AS YOU WANT

"A remarkable and unequivocal study of female sexuality."

—*The Mail on Sunday*

"A very readable and practical approach to the subject. Many women who have orgasm problems will find it very helpful."

—Dr. Andrew Stanway, author of
A Woman's Guide to Men and Sex

"The nicest sex book I have ever read."

—*The Sunday Express*

"Her advice is simple, friendly, explicit, and has worked wonders."

—*The Daily Mirror*

"[Rachel Swift] doesn't pussyfoot around, is never coy and assumes that all women deserve, and can achieve, the big O, over and over."

—*Ludus Magazine*

"An astute and enjoyable read as well as an aid to help improve your sex life."

—*Women Only*

"A sex manual which makes Jackie Collins' novels look tame."

—*The Daily Record* (Scotland)

"Well written, well researched. . . riveting."

—*The Sunday Independent* (Ireland)

"A sizzling new book."

—Sunday World (Ireland)

"The best orgasm of your life!"

—Cleo (Australia)

"As amusing as it is helpful. . . a wonderful understanding of the baggage women bring to bed."

—New Woman (Australia)

"A courageous, witty, and controversial book."

—Nore Magazine (New Zealand)

"A sure-fire bestseller throughout the English-speaking world. . . [Rachel Swift's] frankness and humor make the discussion compelling."

—New Zealand Doctor

HOW TO HAVE AN
ORGASM
. . . AS OFTEN AS YOU WANT

Life-Changing Sexual Secrets for Women and Their Partners

Rachel Swift

MARLOWE & COMPANY
NEW YORK

HOW TO HAVE AN ORGASM... AS OFTEN AS YOU WANT
Life-Changing Sexual Secrets for Women and Their Partners

Copyright © 1993 by Rachel Swift

Published by arrangement with the author. First published in Great Britain by
Pan Books Limited in 1993 as *Women's Pleasure*.

Published by
Marlowe & Company
An Imprint of Avalon Publishing Group Incorporated
245 West 17th Street • 11th Floor
New York, NY 10011-5300

AVALON
publishing group incorporated

ISBN 1-56924-382-4

Library of Congress Cataloging-in-Publication Data
Swift, Rachel
How to have an orgasm—as often as you want / Rachel Swift.
p. cm.
Includes bibliographical references.
ISBN 0-88184-954-5
1. Sex instruction for women. 2. Women—Sexual behavior.
3. Female orgasm. I. Title
HQ46.S96 1993   93-10643
613.9'54—dc20   CIP

10 9 8 7 6 5 4 3 2 1

Printed in the United States of America

Contents

Acknowledgments

The author and publishers wish to thank the following who have kindly given permission for the use of copyright materials.

Virgin Publishing Ltd for extracts from Apollinaire's *The Exploits of a Young Don Juan;*
Hello! Limited for extracts from an interview with Angelica Houston by Anna Maria Bahann;
Little, Brown for extracts from *The Hite Report on Male Sexuality.*

Every effort has been made to trace all the copyright holders; but, if any has been inadvertently overlooked, the author and publishers will be pleased to make the necessary arrangement at the first opportunity.

PART ONE

CHAPTER ONE

What Exactly Is This Book?

This is a selfish book.

I am an average woman in her thirties who, until recently, had never once had an orgasm during sex with her partner. There was nothing wrong with me. I didn't hate sex or find my partners distasteful. I didn't have insurmountable psychological difficulties about men, penises, or letting myself go. I was, physically and emotionally, an ordinary woman. Yet the simple and pleasant experience of orgasm during sex seemed beyond my reach.

One day, after a particularly frustrating encounter, I decided I was sick and tired of it. I'd had my fill of going to bed with men who would climax without any trouble at all, while I was left with no recourse but to tiptoe to the bathroom and finish myself off in secret. So I determined to *teach* myself to have an orgasm *whenever I wanted one*.

This book explains how I did it. It is a straightforward, easy-to-follow, self-help plan that can teach you how to have as many orgasms as you want, whenever you want, with or without the full cooperation of your partner.

Who should read this book? Every woman in the world —and every woman's man. If you have never had an orgasm, this book will teach you how to have one. If you have them "sometimes," it will show you that "sometimes" can be doubled. If you're celibate, then you'll find plenty of fascinating facts and anecdotes to entertain you before you go to sleep. And, if you're a man, it will teach you a thing or two about how to be the kind of man a woman wants in her bed.

This book is also my story. Above all, it is a positive story: sometimes funny, sometimes shocking. It is not written by an impersonal doctor or a soft-spoken therapist, but by a fellow malcontent who faced a difficult problem and found out for herself how to overcome it. It is, in other words, a book that deals with *realities,* not ideals— what sex is really like, not what it is supposed to be like according to the manuals.

What Is an Orgasm?

Some people regard orgasm as the most intense feeling of physical pleasure there is. In describing it they become quite poetic: "poised, pulsating—glowing," "floating," "an ecstatic frenzy of love, energy and emotion, all mixed together," "supreme sensitivity to touch—waves of butterflies in my stomach," "hot," "beautiful and *alive,*" "open and languorous," "electric currents blowing through my body," "voluptuous, elegant, and sensuous," "my whole body burns," "an experience that is somehow spiritual as well as physical," and, of course, "eager for more."

The word itself derives from the Greek *orgao* (to swell). The *Oxford English Dictionary* defines it as a "paroxysm of desire or rage or other passion." Without going into technical language, an orgasm is perhaps best described as a few brief moments leading up to the highest peak of sexual desire, followed by a pleasurable, perhaps overwhelming, sense of release. Orgasmic sensations are concentrated in the genitals but, as the descriptions above make clear, radiate to all parts of the body. Many people experience a corresponding wave of emotion.

It is also true that orgasms—especially women's orgasms—vary greatly in intensity. Occasionally they are mild, even disappointing sensations. Some women are uncertain whether they have experienced one or not, though this is unusual.

There is, however, another answer to the question "What is an orgasm?" For many women, it is a battlefield. Often the man's orgasm is considered a necessary consequence of good sex, while hers is just a happy extra—good news if she has one in time, but not to be fretted over if she's a little too slow, or too tense, or the sex hasn't been good enough. Because it may be difficult for her to climax, orgasm can become an unforgettable issue—certainly not helped by the implicit suggestion that today, unless a woman has an enormous climax on time, in time, and with loads of groans and gasps into the bargain, she has somehow not managed to come up to speed.

Why All This Concentration on Orgasm?

A close friend of mine, who knew I was writing this book, asked a pertinent question: "Is it really such a good idea to write a book that concentrates solely on orgasm? After all, orgasm is only one element of sex—there's so much more to a relationship than orgasm."

I agree with her wholeheartedly. I would never undervalue love, affection, commitment, and understanding. They are essential ingredients of a successful relationship, and very helpful for good sex, too. But it is not my place to talk about such matters—everyone will conduct their relationships in their own special ways, and I'm not about to interfere. Orgasm, on the other hand, *is* something I can help with. I know from personal experience the kind of problems women suffer, and I know from personal experience how to help them.

"But," continued my friend, "is orgasm really that valuable? After all, many women lead happy and fulfilling lives without it."

This is an attitude I came across often during my own training and research, and I think it misses the point. I believe that for sexually active women, orgasm *is* an issue, at some level. At the very least, it's not something we can ever forget about, as one fellow sufferer made clear: "I see *him* do it, day after day; *of course* it means something to me. I want to be able to share that."

Another friend commented, "You'd have to be deaf, dumb, and blind not to think about orgasm. I mean, nowadays sex is just *everywhere*. Why should we, as women, settle for second best, when our potential is so great?"

Shere Hite, who questioned 3,500 women between the ages of fourteen and seventy-eight, quotes case after case of women who felt "depressed," "tense," "cheated and envious," "less desirable," "incomplete," "frustrated," "insecure"—and so on. Hite unhesitatingly concludes: "Almost every woman who didn't orgasm would like to." In a society where orgasm *is* an issue, reinforced constantly by films, books, and endless unsatisfactory sexual encounters, it would be arrogant of me to pretend that I could upset the status quo by claiming that women ought not to take orgasm so seriously. What I *can* do is show that difficulty with orgasm is not so serious. If you want to, you can do something about it.

Although I do not maintain that orgasm is a necessity for good sex, I firmly believe that for women it is important as an *option*. To make an analogy; when education was denied women, it was commonly believed that they were all empty-headed dimwits. Only when education became available could women prove that they were the intellectual equals of men. It is a similar story with orgasm: the myth of male sexual superiority is alive and well, yet the truth is that most women have simply not had the *opportunity* to fulfill their very great sexual potential.

You, as an individual, may choose not to enroll in higher education, just as you may choose not to insist on orgasm every time you have sex. But we all need to have access to orgasm before we can decide whether it is for us or not. Once we have learned all about it, *then* we can decide how important it is in our lives.

What About My Partner?

Although I have called this a "selfish" book, it has a very unselfish result. A satisfying sex life helps relationships as well as individuals. The more a woman is able to enjoy sex fully with her partner, the more the partner and the relationship will benefit. And I don't just mean in the bedroom, but in all sorts of nonsexual ways, because sexual dissatisfaction is, obviously, the cause of a great deal of emotional and social tension outside the bedroom.

This book is as valuable for those who have been married thirty-five years as for those who are just starting to have a sex life. However, it is a fundamental principle of the plan that women help *themselves*. For this reason, the exercises do *not* require a permanent or willing and compliant partner. Let's face it; not everybody has such a person. In fact, much of the program—particularly the crucial early steps—must be done by a woman on her own. The later steps can be done without your partner's being aware that you are following a training program. I have suggested techniques to get your man to cooperate unknowingly. The end result, *for both of you*, will be well worth a little guile.

Those of you who have a patient and caring partner

have the choice whether or not to involve him in your training program. But think about it carefully. The fact of a person of the opposite sex being concerned in such a sensitive, intimate matter may be unsettling. When he is there with you, doing everything exactly as he should, you may feel guilty and unwilling to disappoint him. He may be the ideal man, but if he shares in the knowledge that you are trying to achieve orgasm, the sense of public expectation can make you awkward, as if you were performing on stage. Paradoxically, the very closeness of the relationship can inhibit you. Besides, even if you do have such a partner, you may have been faking some or all of your orgasms up till now, and it would require some pretty delicate talking to get around that! If, however, you feel that your partner's knowledge and assistance in the plan will help you, bring him into your confidence.

Best of all: follow the program on your own for the first three or four steps. Then decide whether or not to tell your partner. Perhaps, once you have seen the great strides you are making, you will feel it important to discuss the matter. Perhaps you will prefer to keep it your secret. That is your choice.

How Do I Use This Book?

Many women—and, I hope, men—will be content simply to read this book through, like any other. There's plenty of interest in it for everybody.

Those of you who also wish to follow the self-help plan should take account of the following:

Whatever your starting point, my method aims to build up your confidence and introduce you gradually to techniques, so that you advance in sensible stages. Each step represents a significant success; at the end of each one I recommend that you *celebrate*. You'll then be in an excellent frame of mind to go on to the next stage.

As I was devising the plan, step by step, I passed on my tips and discoveries to friends and acquaintances. These "guinea pigs," who ranged in age from seventeen to sixty-one and were of very different social backgrounds, reported extremely successful results. During the course of this book, they will be speaking for themselves.

I have also made free use of Shere Hite's two great books, *The Hite Report on Female Sexuality* and *The Hite Report on Male Sexuality*. This is because there are occasions when I wish to make it clear that a particular point is not simply a crazy idea of mine, but an opinion endorsed by thousands. Hite's researches were extremely broad-ranging: she questioned not only 3,500 women, as mentioned above, but also over 7,000 men from thirteen to seventy-nine. Her books do not suffer from the sense of impersonality and scientific callousness that pervades many such studies. Her questions and comments are intelligent and wide-ranging, but not ridiculously cautious. They are without obvious bias. Hite allows the respondents to reply at length, and does not ask them to give merely a yes or no. And, of course, Hite is a woman.

This book contains eighteen chapters.

Part One: Chapters 1 to 4 are introductory. It is important that you read these to appreciate the function and motivation behind the plan and the style in which it is presented.

Part Two: Chapter 5 is a preparation for the plan. Among other things, this includes a very personal questionnaire about some of the issues covered by the book. Chapters 6 to 13 comprise the plan itself: six main steps and two side steps. If steps and side steps sound complicated, let me assure you that, on the contrary, they are arranged like this for the greatest possible flexibility to suit your own needs. Read through these chapters carefully before you begin to get a picture of how the plan works, and to see if you need to make any adjustments in your sexual relationship with your partner in preparation for the later steps which involve his presence.

You must progress through each of the main steps carefully, in sequence. As with learning a language, each step must be practiced thoroughly, so keep on one until you are completely comfortable with it. Your patience will be rewarded in the end.

Once you have perfected a step, move on to the next. *But don't stop practicing the previous step.* Throughout this program you should be consolidating your gains even while you're learning new skills.

The side steps can be introduced at any time after step 2. It depends on when you feel comfortable about them.

Part Three: The remaining chapters are on a variety of issues relating to women's orgasms. Read whichever you feel might be important to you before you begin the program. Chapter 18 has been written especially for men.

Always bear in mind the really good news: the ability to have an orgasm, *whenever* you want one, achieved through careful training and practice, is yours to keep. Like riding a bike. You will need to keep up your expertise by repeating old exercises now and then. Occasionally circumstances will be against you—a really selfish clod of a partner, for example, or too many glasses of wine! But once you have really mastered the art of orgasm, you will not readily lose that ability. This achievement *is yours for life*.

CHAPTER TWO

My Story

**Madame shall we undress you for the fight?
The wars are naked that we make tonight.**

——**George Moore,** *Memoirs of My Dead Life*

There used to be a rather unpleasant girl at my school named Dorothy. She had permissive parents and was president of the Love Club. The members of the club had to rack their parents' bookshelves for any mention of "love," then meet the next day behind a tree in the playground and gloat over the sexiest parts.

"He gripped her passionately," Bobbie read one day in a thrilling voice, from a messy-looking paperback stolen from her father's library. *"His hands slid slowly down her throat, and she could feel his throbbing lips—"*

"Yuck!"

"Shut *up!*"

"Well, it says so here. Look—*'throbbing.'* "

"I feel sick."

At this sophisticated juncture, the Love Club meetings would usually degenerate into fights and giggles. But this time Dorothy only smiled knowingly. "I'll bet you half a Hershey bar you don't know what an orgasm is."

"If it's anything to do with throbbing, I'm going home."

"How do you spell it?" I asked, trying to keep the minutes up to date.

Bobbie haggled over the price. Eventually the bargain was struck, and Dorothy lowered her voice.

17

"It's when your father goes to the john inside your mother!"

We broke up.

At a later meeting, Dorothy—who was an authority on everything outré—announced that she knew what men and women *really* did with each other in private.

"Well?" We all crowded around.

"They go upside-down on the bed and lick each other."

"What?" we cried in chorus, horrified.

"I *know*," she said. "I *saw*."

When we had recovered from this bombshell, Susan leaned forward: "Once you let a man have his way with you, he'll leave you in the lurch," she announced confidently.

"What's the lurch?" Fran asked.

"My mother says never make the first move with a man, or you'll scare him off," somebody else added.

"Men are different from women," said Dorothy. "They have to sleep with plenty of girls before they marry because it's 'in their nature.' Otherwise, if they bottle it up, it all explodes later."

"Explodes?"

"Yes, and they run away with someone else."

I remember looking at my little brother and thinking that surely there must be exceptions. Yet it was he who brought the matter up next.

"What is sex?" he asked plaintively at breakfast one morning. Our parents looked appalled—he was only seven.

"Why do you ask a thing like that?" mumbled my mother.

"Because I want to send off for a cowboy outfit and it says 'state sex.' "

Sex—and particularly orgasm—was a strange, somewhat distasteful subject. My parents used to talk now and then of the male and female sex, but these were subjects quite far removed from the sex that Dorothy knew so much about. The female sex, for example, had "duties."

"However much of a swinger you become, a man likes to be looked after," my father reminded. "After all, it's a woman's duty to make a home."

"We made bullets during the war," my mother muttered.

"This is peace," my father replied firmly.

I had a violent crush on Sean Connery, and couldn't help feeling that the dim-witted starlets with their wiggling hips, high heels, and empty eyes were far beneath him. I particularly admired the way he used to leap out of an open sports car and adjust his tie.

"An awful smoothie," my father said. "Nice girls wouldn't be taken in. I can tell you that much for a fact," he continued, unconsciously adjusting his own tie.

"Oh, be quiet, Peter," my mother said.

But even she, whom I now realize was in many ways a remarkable woman ahead of her time, agreed that it was death to make out with men. "Every man wants to marry a pure woman," she warned darkly, when at seventeen I was flying out of the house to a party.

I was horrified when I overheard an unmarried male friend confide to my father, "What I always say is, if you want a girl for the night, go for the plain ones. They're so grateful for the attention, they'll do anything you ask."

Progress?

Along came the Swinging Sixties, and I let my hair down and my miniskirts crept higher and higher. I remember my first pair of embroidered bell-bottoms—I also remember my parents' expression when I waltzed into their dinner party wearing them. Now I could walk through the neighborhood with a man twice running without our nosy neighbor leaning over the fence to ask my father if I intended "to make a commitment to him."

I brought back boyfriends, then took them away again and fooled around in the back of their car or at a party, before the ordeal of remounting the creaking stairs at three in the morning. "We'll always love you, you know," my parents said, thinking that the whole decade was little more than an extended adolescent rebellion. They tried to take in these developments, although my father couldn't help making his little jokes about the "new *dis*order."

Dorothy's images of sex still haunted me, especially the thought of being used as a *pissoir* by my future husband, but I kept these strange ideas at the back of my mind. One day a boy I'd met in a coffee shop took me to the movies, and afterward we ended up in his back yard. Then he lay on top of me, pressing his penis down on my stomach and squirming about. Pretty quickly he seemed to lose control, which had never happened with my other boyfriends. I wondered if he was having a fit and if I should get him dressed again and call his parents. Suddenly it was all over.

"Did you 'explode'?" I asked.

Then I went away to college in another town. One day a student from the engineering department whom I liked a lot sat down at my table. He was tall and chunky, with a slight swagger about him that impressed me for its independence. He wore dark glasses and had a sort of contemptuous smile that wasn't really directed at anything in particular. I thought this was immensely cool. At a party that weekend, he gave me something to smoke which made me cough and splutter. Then he gave me a drink which nearly knocked me out. I remember dancing and a taxi ride to a distant corner of the city. I remember undressing, and the smell of incense, the sound of Mick Jagger singing "Satisfaction." I remember that we both passed out, but I don't remember whether it was that night that I lost my virginity, or the following morning.

When I went to visit him again, he was playing very loud music and had dimmed all the lights. He got rid of the friend he was talking to by explaining, with an ill-concealed wink, that he had some business to attend to, and then he took off my clothes slowly, holding a glass in one hand, touching every part of me and commenting as he did so. "It was fabulous last night, wasn't it?" he muttered in my ear as he pulled off his underpants. "You enjoyed it, didn't you?" I said yes and felt a little foolish that I couldn't remember anything about it. "I could tell that you did. I could *tell*," he murmured. Then he pulled me on to the carpet, and as he entered me he whispered, "I'll make you come."

To be fair, Jerry was just an egotistic young man who'd been thrown in at the deep end by a decade that had more daring than understanding; he probably matured in time and became a nice, sensitive individual. But it still annoys the hell out of me that it never occurred to him that sex was anything more than a display of his penile prowess. My climax was, in his eyes, a test which either he could pass or I could fail. And, by making me afraid of failure, he pretty well ensured it. All Jerry saw was that he had performed a heroic deed. Therefore, when I didn't groan and wail at the appropriate moment, there must have been something wrong with *me*.

The next couple of years saw a string of casual boy-friends: after all, in those days it was just assumed that you'd sleep together right away. Sometimes it was nice, sometimes just awful, mostly neither. One day I met a man in the library whom I liked a lot. He was elegant, not too studious, and he seemed to like me a lot, which is always a bonus. We went out to dinner a few times, then back to my apartment where we made love for about half an hour in front of a new gas fireplace I'd just bought and was very proud of.

"Did you come?" he asked breathlessly when he'd finished.

"No, but it doesn't matter. I enjoyed it a lot."

"Have you ever come?" he asked, after a pause.

"No."

"Haven't you had an orgasm *ever?*" he asked again quietly. "Not with *any* man?"

"No," I admitted, beginning to think that he seemed quite concerned.

"Oh!" His face lit up with relief. "Then it's hardly my fault, is it?"

Sometimes I didn't tell, but just hoped for the best. Quite often a man would simply ignore whether I had or hadn't come—in those days women's orgasms were not the hot news they are now. But of course if you didn't "confess" beforehand there was always the risk that right in the midst of a passionate moment your lover would mutter, "Haven't you *come* yet? We've been doing it for twenty minutes, you know."

Why didn't I fake an orgasm? Quite simply, it never occurred to me. And by the time I was tipped off about this by another woman, I didn't have the confidence. To begin with, I was not sure *how* you faked one. Secondly, I was quite convinced that a man would be able to spot it immediately. After all, men were the ones who had all the experience, weren't they?

Naturally, not all men were like this. The bad ones stick out in my memory simply because they played heavily upon my sexual sensitivity. My first husband, on the other hand, was a wonderful man: kind, considerate, and a real expert in bed. He made me feel better between the sheets than I'd ever felt before and introduced me to sex that seemed almost indecently hot. Thinking about it even now gives me a tingling feeling—I hate to think how many times we got close to being caught at parties and official functions. And I enjoyed the sex. Often I enjoyed it so much that I reached a peak of agonized and unrelieved frustration, constantly (as it seemed) on the brink of relief but never getting there. I could have screamed. But I never had an orgasm.

Nowadays I sometimes *choose* not to reach orgasm during sex—if I'm feeling lazy or particularly mellow. And that in itself is pleasurable because I know that I can come when I want to. But, until recently, I found it deeply frustrating to feel I was unable to climax, no matter what my desires.

My Fault, or His?

The more I observed my partner lying in blissful contentment beside me, the more I was convinced that there was something wrong with me. Not something obvious that could be fixed but something secret, deep down, that was stopping me from climaxing and that perhaps I could never ever cure. Films, books, magazines, articles all testified to the fact that I was the odd one out. Other women climaxed happily without any difficulty. None of my friends gave any signs that they were ever dissatisfied with the way their bodies functioned in bed. If I pressed for details—pretending, of course, that I just wanted to hear a titillating story—the happy woman either went coy or boastful, assuring me that she'd enjoyed it like there was no tomorrow.

I remember getting into intimate conversation with a special friend of mine, who seemed just the kind who might also have trouble—she'd been anorexic for a long time and was generally nervous and unconfident. She'd been having an affair with a man about twelve years older than herself.

"Well, tell me all," I urged. "Is he good in bed?"

"Oh, he's really decent," she said quietly. "He always waits for me to climax before coming himself."

One more blow.

Sometimes I wished I were truly "frigid"—unable to feel anything at all—then at least, I felt, I could either give the whole thing up as bad news and lead a pleasant life on my own, or find some really obvious difficulty I could grasp hold of.

It wasn't even as if I was a meek little thing who was accustomed to accepting second best. In other aspects of life, I was pretty demanding. I could do just about everything that a man was traditionally supposed to be able to do, so why not this? I could fix a car, run a house, build shelves. I was intelligent and resourceful. I could run faster than anyone in the office. (I found that out when we had a charity sports day. I also won the egg-and-spoon race.) I once even beat up a burglar—not with my handbag, but with a jab from my elbow and a kick at his kneecap. There wasn't anything obviously wrong with my childhood. I read of women who had suffered trauma, either physical or mental, and lost the satisfaction they had once been able to have, or had never gained. I even read of one poor newlywed whose husband had dropped her when crossing the threshold and knocked her out as well as her orgasm! But I had none of those excuses. And the most maddening and inexplicable thing of all was that I could make myself come as many times as I liked when I was on my own.

Then, in the mid-eighties, came the fear of AIDS. Suddenly the *quality* of sex—not the quantity—became important as never before. Many of my friends felt that they had had enough of wild promiscuity; some had settled down. Though divorced from my first husband, I myself had a flourishing career which took me to a lot of conferences—where, in turn, I met a lot of men. Soon I was again settled into a comfortable relationship. I had matured a lot, felt more at ease with myself in a variety of ways. I had learned something of the kind of lovemaking I enjoyed. *But still no orgasm.* However satisfactory, and however long my partner was able to continue, I knew that orgasm was a long way away. I was, I realized bleakly, one of those women who would never have an orgasm.

And I didn't like it one bit.

Revelations

Then I began working among a group of women. After a pleasant partnership of several weeks, we went for a celebratory supper at an Indian restaurant. The wine flowed very freely and we began chatting. In the early hours of the following morning, we had moved to someone's apartment and were still chatting. Our subject? Sex. Tongues loosened by this time, the women talked about their husbands and lovers.

They talked about the size of their men's organs, of their fantasies, and of their sexual escapades—all the usual things. But unusually for me, who had always remained secretive about my sense of failure, they talked most of all *about their lack of sexual fulfillment.*

What was *doubly* astonishing to me was that they talked about sexual *unfulfillment* as if it were an obvious fact of life! They described unblushingly nights of frustration, of masturbation alone, and of faking orgasm—as if it were the most natural thing in the world.

It was a revelation. How naïve I had been! And those women were only the beginning of my understanding, because I was certain there was nothing very special about them. If they didn't enjoy sexual fulfillment, then the world must be full of women who didn't. I thought back to all those previous girlfriends of my partners, those enviable women who "always had an orgasm," and I realized that of course they didn't *"always."* Often as not, they would have been faking, or probably the men simply assumed they had been satisfied without bothering to find out. I began to think of this problem in a brand-new light.

After that, whenever I got the opportunity, I deliberately steered the conversation with other friends onto sexual matters. Now I asked them what I wanted to know directly. Sure enough, among all the accounts of successful or remarkable sex—and there were quite a few of these —story after story poured out of disappointments, frustrations, and distaste. Quite a number, like me, had never had an orgasm; many *were* able to have one, but only some of the time. "It's a terribly hit-and-miss affair," declared one woman. "I just have to take pot luck." A lot of them, like the women in the restaurant, were very funny about it —not in the least tragic, but treating it as a situation they had to accept. What *did* bother them was that they felt it was more than just a personal predicament: that so many men still regarded women in general as sexually *inferior*. Others felt resentful and bitter. All of them would have liked to change things.

At long last, it was no longer my story—it was *our* story.

The Real Truth About the Situation

I decided to *act*. At first I had no plan at all. I simply read more sex manuals, plowed through page after page of women's sexual "confessions," sought out statistics, and labored over the deadpan prose of scores of sexologists. I read feminists, sociologists, anthropologists, ethnologists, biologists, and plain old doctors. I went to clinics and self-help groups, even if they were only vaguely related to the topic in question, and I steered the conversation around to what interested me.

26

I was astonished: the women I had talked to in the restaurant were only the tip of the iceberg. The picture that was emerging was much more dramatic. Every time we turn on the television, open a magazine, or pass a bookstore, sex stares us in the face. Facts about sex, stories, advice, and techniques. The overall impression is that every adult—and a good many children, actually—in the Western world is highly educated about sex and, by extension, highly expert in the bedroom. But the truth is that there is still an astonishing level of ignorance about sexual matters. And it makes life unhappy for thousands of men and millions of women.

The more I read and the more I talked, the more I appreciated just how vast a body of women needed help, either to climax *whenever* they wanted, or to climax at all. And, I should add, how vast a body of men needed educating.

Then I discovered *The Hite Report*. Hite's statistics reveal that, of her volunteer sample, only 30 percent have an orgasm regularly from intercourse. And 29 percent have never reached orgasm during intercourse. The rest lie somewhere in between. Later surveys of 4,000 came up with even lower figures. I was shocked and (I have to admit) a little pleased—there's nothing like solidarity in adversity to improve your spirits.

Furthermore, it's a pretty safe guess that the statistics are worse than that. Because, if it's a volunteer sample, the women most likely to come forward and be candid about sex are likely to be those who are also successful with sex. And while many people might be tempted to pretend they *do* have an orgasm when they *don't,* few are likely to pretend that they *don't* when they *do.* That's about as probable as a woman claiming she weighs 140 pounds when she actually weighs 125.

These revelations left me feeling dizzy. It was Christmas time, and everyone else seemed very happy. I remember wandering listlessly about my apartment, vaguely trying to pin the angel on the Christmas tree and thinking that perhaps, after all, women weren't meant to have orgasms. Never mind the Nativity story—all I could think of was the Old Testament: Genesis, Adam and Eve, The Fall. That's it! I decided. The Bible was right; it's all true, really. This is God's punishment for Eve and that damned apple. I took the angel off the tree and hung up a snake instead.

Two days later, I had a lucky break.

The first stage of my liberation came on the day I met the Mangaians. . . .

Those Marvelous Mangaians

I remember it well. It was 1981, and I was musing over one of my Christmas presents: an enormous illustrated royal wedding album of Charles and Di given to me by a well-meaning aunt. Weddings, I thought—honeymoons—sex—orgasms. Do royalty have orgasms? I wondered. Shall I write to the Queen and ask her?

My speculations were interrupted by the sound of my boyfriend wolfing down his bacon and eggs. He had done himself proud the night before and climaxed twice in under an hour. Now we sat at breakfast the morning after. I picked dejectedly at a croissant, while he congratulated himself.

Before you start thinking that he must have been a monster of conceit, wait a moment: I *don't* mean that he sat there saying, "My God, I did it well last night. What a stud I am!" Believe me, if this had been the case he wouldn't have been sitting there in one piece for long. What he *actually* said was, "Mmmm, it was good last night," leaning over to give me a kiss. "One of the really great fucks. I feel ready for anything this morning"—all uttered with a charming smile and a (slightly absent-

28

minded) ruffle of my hair. A very typical morning-after scenario, in fact.

The trouble was, I hadn't climaxed at all. We'd been together several months, and he seemed very happy with the relationship. Either it never occurred to him to wonder how *I* was enjoying the sex; or, more probably, he didn't really want to hear if I had any complaints and thought it best not to ask. After all, if there was something wrong, wasn't it up to me to mention it?

This particular boyfriend was an anthropologist, due off on another trip to darkest Africa. I wasn't especially sorry to see him go. He finished his coffee and went off to take a shower. He'd left some of his books lying around, and I picked one up idly. In it there was an article about the sexual life and education of the Mangaians.

What I read changed my life: because on Mangaia, all the woman have orgasms all the time.

Mangaia is one of the Cook Islands in Polynesia. It may be a long way off, and it may be small, but the fact is that fundamentally the women there are just the same as you and me. They don't have different anatomies; they don't have orgasmic drugs; they don't undergo hypnosis—the only difference is that in their culture women and men are *trained* to get maximum satisfaction from sex.

Their approach is straightforward. In my more frustrated moments, I've often wondered what it would take to get it adopted in all its glory over here. Boys begin their sexual education when they're thirteen or fourteen with an older, experienced woman. She teaches them techniques of foreplay and cunnilingus, skills to be practiced briefly, and with the sole purpose of arousing the woman sufficiently for coitus. Intercourse lasts—oh, the bliss of it! —from fifteen to thirty minutes, during which the woman, who has also been trained in sexual proficiency from an early age, climaxes two or three times. The man withholds his orgasm until the very end.

If a man is an unsatisfactory lover, the woman may leave

him and spread news of his inadequacy throughout the island. He quickly gets a "reputation" and will then find it hard to get another woman to have sex with him.

This remarkable evidence for the importance of *learning* in sexual relations is to be found by studying the few societies in the world where sexual training is an integral part of the culture. Just recently I was reading about a similar community in the Himalayas called the Lachas, and another one in the South Seas—there, too, all the women have orgasms during sex.

I was thrilled to pieces. It seemed just the omen I needed to reverse my gloomy thoughts. Of course I was well aware that my lifestyle and upbringing were a world away from that of the Mangaians. But their story convinced me that given the right training, *any* woman can *learn* to have an orgasm. *They gave me the confidence to start training myself.* There and then I began to devise my plan.

I have never looked back.

CHAPTER THREE

Our Story— Success

So, if you have trouble with orgasm, you now know that many of the women you see when you walk down the street are in the same boat, although they'd be loath to admit it.

The mistake that is so often made, however, is to assume that ability to have an orgasm is simply a personal characteristic which you've got to accept willy-nilly, like having a big nose or short legs. So many women worry that they cannot have an orgasm because they weren't born that kind of person, or because there was some factor in their upbringing that upset their chances forever.

This is nonsense. Not only the Mangaians, but science, theory, and practice, all show that women can *learn* to have orgasms.

Women as the Subtler Sex

It has long been known that whereas a man's orgasm is a simple affair; a woman's orgasm is much more sophisticated. It has nothing to do with failure or inadequacy, it is simply a feature of our existence. In evolutionary terms, men *have* to climax quickly. If, several hundred thousand years ago, they couldn't produce a pretty fast ejaculation, they probably would have been eaten by saber-toothed tigers, and the human race would have died out.

Unfortunately for women, the survival of the species never depended on *their* climaxing at all. One of the really fascinating things about female orgasms—or maddening, depending on your point of view—is that nobody really knows *why* they happen at all. And if nobody knows why they happen, it's hardly surprising that we can't agree why they *don't* happen.

In Chapter 16 I discuss the different theories that specialists have devised to account for the existence of female orgasm. Suffice it to say here that the great gulf between men's ready ability and women's difficulty has not been helped by the fact that, even in our advanced, sexually "enlightened" era, ignorance of women's sexual needs still predominates. Researchers are constantly amazed and fascinated by the great sexual potential of women. Too many women—precisely because of the complexity of their sexuality—do not appreciate how to make use of these qualities. And, perhaps more importantly, too many men do not appreciate it either.

Scientists agree that in evolutionary terms a woman's orgasm is much more advanced than a man's. In the females of most lower species, it is absent. But whatever polemical point you want to make about this, no one can deny that it *is* interesting, and it sheds an enormous glare of light on the problem of why women have more difficulty with orgasms than men. The male and female orgasms may be similar sensations, but they represent very different degrees of evolutionary sophistication.

What's Wrong with Me? Nothing!

Whatever your reason for wanting an easy orgasm, or just any orgasm during sex—be it personal satisfaction, to prove a point or just out of interest—this book can help you to achieve it. However much we are told not to worry about failure to climax, orgasm-related anxieties will not vanish, any more than dieting-related anxieties vanish because we are told we should "learn to live with ourselves."

The terms "frigid" and "cold" may have disappeared from the sex books, but unfortunately many women are still tormented with them. I recently read in a popular women's magazine of a sixteen-year-old girl who, after having had sex for the first time with her "experienced" boyfriend, was taunted about being "frigid" because she found it painful and distressing. Or, as one married woman commented to me, "What a crazy, ironic description. Here I am lying in bed, almost *boiling over* with frustration, and he calls me *frigid!*"

After the sex researchers finally realized that these labels were not only repugnant, but scientifically untenable, they congratulated themselves on the introduction of a new term: "dysfunctional." Not a great improvement, but it was a small step forward. To my mind, it still manages to capture most of the unpleasant overtones of the old words, but dilutes them a little with the cold objectivity of science. It's a term divided into two parts: "primary" or "secondary." If you've never had an orgasm, then, says the sexologist, you have a "primary dysfunction." If you've sometimes had one, but less than 50 percent of the time, then you have only a "secondary dysfunction." In my case when I began my self-help program, I was resoundingly "primary."

But things are changing again. Because now, in answer to that nagging question, "What's wrong with me?" scientists are finally beginning to realize that the answer is "Nothing." Moreover, since it is the great majority of women—something like 70 percent—who have trouble achieving orgasm, it is simply inaccurate to consider them abnormal. As sexologist Martin Cole wrote recently, "The terms 'frigid' and 'dysfunctive' when applied to women who do not achieve orgasm are simply 'intellectually unacceptable.' " It makes no more sense than to label the minority of people who practice foot fetishism (for example) "normal" and the rest of us who prefer plain old sexual intercourse "deviants." Women who were once called "frigid" and more recently "orgasmically dysfunctional" actually have nothing wrong with them at all. All that is the matter is that they have not yet been able to fully develop their orgasmic skills.

So let's get rid of those repressive old terms like "abnormal," "failure," and "inadequacy," and start thinking about our sexual state as being "preorgasmic"—a term that is gradually becoming accepted in the scientific world. It is not only more pleasant, but it is also scientifically more accurate to do so. You are no more an "abnormal" person because you have not yet learned to make the most of your sexual potential than you were "abnormal" before you learned the skills of reading and writing, riding a bicycle, playing a musical instrument, painting a picture, or speaking a foreign language. Just as you learned these sophisticated skills, so you must *learn,* by means of simple, easy-to-follow exercises, to have an orgasm.

Why Are Some Women Preorgasmic and Not Others?

This question is, of course, the one that everybody would like to be able to answer. As with many sciences, in sexology ignorance is the general rule. I am not being flippant or damning. The average person thinks of science as all-powerful: it takes a physicist to tell you just how *little* is known about the universe, what a small drop of certainty our knowledge really amounts to.

So it is with sexology. The fact remains that for all the shelves full of sexology manuals—and I have plowed through a good many of these—there are vast areas which nobody adequately understands. And women's sexual response is particularly difficult to monitor—not least because we don't have erections to give out loud and clear signals of our arousal and climax.

In fact, reading about the methods of early researchers and their primitive devices for measuring female response is quite entertaining. Shortly after the First World War, the sexologist John B. Watson, decided that sex was too important to be left to the medical profession and devised his own set of instruments. Watson connected his own body and that of his female partner to his very primitive equipment while they made love and produced what were quite likely the very first reliable data on human sexual responses which he cataloged carefully in a set of files. But the story ended dramatically when his wife discovered why her husband was spending so much time in his laboratory. She sued for divorce and confiscated all his scientific records. The case made lurid headline news, and Watson ended his days in an advertising agency.

Nowadays sexology equipment is sophisticated. But, because there are so many factors influencing our sexual responses, studies tend to concentrate on tiny areas and have small numbers of participants. Almost invariably their conclusions are tentative and likely to be disproved or challenged the following month. Sexologists simply cannot agree.

So it is not surprising to learn that the causes of orgasmic difficulty in women are still not understood. In some cases, the partner is not sexually suitable for the woman; in other cases, the lover may not know how best to stimulate her clitoral area. But, in general, difficulty with orgasm is due to a mixture of causes, including psychological ones. What researchers do agree about is that in almost all cases there is no *physical* reason why a woman can't have an orgasm. (Those rare cases when a medical condition is to blame—and what can be done about it—are discussed in Chapter 17.)

In individual cases, there can be dominant influences. Fear of inadequacy is a major inhibiting factor that many of us have felt at one time or another. But surely even women who *do* climax sometimes feel this, too? The trouble is, the woman who fails to have an orgasm risks getting into that vicious circle: "failure," which causes fear of "failure," which in turn induces anxiety and therefore certain "failure."

Some women cannot climax because, deep down, they fear orgasm. They see it as a loss of control and have even described it as "having a fit," "going wild," "losing hold of myself." This program will help to allay such fears because cultivating a sense of *control* is fundamental to it. Control over your own body, control over your own sexual responses at all stages, even when you are being penetrated by a man. Far from being out of control during orgasm, you will learn to be *in control* as never before.

Perhaps the most overriding belief is that women's lack of orgasm is a legacy of our cultural past, the result of our society's attitudes to women, built up over the centuries.

Broadly speaking, our society says that whereas men have powerful "sex drives" that need satisfying, women do not. More than that, women *should* not. For centuries women have been told that to be anything but passive is dirty, unladylike, altogether undesirable. Because women's orgasms are much more dependent on psychological factors than men's, these causes can have profoundly inhibiting effects which we must learn to overcome.

Even though this repressive attitude is slowly disappearing, its influence is still strong and should not be underrated. It colors women's childhoods in numerous small ways, both at home and at school; it is reflected in the media, in endless social conventions—each of which appears insignificant when considered on its own, but which in total has a devastating effect—and it colors men's attitude to women in the bedroom. If women's orgasms were as straightforward as men's, these influences would be annoying but not dramatic; but because women's orgasms are complicated and subtle, the influence can be a significant obstacle to the natural learning process.

What Type of Woman Has Trouble with Orgasm?

Now that we know that the majority of women are, to some degree, preorgasmic, the question of what *type* of woman has trouble becomes increasingly meaningless. Princess to pauper, it affects us all.

Even if we try to narrow the field and ask what type of woman has *great* difficulty with orgasm—the woman, for example, who has never climaxed—it is very hard to pinpoint the answer.

Needless to say, hundreds of studies have tried to do just that. One researcher, for example, concluded that the only consistent factor among women who had trouble with orgasm was the quality of their early relationship with their fathers: those who perceived him not to have invested a serious or dependable interest in them were more likely to report orgasmic difficulties. There was no such correlation with relationships with mothers. But is this universally the case, or simply the oddity of that particular study? There has been some—undramatic—support for this idea, but, as always, the conclusions are cautious. Having thought about it in relation to myself, it seems credible to me that the woman who is accustomed to a relaxed, stable relationship with a man might well do better in bed.

I had always believed that women with repressively religious upbringings had difficulty with orgasm because of inherent guilt, and also that women who've undergone trauma, such as rape or incest, would have trouble climaxing. But, according to a number of detailed studies, there is no evidence for either association. In 1966, in an unpublished doctoral dissertation mentioned in Fisher, D. F. Shope even discovered that, in the sample investigated, unmarried orgasmic women had *more* traumatic sexual encounters before the age of sixteen than their nonorgasmic counterparts. The sexologist Seymour Fisher also claims that education has some influence—better-educated women have a little less trouble than their uneducated sisters, although this may be because educated women demand more from their lovers and are less content to settle for second best. My favorite result is that of a group of researchers who discovered that churchgoing women tended to have less trouble with orgasm than the impious ladies who went elsewhere on Sunday—a sure suggestion that hell's delights might not be so great after all.

Among all the many women I've spoken to, I have never come across a "type" of woman who has difficulty with orgasm. It is a problem which affects rich women and poor, successful and unsuccessful, thin and fat, glamorous and homely, healthy and unhealthy, old and young.

All in all, the only really predictable factor is their diversity!

Does Therapy Help?

Some women may find therapists, psychologists, and counselors helpful regarding sexual difficulties. They didn't work for me at all. And, looking at the results of many women I've known, I tend to be skeptical. Whereas I've heard success stories when it comes to family problems, self-confidence, anxiety, and phobias, sexual problems can be maddeningly elusive and difficult for the professional to treat. (Besides, whenever I see the word "therapist," my punning eye changes it to "the rapist.")

My first therapist was nicely mannered, with limp advice and endless euphemisms. "How can I be sure of faking my orgasm successfully so that my boyfriend won't start calling me 'frigid'?" I asked her innocently one day. Ms. Therapist almost fell backward off her chair. She spluttered a bit and then began burbling on about love, honesty, and understanding.

"Look"—I *had* to interrupt her—"I *have* tried that, actually. Oddly enough, I, too, like love and understanding in a partnership. But it doesn't always make you come." I crawled home feeling more than usually guilty about faking, and scared that I was about to be found out.

After her, I moved to a stern young man who sat up stiffly as if glued to his seat in the wrong position. Each week I steeled myself to face his grim expression. It didn't encourage me to open up. I soon formed the impression that he was feeling his way in his profession, yet tried to cover this up by being assertive. It did not inspire confidence when I came in one day to find him quickly shuffling a "how-to" textbook into his drawer behind a half-eaten Mars Bar. Another of his tricks was making an elaborate pretense that he wasn't looking at his watch, but was pulling up his shirtsleeves and scratching his wrist. I watched this performance for several weeks before I interrupted him:

"Why don't you just look at the clock on the wall if you want to know the time? Have you any idea how hurtful all that subterfuge is?" After all, it's not easy to talk freely on delicate topics when you are worrying that he is longing for the session to end. When he didn't like what I'd said, he simply fell silent, with a Buddha-like smile on his face.

My respect for him really plummeted when I went away on vacation. He knew my hobby was natural history, so I selected a dramatic postcard of a spider to send to him.

When it came to our next session, he lay in wait, fingering the postcard.

"I think you want to eat me," he blurted out.

"What?" I replied incredulously.

Immediately his face fell. "Isn't that what female spiders do? Eat their mates?"

For Christ's sake! I thought. He doesn't even know. Very helpful for my problems.

The worst of all came two weeks before I was due to be "terminated" (nice expression, that). I'd missed a session because of a crisis at home, but forgot to telephone him to say so. He jumped to the conclusion that I was "running away." The following day, a letter arrived in the mail, informing me that I had some "very serious problems" to sort out, and warning me against missing the last two sessions. It seemed astonishing to me that, in my apparently "fragile" state of mind, he could think fit to taunt me with it.

"What panacea do you think you can offer in two hours that you've failed to do in two years?" I demanded. He, of course, chose to remain silent, nodding his head like one of those plastic dogs people used to have in the back of their cars. It was an unnecessary and upsetting end to the therapy, made worse when he informed me that I was "unable to open up and confront my problems."

"Yes," I agreed. "Unable with you." I knew this was true because, on several occasions when he'd been ill, I'd felt quite relaxed with his replacement. But he wouldn't admit that. I left with my confidence lower than when I'd started. I see now, with hindsight, just how irresponsible his attitude was. We were mismatched, and he preferred to blame me. At the time I was particularly vulnerable, and I trusted him. I did not have the self-confidence to get angry, so I grew depressed.

I mention this episode because so often therapy is regarded as a universal cure for all problems. And not enough is said about the frightening way in which an incompetent or even mismatched therapist can do harm.

Of course, this is not to say that psychotherapy cannot be helpful. Although sex researchers have found little evidence to show that therapy is effective in treating sexual difficulties, some people find the involvement of a third, objective, professional person in their sex life comforting and encouraging. In individual cases, if not in general, psychotherapy can then be useful. If you are lucky enough to be able to get a good therapist, then by all means take advantage of the opportunity.

Behavioral sex therapy, such as that developed by Masters and Johnson, is far more successful. Instead of trying to approach the problem negatively by concentrating on resolving "inner conflicts" (just what these are depends on the school to which your psychotherapist adheres), the behaviorist takes a positive approach. By informing the woman about the true nature of her sexuality, and by training her physically to make full use of her sexual potential and overcome her inhibitions, these therapists have reported remarkable results. But it is important that you be the right sort of participant in such a program: if you can afford the fees, and the time it takes, and if you have the peculiar sort of nerve required to go through with such a program wholeheartedly, *and* if your partner is equally willing (most behaviorists will treat only the couple together), then you might consider it.

There's one other thing, too. Although these therapists have very good results, you must keep going. Often after a participant has left the program, her earlier difficulties return slowly. In my opinion, this is because the programs frequently don't concentrate enough on developing the individual woman's capacity to learn. They place too much emphasis on the importance of both partners—an admirable approach, but not always a practical one. Relationships change and, outside of the supportive atmosphere of the sex clinic, the gains may soon be whittled away.

Personally, I knew I had to do it alone.

CHAPTER FOUR

Women Take Control

Women's ability to have an orgasm is a skill which—like all the skills of civilization—we need to develop. All that is required is a willingness to learn. Both women and men will benefit.

I have already stated that there are various possible reasons why women find themselves unable to have an orgasm: our cultural heritage, personal upbringing, lack of adequate stimulation from our partners, and so forth.

To all these I have something important to add—something to which the sex therapists give scant attention: control. I believe that a sense of control is the most important feature in achieving orgasm. By control I do not mean domination: I mean a sense of taking charge of your own life, your own body, and your own orgasm. And control is something that women still do not have enough of—especially in the bedroom.

The Problem of the Invisible Barrier

Sounds like a Sherlock Holmes story, doesn't it? Let me explain what I mean.

All during the time I was agonizing over why I didn't have an orgasm, and while trying to develop my training program, it struck me as particularly significant that, with few exceptions, women can easily achieve orgasm by masturbation. Indeed, the majority of women in sexologist Alfred Kinsey's study masturbated to orgasm within four minutes. Yet most of these same women have difficulty achieving orgasm during intercourse; many of them have great difficulty; and some, like myself before I began training, don't have them at all.

To some extent, this vast discrepancy is explained by the fact that the men do their part inadequately. They don't provide their partner with enough stimulation, they ejaculate too quickly, they are too rough, their position is wrong, etc. These are what I call the "technicalities" of sex, and they *are,* of course, very important.

However, this is not a sufficient explanation for women's lack of orgasm. There are many times when the partner is all attention and understanding, but still no go. Lisa's problem is typical:

This guy was a god, as far as I was concerned. Nice chunky legs and a gorgeous behind that came in at the sides. Strong arms, and a face that made me want to come just to look at it. He was also an excellent lover—gentle, patient and inventive. Did my pussy pay any attention? No, it didn't. But the most annoying thing was that as soon as he'd finished (we'd do it for an hour and a half, probably more) leaving me still desperate, all I had to do was run into the john and do it to myself in a couple of minutes. Now, what foul trick of nature is that?

And, quite apart from this, women *should* be able to achieve orgasm even when conditions are not 100 percent ideal. They can quickly learn to have an orgasm through masturbation even in the most adverse circumstances, as Deborah's story shows:

My masturbation techniques are quite crude and unimaginative, really—I realize that since reading *Hite*. Just a short rub *anywhere* around there,—it doesn't even have to be on target—and I come. Yet Vince, who really has a lot more patience and skill, has to work for a *long, long* time before I can even think of coming. Even then it's only about 50 percent success.

What happened between Deborah's own sexual attentions to herself, and the attentions of her boyfriend? *What happened* between Lisa's own sexual attentions to herself, and the attentions of her boyfriend? The story is the same for thousands of women. A *barrier* appeared; an *invisible* but powerful one. This invisible barrier is a maddening phenomenon. Perfectly ordinary women with no physical or psychological handicaps are simply not able to have an orgasm during sex, for no apparent reason.

How do we explain it? I believe the answer is that this invisible barrier represents a *loss of control*. In both Lisa's and Deborah's cases it was not simply a technical difference between masturbation and sex with their partner—it was the difference between having total control over the situation and having only partial control. For many women, the sense of "another" is deeply—perhaps unconsciously—disturbing. We do not readily allow another person to "control" us. Especially when that "other" is engaged in something as intimate as sexual stimulation.

When I began devising this plan, I realized an important truth about myself: I had only really begun to enjoy sex when I realized that the man did not have to be sexually dominant. In other words, the more control I gained in the bedroom, the closer it brought me to satisfying sex, to overcoming this pernicious invisible barrier.

In my case, this feeling came to me as part of my growing confidence as I got older. Before then I had had good times and bad times in bed. I had certainly gotten sexually aroused. But I had rarely felt totally *at ease.* There was always the feeling that the man led and I followed. I didn't want to follow, and I didn't particularly want to lead. *I wanted to be equal.*

I began to analyze why my early sexual encounters had been so unsatisfying. With experience I had achieved a greater degree of coordination of the situation. I was less a "subject" of my partner, more psychologically comfortable with him, less self-consciously aware that he was a "separate," potentially critical, individual. And, of course, I was more confident of making sure that he pleased me as much as I pleased him.

I discovered that among my friends it was often the older women who had more success with sex. Several had had bad times when they were young, but later had managed to find satisfaction, or at least to get a lot closer to achieving orgasm. And the reason? Because these older women had learned to get over their youthful worries and insecurities. They were more at ease with their sexuality and more confident about themselves.

This feeling of lack of control during sex is difficult to pin down in words. Think hard about your own situation and you will begin to understand what I am driving at. In fact, I use the word "driving" advisedly, because the most helpful analogy I can make is that of learning about cars. When you begin to learn how to drive, you feel as if you are holding the steering wheel of a malicious-minded metal dinosaur. It seems as if at any moment the car might simply decide to stop paying attention to you, and do something horrible of its own accord. Getting from A to B seems like a matter of luck. Gradually you become more and more familiar with the beast until that marvelous moment—usually long after you have passed your driving test—when you realize that *you* have complete control of the car, not the other way around. Gone is that element of chance in how the car moves. Now you have really mastered it.

This gradual growth of confidence applies to anything else you have learned to do successfully; ride a bicycle, operate a word processor, bake a cake, even take care of a baby. That feeling of *total* control, total *ease,* a professional sense of what you are doing, is what you are aiming for sexually. Not in regard to your partner, but in regard to yourself and your partner*ship*.

A sense of control is a vital factor in women's sexual fulfillment. Yet so many women lose control in the bedroom—often without realizing it. In fact, the idea of control is so important that, although the distinctions are not watertight and sometimes overlap, I have divided it into two types: Visible Control and Invisible Control.

Visible Control

The first kind of control you will learn in the program is "Visible Control." I call it that because it is control over the visible, tangible parts of yourself: your own body and its responses. You will train your body, step by step, to respond sexually. At the end, you will know precisely *what you like* and what you don't—regardless of what sex books tell you is enjoyable. Barbara gives a good example of this:

How many times have I read in books that earlobes are erogenous zones! So I thought, Okay. I let men keep on playing with them, hating every minute, but thinking I must be abnormal. I thought that if I kept on, maybe I'll start to like it. It made me wince.

At long last I realized: that's not me. I had the confidence to say no, I hate it and I'll always hate it, and it doesn't matter in the least. Because what

I *do* like is having the back of my neck nibbled. If that's odd, I don't give a damn!

Sex will no longer be a "lie back and hope for the best" affair as it was for Rosalind, who

just used to think that if I could only really relax, let the guy take over, it'd all be OK. Relax, relax, relax—my counsellor used to use that word ad nauseum. She said I was "fighting" sex and must learn to relax. I used to twist myself in knots trying to relax. I relaxed so much I went to sleep. I felt it was a mistake for me to try and guide him, and that I should gracefully accept what he did and not change it. Well, I kept this up for two years and it got me just *nowhere*. "Lie back and relax" is *the* biggest sex myth.

Nor will it be a "try everything and hope for the best" business as it was for Carol:

After I realized I had problems with orgasm, I thought it was because I was too conventional. Every book I picked up showed couples doing outrageous things to each other and having wild orgasms. I really did believe that if I could be more adventurous I would succeed. I was completely wrong; in fact, I hated it most of the time. I can tell you, categorically now, the *only* way to enjoy fancy sex is after you've really mastered the basics. I just wish someone had told me that years ago.

Rosalind and Carol are right. In learning to have an orgasm *every* time you want one, it is *not* enough to lie back, relax, and let the man take over. Nor is it a wise move to be shamed by advanced sex manuals into exotic options. The way to permanent, constant success with orgasm is gradually and carefully—with *you* taking a major role.

Invisible Control

Invisible Control is something more subtle and elusive—a state of mind, which means it's harder to pin down.

I think we are all getting familiar with the ways in which, in ordinary life, so-called equality for men and women can mask a range of inequalities. For example, women have won the right to enter previously male professions such as medicine and the law; they have won the right to equal pay and, theoretically, to equal prospects. Where they exist, these are clearly defined "equalities." Now we have to tackle all the subtleties of inequality that legislation cannot handle: the fact that in many of these jobs women must be twice as good to be accepted, that again and again they get passed over for promotion; that undermining sexual harassment still goes unchecked. Angelica Huston put it well when, shortly after the release of *The Addams Family,* she was interviewed by a magazine:

"You have said before that women are trained to yield to men, to defer to them, so to speak. Is this true in your case?" they asked.

"Well," she replied, "it's not so much about yielding, it's more a sort of acquiescence, like this is more important for him than it is for me. I just won't do that, but women feel that in order to be feminine they can't be aggressive, and it's a fine line."

Now translate these kinds of attitudes to the bedroom. Again and again in sexual situations female equality is seen as female stridency—by the women themselves, often as not.

To begin with, what I have described as Invisible Control is not feeling yourself duty bound to place his needs before yours.

"Well, that's obvious," the more enlightened readers might protest. I thought it was obvious, too—but I am *still* realizing just how difficult that is to put into practice. In fact, my own views were very similar to those of Veronica:

I think of myself as utterly liberated—in *every-thing*. And yet so often I catch myself making little concessions to his pleasure in bed. I feel I have to give his genitals more attention than he gives mine. If he's getting really excited and close to orgasm, I feel I oughtn't to stop him so that I can catch up—I let him go right ahead and enjoy himself—and so I'm left frustrated. And, even when he *does* give me lots of attention, I often feel slightly guilty, as if I'm having a treat, not something that's due to me. It's almost as if these responses are programmed into me. When I notice them, I get very angry with myself—yet I find it hard to stop and really enforce my equality.

Again and again I have listened to this response from women—I quote only Veronica precisely because the others are so similar. I, too, believe passionately in women's rights—but it is not a feminist obsession to recognize that women are encouraged from birth to be second to men *sexually*. This is a conclusion I have come to after years of speaking to both men and women. To make the point, I quote here a selection of men I have recently interviewed:

I have to admit that however forceful a woman is outside the bedroom, they're usually pretty accommodating in. All the women I've been to bed with just lie there and wait for me to get it on. I wish they wouldn't. The only exception that I can recall is a French girl I met in Paris.

50

Goodness, I wish women *would* be more assertive. It's sexy. [This man was laconic—he blushed and wouldn't say any more.]

And the only one out of twenty who showed a definite preference for "passive" women:

Thank God, yes, women seem to have an inbuilt sense that men come first in the bedroom. Even aggressive ones? Yeee-ees . . . yes, definitely. In fact, the only woman I've ever bedded who was bossy in bed was pretty low-key outside. Must have been. If I'd guessed, I wouldn't have seduced her!

However, the real difficulty of sexual equality in the bedroom is that of *identifying* it in the first place. This vague but undermining feeling of sexual submissiveness—of not feeling fully in control in a relationship—creeps in in all sorts of insidious ways, however "liberated" we feel. As Veronica (above) has made clear, it takes sensitivity and vigilance to spot our inequalities, and it takes a great deal of self-confidence to eradicate them.

A lot of different factors combine to give women a bad start in sexual equality. First, the ease with which men can have an orgasm means that many women feel themselves less sexually capable, and therefore something of a sexual underling by comparison. (It is precisely this feeling that this book seeks to redress.) It is for the woman that the man waits; it is for the woman that he extends his foreplay, etc. *He* doesn't need these things for himself. Because women are sexually more sophisticated, they take longer to warm up, and they require more skilled love-making than men. In fact, many sexologists believe that a woman's lack of orgasm simply reflects the man's incapacity to retain his semen.

51

Second, men often *are* more sexually experienced. This doesn't mean simply that they have had more partners, but that they, finding sex so much more readily gratifying, have quickly learned how to make the most of it. A recent article in a woman's magazine revealed that 48 percent of girls have had sexual intercourse before the age of sixteen. Almost invariably, these early sexual encounters are more pleasurable for the male than for the female. The race for sexual satisfaction has begun, and already men have a head start. It can take years for a woman to catch up.

Sex manuals don't help much, either. Many women have pointed out to me that the one picture they could remember from sex guides was how to rub a man's penis, or how to suck him off. This is partly because women's genitals are smaller, more discreet than men's—or, like the clitoris, hardly visible at all. Cunnilingus is usually a picture of a man's head with a little twizzle of pubic hair poking out around his mouth. But fellatio is a huge phallus, "rubbing his penis" is a huge phallus, and "delaying ejaculation with your finger and thumb" ditto. Small things on their own, but they add to the general feeling that the man is the more important partner. The very size and visibility of a man's sexual parts compared to the discreet female genitalia has an effect. When we look at old Greek vase paintings of erotic scenes, the men have huge erections and give the obvious impression of "feeling horny." As for the women, whatever position they are in, how can we tell whether or not they are highly aroused?

Economic factors also play a part in limiting women's sense of control in the bedroom. Many women feel that they must put their partner's sexual needs before their own or they will lose him. As long as women are economically dependent upon men—which with children they often cannot help but be—this situation will continue. As one mother of four told me, "I don't enjoy my husband's lovemaking. But what can I do? If he leaves, I'm left with four kids, no money and little prospect of attracting another partner. Looked at like that, bad sex is a small price to pay."

Another reason for loss of control in the bedroom is that during sex we are always keeping half a mind on how we look, constantly asking, "Am I alluring enough between the sheets? Slim enough? Pretty enough?" And, of course, "Am I a good lover?" But most of the men, when I asked them, said they worried about such things only at the very beginning of a relationship. Just the simple fact of being able to walk around the bedroom naked and unembarrassed, as men always seem able to do, gives them an advantage. So many women, anxious to look "perfect" for their lover, feel they must grab a robe to hide their "defects". The fact that the man may not mind these "defects" doesn't make much difference. A recent survey in a woman's magazine revealed that a massive 84 percent of women believe they are too fat. Translate that to the bedroom, where we cannot hide behind a well-tailored jacket or a loose skirt, and you can begin to calculate the damage to women's self-esteem.

Countless studies have shown that men have a far more positive self-image than women. For example, when a group of people were asked to comment on their physical attractiveness, almost unanimously the women tended to describe themselves in terms of their defects—"My butt's too large," "I'd like to change my mouth," and so forth—while the men described themselves in relation to their positive points: "I have good legs, nice hair," etc. The woman's magazine survey also revealed the astonishing and somewhat tragic fact that only 7 percent of women are confident enough to want to look like no one but themselves. Princess Diana and Victoria Principal were the top two preferred ideals. Of course, this kind of self-doubt takes its toll in the bedroom.

There is also the much-held popular view that whereas a woman is content with one partner for many years, men need a variety of lovers to keep their interest. This "seven-year itch" has been the subject of numerous films—most famously that of the same name in which Marilyn Monroe plays a (guess what?) curvaceous blonde tempting a man away from his staid wife. So that for many women the very time when after several years with their partner they should be feeling most at ease physically and emotionally, they are also beginning to worry that their partner will tire of them.

Before you begin to wonder whether you wouldn't rather go and take the dog for a walk than read all this gloom and doom, let me stress that I am not necessarily talking about what *is*—but about the kind of things women *fear*. The very fact of recognizing such things is the first step to eradicating them.

Outside the bedroom there is another undermining factor which can cause you to feel loss of control in a sexual sense. This is the feeling of being the "prey" of a man, under his scrutiny. Still, it is men who are usually the ones to seek out, size up, and make proposals to women. However high our self-confidence, an aggressive pickup approach can make us feel less of an individual, more of an anonymous female.

My friend Liz had had a bad experience with a sexually domineering partner. Fortunately, she found an excellent —and unexpected—way of getting over her feelings of loss of control. She was invited to the Kentucky Derby, but became separated from her party. Longing for some refreshment and finding all the tables occupied, she sat down next to a single young man. He, some years younger than she, looked quiet and nervous; after a while, they began talking. He invited her for a drink, and then— somewhat abashed at his own boldness—to dinner, which he didn't have enough money to pay for, so they split the bill. With most men she would have been on guard right from the start, but this one seemed to have to muster up so much courage for each stage of his courtship that she felt not in the least bit threatened by it. As she said, "He was not one to start lunging, and even if he had, it wouldn't have taken much to push him off." Back at her hotel, he lost his nerve. He was charming, intelligent, nice looking, and Liz really began to be attracted to him, but he was rooted to the spot for fear of affronting her with any bold advances. So in the end she leaned over and kissed him . . .

I can still remember the surprise I felt and the liberation. Even when we were lying together making love in the most ordinary manner possible, I felt that the whole scene was containable. He was the one doing the worrying; if I was not satisfied, he would feel it must be his fault, not mine. And because he was so obviously young, nervous, and inexperienced I didn't have the feeling that I was under scrutiny. I had no intention of making him feel submissive, but I relished his complete inability to behave dominantly. Clearly he had no inherent assumption of his superiority. I knew I could encourage him to satisfy me; my pleasure was no longer accidental.

Liz's story describes well the importance of sex in which the woman feels relaxed and not under scrutiny. Of course this does not have to be a situation in which she is dominant:

The trouble for me was that I wanted more than anything for Mark to fling me down on the bed and force me to have sex with him while he held my arms back. I loved the feeling of being pushed around during sex. But I didn't want to also submit my enjoyment to his. If he came, then I wanted to come, too. As far as having an orgasm was concerned, I wanted to be an equal—in that sense, yes, I wanted control. I didn't want to feel

that my pleasure was inferior to his, just the sex role that I played. After I'd gotten Mark to understand that, everything was dandy. We have plenty of "male dominance" scenarios together. But I never feel subordinated in my mind. It may be a subtle difference, but it's very important.

In a recent study, an erotic story describing a male and a female engaging in sexual activity was presented to college students. The female subjects "reported more sexual arousal and less negative effect when the female character was described as dominant." Another researcher, with the charmingly appropriate name of Heiman (sexologists these days have *delightful* names—Seamen, Horney, and Hyman Rodman to name just three) found that "a female-initiated, female-centered narrative was significantly more arousing for female subjects than any of the other variations."

The sense of being "prey" to a man is something that many women live with day after day. Let me give you a different example. For years I was hugely flattered whenever a workman wolf-whistled at me, yet I also felt an uncomfortable sense of threat. Then, in my thirties, I grew less obsessed with my appearance and began going out deliberately unmade-up, wearing comfortable (some would say frumpy) clothes. After the initial disappointment of passing a building site in silence and not drawing the occasional admiring glance down the street, I began to see my power. For the first time, I felt like a real person, not simply a being who existed only in relation to other people's views of me. Sheila Kitzinger quotes a woman who, because of being pregnant, was no longer regarded as a viable sex object:

Strangely, once I was no longer bombarded with sexual advances, it struck me how in one way it

gave me a sense of power, of attractiveness, and, more importantly, a sense that I existed.

Germaine Greer's sharp and inspirational *The Change* tells how, on a trip to Sicily, she decided, as an expression of mourning for her father, to dress in black, with her hair covered:

I found the new freedom from men's attentions exhilarating rather than depressing. There was also tremendous liberation in not having to think what to wear. Black goes with black. One has only to think of textures, of the part of one's clothing that matters to oneself.

Of course we all like to feel we *can* look attractive for the right person, or when we *want* to draw admiring glances. But this "invisible" independence can be, I now realize, a far more powerful feeling than the "power" of sexual attractiveness. Try it sometime —I'm sure you'll appreciate my point. Most importantly, it helps build up that all-important sense of *control*.

Try to familiarize yourself with Visible Control and Invisible Control—each will have some special meaning to you and your relationship. Once you are conscious of the little ways in which we lose control in sexual relationships, you'll be on the way to helping yourself. The plan has been specially formulated to take them both into account. It works by making use of all the best of the "technicalities" of sex, while at the same time breaking down the invisible barrier step by step. Taking more control is, therefore, *prescribed*.

The Myth of the Passive Woman

I want to end this chapter on what I think is a particularly cheerful note.

I have talked about our cultural heritage, which for so long has seen women as sexually passive, and how for all the sexual liberation of the 1990s, the myth that women are—or should be—essentially passive still exists. Indeed, I'm a good example of it myself. In my family, a woman could be all sorts of things—confident, pushy, career-minded, she could yell at a man in an argument, refuse to do the cooking, slam the door in his face. What she could never do was be sexually forward. If a woman asked a man out, or made the first move, she was considered "cheap." I'm in my thirties, but the old Victorianism lingers on. In a sense it's hardly surprising. The celebrated sex researcher Krafft-Ebing's *Psychopathia Sexualis* was originally published in 1886. I've got a 1931 edition. Nearly half a century later it's still being recommended as a textbook for the medical and legal professions. It states:

Woman, however, if physically and mentally normal and properly educated, has but little sexual desire.

"Oh," you may protest, "that's 63 years ago. No wonder it sounds old-fashioned." Not at all. Both my parents were growing up at that time. "Old-fashioned" ideas pass easily down the generations and die slowly, very slowly. The new ones hit the headlines and the more outré cable TV shows, but the old ones live on for a long time after.

Take a look at so many books and films, and you'll see that true romance and love still belongs to the woman who is—in the last analysis—submissive to the man. She may have had oh-so-many adventures/tantrums/escapades/ revolts—but when she settles down with the man, it's well understood who's actually boss. To take a recent example, the film *Working Girl* purports to portray a modern woman's rise to power. What happens? Lo and behold, it ends with two women fighting over a man. Harlequin sells millions of books worldwide. In every one—at least of the many I've read—the woman, after a period of revolt or individuality, ends up more-or-less subservient to a dominant man. In many cases, he's offensively dominant, almost to the point of rape (avoided only because she "enjoys it really").

The trouble is, outside of the celluloid, fictional world, the passive woman is usually not so lucky. For one thing, it's a serious impediment to achieving orgasm. Lack of control over one's lovemaking leaves you no time to be free to relax, enjoy sex, and make sure it satisfies *you*.

And never confuse refusal to be "passive" with being loud, aggressive and "unfeminine." I personally think the limited notions of what is acceptable "feminine" behavior are laughable. After all, strong, dominant women can be as hugely attractive as frail, feminine men. But that is not my point. You can be as firm and insistent as you like, as quietly as you like. In fact, quiet insistence, or refusal to give in or compromise, is often the most effective.

Now that I've made my point about refusing to be sexually *passive*—what will your partner think?

"I couldn't possibly be more assertive sexually," said several women I've spoken to. "Men hate women like that."

I used to think so too. In fact, as I've said, it was the mainstay of my upbringing.

Now listen to this:

I *hate* making sexual advances. It makes me feel vulgar and crude.

I usually make the initial sexual advance. How do I feel about it? *I feel precisely that I am less desirable to the woman than she is to me;* **and fairly often I feel I'm frightening her. That is one hell of a way to begin. When the woman does make the sexual advance, that alone gives me very positive feelings.**

I almost always make the initial sexual advance in all my relationships and I hate it! I feel like I am stealing something or forcing her to do something she may in fact not want to do.

I have a lot of trouble making the initial sexual advance. If I think about it long enough, I always come up with enough doubt to keep me from doing anything.

As you have probably gathered by now, these are all men speaking. The quotes come from *The Hite Report on Male Sexuality,* and there are scores more. I begin by quoting Hite precisely so that you will *know* I am not making this point to suit my own purposes. In fact, Hite identifies the main male complaints about sex as first that women don't want sex often enough, and second that *women are too passive.* She shows that, while there are always exceptions, a major sexual dissatisfaction among men is that women do not take the initiative or participate eagerly: in short, show a degree of control.

After Hite had ascertained men's objections, she asked outright: "Do men want women to make the first advance?" Here are just three of the responses:

A very aggressive approach by my wife would really be great. For example, if she were to unzip me and pull out my genitals and start to play with

them or if she would start undressing me, I would love it.

I'd love to be a sex object at least for a while. I think I'd probably have a heart attack if some woman said to me, "You turn me on and I'd like to make love with you."

I often wish they'd be more up-front and tell me what they have in mind. I wonder if they tell Redford in advance.

Hite concludes that while "only a handful of men said they always preferred to be the aggressor . . . *Over and over again . . . men said they wished the woman would make the first advance.*"

Have *you* ever seduced a man? By which I *don't* mean have you led him on to seducing you—"I chased her till she caught me," as some wit once remarked. I mean have you ever been in a situation with a man where you had the upper hand? Have you ever felt *really* in control of the evening, from the moment you stepped out of the front door to the moment you fell asleep beside him? It's a wonderful, heady feeling. And, believe me, it works wonders for your sexual ability.

PART TWO

CHAPTER FIVE

Preparing For Orgasm

The only thing you really need to prepare for my program is one vital ingredient: *yourself*.

This chapter outlines a few considerations that will complement your training program. It is a long chapter not because there is a lot to do, but because every woman's requirements will be different.

How Does the Plan Fit into My Life?

The first thing to decide is exactly how you will relate the plan to your normal sex life.

You can, if you like, take a drastic approach and call a halt to your normal mode of operations while you follow the plan through step by step without interruption. This is the approach that most sex clinics would require if you chose to join a professional program. It is also, to my mind, the least productive and most awkward.

One of the great virtues of this plan is that it does not have a rigid structure. Make absolutely sure that you do not feel under pressure from yourself or your partner to get it over and done with as quickly as possible.

A much more profound approach is *gradually* to *replace* your ordinary sex life with stages from the plan. To put it another way, by the end of the plan, your new sex life will have replaced the old; but, in the meantime, you must concentrate on bringing them closer together.

I have said that this plan is suitable for every type of woman—those who have been in long-term relationships as much as those who have not. The long-term partnership will probably have the advantage of a greater sense of ease between you and less impatience to "get it on." On the other hand, if you are in a sexual rut (excuse the pun) you may find it difficult to initiate such a program. The method that the more routine-bound women who tested this plan found worked best was to make a number of different changes. If all kinds of new beginnings gradually start taking place in your life, then sexual change will not stand out to your partner so glaringly. Just about anything at all can fit into this category, depending on your circumstances: a new job, beginning volunteer work, a refreshing vacation, enrolling in evening classes, a new style of dressing, redecorating the house. Then, into the whirlpool of small changes you can introduce sexual change.

How Long Will the Plan Take?

If this were a magazine, I'd scold you for being impatient. But how well I understand the desire to see quick results! The best answer I can give you is: it depends. On your partner, on the circumstances, on the point you have reached before you begin the program, etc. But principally it depends on you. As with dieting, every woman is different, and it would be dishonest to try to put a time limit on any part of this program. Sooner or later, if you work consistently, you can make the break. One woman I know went from never having had an orgasm to a state where she could succeed 60 percent of the time in just four weeks. Others have taken the same time just to complete step 3.

But there is one thing I can guarantee: every small success will feel like an enormous breakthrough and will increase your confidence tenfold. To talk of the pleasure of learning may sound corny, but in this case it's also true. In the context of a good relationship, each small success is infinitely more intimate than if you'd both been able to do it perfectly from the start. And if you change your partners regularly, these pleasures will be all yours. *That I promise.*

Acknowledge Your Worries and Grievances

Because your sexual success is dependent to a large degree on your mental state, it is important to do whatever you can to build up your self-esteem and rid yourself of anxieties. Of course, what you find most suitable will depend on your own personality and state of confidence. But there are a number of possibilities and factors which you should bear in mind.

When you begin this program, it is a good idea to draw up a list of your worries and grievances about sex. If you are really honest, you may find the list gets very long indeed. I know mine was. Don't be disheartened. By the simple fact of acknowledging that anxieties exist, you have taken the first step to curing them. In fact you may find it helpful also to make a list of the things that you particularly enjoy about sex. You can then learn to maximize these.

Pay particular attention to what you feel might be inequalities in your sex life. Perhaps your partner frequently demands a blow job, but is unwilling to give you oral sex in return. Maybe he likes to come quickly, but doesn't put enough effort into your own satisfaction.

The following are just a few examples of what might appear on your list:

> **I feel uncomfortable making love with the light on.**
> **I dislike the look of my partner's penis.**
> **My partner always hurries through sex.**
> **I worry that he wants to get it over with.**
> **I worry that I'm not thin enough.**
> **I worry about not having enough lubrication.**
> **I always feel very slightly manipulated by him.**
> **I can never fully relax during sex, unless I am a little drunk.**

Once you've made the list, start to describe each of the entries in more detail. For example, if you have written "I dislike the look of my partner's penis," try to pinpoint what it is that displeases you. Is it really the penis itself, or is it perhaps the way your partner uses it? If he is pushy and aggressive about his lovemaking, a penis can seem a very threatening object indeed. Or is it that you don't like the feel or taste of it in your mouth?

Try to figure out the strengths and emphases of your worries and think how they might have originated. Give them an order of importance, and consider how to minimize their influence. If there are things that your partner insists upon but that you don't like, decide that at least for the duration of this plan *you will not do them.*

This may not be easy. But now is the time to make a stand. Be *strong* in telling your partner that you don't want to do sex in such and such a way: don't apologize, and don't be surly about it. Just be firm. Haughty, if you like. As one male friend of mine remarked:

There is actually something terribly sexy about a woman making it quite clear she knows what she wants and what she doesn't want. It makes her seem unattainable, not to be taken for granted, and therefore doubly desirable. I'd far rather have a woman who pleasantly told me in no uncertain terms that she *hated* performing oral sex, than one who submitted grudgingly.

It's amazing how your own enjoyment of sex can increase simply by eliminating the pressure to do something you don't particularly like. With any luck this will communicate itself to your partner, thus canceling out any resentment he may feel.

Before you get angry about his annoying habits, try being inventive in stopping them. If necessary pretend to like something that you know he dislikes; then negotiate a trade. Anger builds up tension and a combative atmosphere which you want to avoid just now.

Robert thought his designer stubble looked rakish. "Yes," agreed Jacqueline. "It rakes my face and breasts." He wouldn't shave it off. Jacqueline begged, glowered, and threw tantrums. No success. In the end, she found a beautiful cure for Robert's stubbornness: she stuck large Band-Aids all over her chin and kept turning up at his office. Robert was embarrassed into surrender—and they actually ended up laughing about it.

All in all the most important thing with your various worries and grievances is beginning to examine them. It is very important that you don't embark on any of the exercises pretending that this time everything will suddenly be different.

Preparing Your Body: Some of the Troubles

For the purposes of this program, "preparing your body" is really another way of saying "preparing your mind"—because our attitude to our own bodies can be one of the most bothersome disruptions to our mental relaxation.

Feeling at ease with your own body is the keystone to sexual fulfilment. Nobody who is embarrassed about being seen nude, anxious about being overweight, or encumbered with uncomfortable garments is going to have an easy time.

Now, I am aware that this is simple to say, but very much more difficult to achieve. Let's face it; most women worry to an uncomfortable degree about what they look like. Even the most exquisite woman is very rarely flawless in her own eyes.

It is, of course, a cliché now to observe that from birth women are undermined about their bodies. We are constantly exhorted to be slender, alluring, fragrant, beautiful, sultry-lipped, wide-eyed—whatever the fashions of the day demand. Glossy magazines scream glamour, and *Playboy* cover girls give us all a complex by displaying flawless breasts every issue. As one usually self-confident woman remarked: "Just going to work on the train each morning upsets me. There you are, surrounded by twenty editions of the 'perfect girl' and you're uncomfortably conscious that the man you're going to strip for this evening might also have been gazing at those oh-so-perfect breasts. Nice way to start the day, isn't it?"

The day I become president, the first new law I'll draw up is "cover boys"—so that a handsome hunk with a perfect body and huge, beautifully shaped penis stares at every man on the train each morning. That would certainly be an effective way of showing male readers just how withering to a person's self-confidence this constant reminder of the currently "desirable specimen" can be.

There are certain places where you expect perfect-looking women—*Vogue,* for example. But just to illustrate how all-pervasive this nonsense is, the drawing on page 72 is taken from a popular sex manual written by two long-standing and highly reputable American sex therapists—a manual currently recommended by most marriage counselors. And—would you believe—*on the facing page* the writers advise women to

> **pay particular attention to where your standards are coming from. . . . Chances are that your ideals have been adopted from television, magazines, and films in which the stereotypical woman is still *large breasted, slim, flawlessly complexioned, stylish, somewhat athletic, and barely twenty-three.* [My italics.] The image is as fictitious as an afternoon soap opera.**

Feminists, of course, urge that we should not try to please men, but learn to live with ourselves. Very good advice, if only we could take it. But what is sound in theory is often very hard to do in practice.

You may be lucky and feel perfectly at ease with your own body. If not, *for this program, the important thing is that you strike a balance*—that is, a balance between coming to terms with what you consider your less-pleasing features and making an effort to change them. You must strive to feel as relaxed as you can about your own body, without getting into a tizzy about how to change it.

Self-help groups and assertiveness training can be encouraging. I found that the most helpful thing was exchanging views with other women. Knowing the kinds of problem they suffer, problems one very often never sus-

pected, is a simple but effective counter to the "perfection" of magazine images.

"O! That This Too Too Solid Flesh Would Melt" (H Act I Sc II)

Shakespeare's lines were not meant literally, of course. After all, Hamlet had problems other than his figure. (He's usually played by a skinny little actor, anyway.) But they fit the facts here.

I grew up in the era of Twiggy and during those years never ceased to worry because I was not a sylph. I remember how, because Twiggy and other models of the period were as flat as an ironing board, I used to try to squash my chest with tight clothes; and, when that failed, I never went anywhere without clutching a large book to my chest.

It makes me hoot with laughter now. God knows what the neighbors must have thought!

What a ludicrous situation! I wanted to be "attractive," but I didn't have the knowledge or sophistication to realize that even if fashion dictates we all look like broomsticks, fashion rarely dictates men's sexual preferences (at least not from year to year). And I certainly didn't have the self-confidence to realize that I could live without every man's approval anyway.

Like most other women, I've been on and off diets for years. Some work, some don't, some are sensible, and some absurd. Now, whenever I begin a diet, I think of Christina Rossetti's lines:

Better by far you should forget and smile
Than that you should remember and be sad

It's not just an admirable sentiment, it's an extremely useful dieting tip. The surest way to fail on a diet is to be constantly preoccupied with it. Because they want to lose weight quickly, dieters cannot stop thinking about food. They're constantly mulling over what foods they're allowed, pining for those they're not, and every few hours jump on the scales hoping to see a difference. The outcome is—almost always—giving up. The results just aren't quick enough, and the continual concentration is exhausting.

So begin your diet, then "forget and smile." Don't let dieting preoccupy you. You *can't* change your shape in days, however maniacally you try. To see results will take weeks. Accept this fact. Draw up a list of your favorite dietary principles, the ones that suit you. That way you're far more likely to stick to them. Then forget.

In the Bedroom

Exactly what you wear in bed and how you arrange your bedroom are, of course, personal matters and not my business. However, for the purposes of this plan, let me suggest the following general points:

1) *Don't* wear a lot of makeup in bed—a small part of you will be worrying that it will smudge. Besides, the lights will probably be dim enough not to need it.

2) Dress carefully for bed. Wear something that you *know* you feel at ease in. New outfits—even sexy nightgowns—can prove uncomfortable in all sorts of ways. Dress flatteringly, but don't be afraid to cover yourself up. A man's long shirt or pajama top never fails to look attractive and is extremely comfortable. It covers you well if you feel you need that, but you can undo as many buttons as you choose, either at the beginning of the evening or as things heat up.

Don't get yourself done up like a sacrificial victim in the regulation black stockings and garter belt. Not only are they dreadfully uncomfortable, but you are shifting the emphasis onto *his* gratification. And that breaks one of the fundamental rules of my program. Besides, *he* doesn't *need* any help to climax. The last thing you want is to encourage him to do it more quickly. It's your turn now.

3) An attractive, comfortable bedroom will help your confidence. As I've said before, and will say at least another dozen times, don't underestimate the importance of apparently peripheral things like this. If your bedroom doesn't look right or makes you feel ill at ease, then change it. Don't compromise. But arrange it *to please yourself.* Don't get black silk sheets and a leopardskin rug because you've heard that Mata Hari was successful this way.

The chances are you'll feel self-conscious rather than sexy (and so will he). Spend a week or two planning and arranging it exactly how you've always envisaged it. Don't agonize about the color. If you don't like it as it is, choose another—it's worth the price of a can of paint to set yourself at ease. Hang up the pictures you like, and revitalize it altogether. Never mind the rest of the house. Make your bedroom a room where *you* feel comfortable, not a boudoir designed to kill.

4) From the point of view of this program, the most important aspect of your room is lighting. Make sure that you are comfortable with it and that it shows you up in the way you prefer. You should have a couple of table lamps, with 60- or even 40-watt bulbs—a dim, low-angled light with plenty of suggestive shadow is just the thing. If you worry about your appearance, then this simple arrangement of lighting will help to relax you. But remember: make changes only for *your* comfort. If you feel good as you are, don't fuss. Go on to the next section.

5) Most important of all, always try to arrange that your lovemaking takes place at your house, not his. (That is, of course, assuming you have a bedroom of your own.) You will feel more at ease in a room that is familiar. When you have to go to the bathroom, you will feel relaxed walking down your own corridor, with your own things handy. To use a rather macho analogy—but a useful one—in sports, the home team usually has the advantage.

Contraception

It is vitally important to the success of your sex life that you are happy with your contraception. Anxiety about getting pregnant is one of the commonest reasons for failure of orgasm. In fact, there are authentic cases where anxiety about getting pregnant was the *only* barrier to the woman's orgasm; as soon as she was really able to set her mind at rest, she found she could climax. I cannot over-emphasize the importance of finding the method of contraception that is *comfortable and convenient* for you and—above all—*safe*.

AIDS & Sexually Transmitted Diseases

It is vitally important to the success of your *life* that you are protected from sexually transmitted diseases. Don't forget, there's not only AIDS but also herpes, gonorrhea, and syphilis, to name just three of the many nasties.

As with contraception, even the faintest worry can spoil your chance of orgasm. I remember in the '70s, when everyone was on the pill, only dirty old men in raincoats were thought to use condoms. Nowadays, one of the very few benefits that have arisen from AIDS is that it is no longer uncool to insist on protection.

Don't wait for him to suggest it: carry your own condoms. And make sure you are absolutely familiar with *all* the safe and nonsafe sexual practices.

Successful Sex: A Golden Rule

This is something that, if it's unusual in your relationship, you may find hard to do at first. It is worth every effort to put it into operation as soon as possible:

If he does something in bed that you don't like,
say so at the beginning.

For example, if his method of rubbing your clitoris is painful, *don't* be shy about telling him. I know it's awkward; but, believe me, it'll be a thousand percent more awkward when he's been doing it like that for six months.

First, you don't want to have to endure it for six months, or until you know him well enough to mention it. It's no good for your nerves, and it's rotten for your progress during this program.

Second, if you tell him immediately, then it's barely embarrassing at all, providing you say so kindly. And, by setting up a situation of frankness, he may be relieved to feel that *he* can tell *you* that you're pinching his balls when you fondle them. Imagine that you'd been doing your special technique for six months, and then suddenly he tells you that it has been uncomfortable all along. The dreadful embarrassment! You might well feel that there are other things you've been doing wrong. Your whole confidence would be undermined. So, for both your sakes: *tell each other at the beginning*.

Third, it's wrong on principle. Start making little concessions, and you'll undermine your sense of control. Having the courage to tell him means you're well on the way to greater self-control.

Learning to Say No

Learning to say no to sex when you don't want it is really part and parcel of the section above. But, because it is so important for a woman, I have given it a section of its own.

Nobody has the right to demand sex from another person. It doesn't matter if they have been married for sixty years. Remember: if *he* didn't want it, he wouldn't *be able* to do it.

How you say no is important. Be pleasant, but firm.

Don't get into the habit of making excuses such as "head-ache"—*you don't have to make excuses.* It may seem simpler at first, but it's seriously undermining your position in the relationship. If you really have a headache, then say, "I have a headache." If you are tired, say "I am tired." Remember you are an *equal,* and you have the perfect right to say no if you don't feel in the mood. By making excuses, you are belittling yourself and your rights.

Also, it *is* hurtful to the man when he realizes (as he will sooner or later) that you are making excuses. It's hurtful because there is nothing he can grasp hold of—just an undermining sense of your dislike of sex, which is far more sinister and threatening than a truth that he can attempt to remedy. If you make a habit of being perfectly open, at least he has the opportunity to understand *why* you may not be feeling like it.

No Orgasm: To Tell or Not to Tell?

A major issue facing women who do not climax at all is: "Do I *tell* a new man that I've never had an orgasm?" As I have described at length in Chapter 2, this was a question I used to dread.

In general, my advice is not to mention it. As always, ultimately the details of your disclosure or secrecy will depend on you, your partner, and the relationship you have. If he is understanding and his concern about your lack of orgasm will help you, then, by all means, sit him down, begin with something like "Nobody else has made me get so close," and then spill the beans. But do it *before* you have sex, not during.

In the meantime, ensure that your sex life suits your requirements as much as possible. If you want more time during sex, remember that it is one of the standard fears of a man that he is too quick. Make use of this. After all, successful intercourse depends on mutual enjoyment—if it's not slow enough for you, then he hasn't met his side of the bargain.

In a long-term relationship, the question "Have you had an orgasm?" may well have cropped up already, and you will have your own way of dealing with it. It is really a burning issue only in a new relationship. I believe the best possible answer is to look critically at *him* and reply, "We'll see," thus shifting the emphasis from your ability to his performance. Never look flustered or guilty. Make it quite clear that the question is meaningless in the abstract like that—that the answer depends as much, if not a good deal more, on him as on you. Similarly, if, while you're in the middle of having sex, he asks, "Haven't you come yet?" with a nasty edge to his voice, give as good as you get— "With *this* performance?" Shrug the blame off yourself and onto him. Always remember; sex is a two-way relationship.

Alternatively, you can say, "No, I haven't had an orgasm yet, but don't let's get worked up about it." Try to avoid making it an issue of great importance at this stage. This leaves you free to pursue your own training as freely as possible.

Or you can fake an orgasm. If you feel the need to do this, then you should familiarize yourself with Chapter 14.

The Sexiest Days of Your Life?

Which part of the month do you feel most sexy?

Unlike other animals, women have the great advantage that they can mate and, a more dubious bonus, conceive all year round. However, some days in the month you will feel sexier than others. And since, in terms of sexual

79

arousal, we welcome all the help we can get, it's well worth noticing which days out of the twenty-eight you feel most sexy.

Shere Hite reports that most women who answered her questionnaire found that they noticed increased sexual desire before and during menstruation. Her conclusion, however, is the only incidence where I disagree with her. She says: "Women are generally more interested in sex during times of the month when they are not fertile. This agrees with findings of other sex researchers." To put it bluntly, sex researchers rarely agree about anything, and matters concerning the menstrual cycle are no exception. Whichever book you pick up seems to say something different, as a recent paper by two Canadians (Markowitz and Brender) confirms. Summarizing the research of the last few years, they note that some investigators have found the peak of erotic desire to be just after menstruation, others just before it. Others still suggest that it is around the time of ovulation; and some have found two or even three peaks. Then of course there are those who report no particular period of female sexual interest. (It's worth bearing in mind that while many women say they feel particularly sexy just after their period, this may be due to abstinence during their period, and not to any special "peak.")

Here's an excellent opportunity for us to do our own research. Note that the double digit—5.1—refers to the chapter and to the exercise itself, for easy reference.

Exercise 5.1 Using Chart A on page 83, keep a record of your monthly cycle. Day 1 represents the first day of your period—and so on. All I want you to do is mark with a cross those days when you feel particularly sexy.

Don't start racking your brains each day to try and work out whether you feel sexy or not. The chances are you won't be able to decide, and you'll end up confused. Forget about it overall, but on those days when you notice that you quite definitely *do* feel horny, then jot it down.

After a few weeks, you may well find that you notice a pattern. If so, it's silly not to arrange to see your lover on those days. Of course, if you live with your partner permanently, you may decide there is no advantage to knowing which days you are most likely to feel horny, since any time you do you can inveigle him into bed. But it's still worth doing the exercise, as any little piece of information about your own sexuality is helpful. You never know when it may come in useful in the future.

But, more importantly, you may decide to introduce new exercises from the plan on those days that find you at your most responsive.

Naturally I am not suggesting that the thing works like clockwork. Many of you will find there is no pattern whatsoever, and that doesn't matter one bit. Besides, our attitude to sex is affected by all sorts of other factors: our personal state of mind, our relations with our partner that particular day, how we feel about our own body, even the weather. In olden times, it was generally believed that desire peaks in the spring, when birds and animals are merrily breeding.

A friend of mine worked in the ticket office of a large opera company. A certain woman—large, red-headed, flamboyant—and her shy male escort used to visit the opera once a month. As they arrived, he always stood quietly nearby, while she went straight to the advance booking office and, after some preliminary counts on her fingers, requested two seats exactly twenty-eight days hence. Eventually this fell on a Sunday when there was no performance. Full of curiosity, my friend inquired whether the date really needed to be so exact. "Oh, well, a day or two won't make much difference," replied the lady, beaming, and then proceeded to explain that she was a married woman who lived out of town. On the pretense of staying overnight with a female friend, she visited the opera with her lover. "And," she concluded with a flourish, "it's so much more successful if I see that it coincides with the *sauciest time of the month.*"

You may not be able to plot your "horniest time of the month" as accurately as she did; but, like her, the secret is to become familiar with yourself. Learn to recognize those moods and sensations that indicate you are ready for sex, not because *he* decides he wants it, but because *your body is telling you.*

Chart A: Your Sexual Desire

Day 1 represents the first day of your period. Mark X if you feel noticeably sexy that day (regardless of whether you've actually had sex or not). Compare your results over three months.

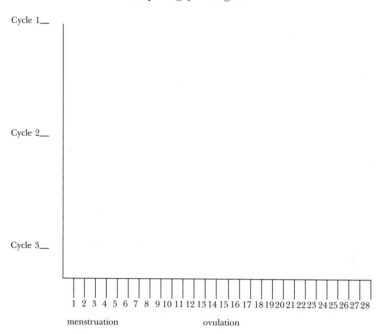

Exercise 5.2 Chart B is for recording your responsiveness on days when you have had sex. The idea is to evaluate your degree of arousal. For example, if on Day 1 you feel highly aroused, mark the appropriate level on the chart. Once you have gathered some data, you can compare your findings with Chart A.

Chart B: your sexual responsiveness

For every day that you have sex, mark a dot against one of the following levels on how you enjoyed the experience. If you achieve orgasm, encircle the dot.

Did not enjoy it
Medium quality
Good quality

83

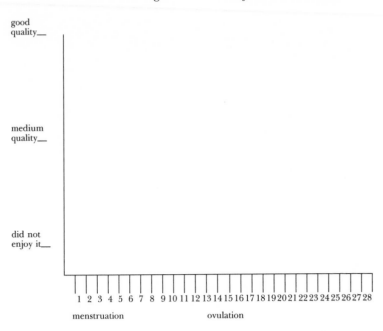

Supertip

Have you ever wished you could make love during your menstrual period, without all the mess? You can! Ask your doctor to fit you with a diaphragm. Whenever you want to have sex during your period, just put it in—not, of course, as a contraceptive (you *must* use your usual method as well) but simply to stop the blood.

If your flow is especially heavy, you may notice a little staining on the sheet, but nothing more. But take care when you remove the diaphragm afterward—do so over the toilet, or squatting in the bathtub—because the blood collects in the hollow.

Kegel Exercises

It has long been known that a well-toned vagina greatly increases the pleasure of the male, as the following somewhat exaggerated description of one woman's "nutcracker" technique, taken from a nineteenth-century French work *Tableaux Vivants,* makes clear:

> **I entered, I thrust—Ai'e! Heaven! What pleasure! The coynte of this chambermaid was like a rasp! This waiting-maid had that which Duchesses had not, that which I had vainly sought in Marquises— the CASSE-NOISETTE. It tightened on me, it pinched me. And these pinches and this vise, acting as a furious suction pump on my surprised member, astonished me. I enjoyed, I discharged, I sank with all my weight . . .**

The really good news, however, is that *women* also benefit.

In 1952 Dr. Arnold Kegel developed a series of exercises for women who needed to improve urinary control by strengthening the pubococcygeal or P-C muscle, which controls the size and tension of the vaginal opening. Much to his patients' delight, the exercises increased their ability to have orgasms; it also increased the intensity of them. By building up the strength of the muscle, they had increased the blood flow to it; and, since good blood flow plays a very important part in sexual arousal, the result was greater sexual sensitivity and responsiveness.

Kegel exercises are not as popular as they once were, but some sex therapists still recommend them. I am convinced that they work and that good muscle tone in the right place really does help orgasm. By carrying out some simple exercises, you can significantly increase the quality and the quantity of your orgasms. So, if you don't have a well-exercised P-C, then start working out.

First, make sure you know which muscle I'm talking about. The way to do this is by interrupting your urine flow when you go to the toilet—the muscle you use to control the flow is the P-C muscle. Make sure you've got the right muscle by checking that your control doesn't depend on your legs being close together. You don't want to build up big thigh muscles by accident!

Once you feel you've got a hold on the P-C, then start exercising it. The wonderful thing is that you can do these exercises at any time; in the middle of the supermarket or in the privacy of your own bedroom, standing, sitting, or lying. Like other exercises, they'll be a little tiring to do at first, but they'll quickly become much easier.

Exercise 5.3
1. Contract and relax the muscle. Do this twenty times.
2. Contract the muscle, hold for three seconds, and then relax. Do this ten times.
3. Contract the muscle while inhaling. Try to avoid contracting your stomach muscle at the same time. This will be difficult at first, but it becomes easier with practice. Do this ten times.

That's it. Do them three to four times a day. For both you and your partner, it will be well worth the effort.

The Questionnaire

Pick up a pen and a piece of paper. In just a moment, I want you to answer a very personal questionnaire.

It is important that you answer carefully and in detail. If

necessary, illustrate your replies with stories and anecdotes, even drawings. But, most important of all, you must answer with complete honesty. This is not always easy to do with such a sensitive matter as sex, let alone orgasm. So, if you're sitting in a public place, turn over to a later section of this book and come back to this part only when you're truly on your own. If you're with someone else who's insisting that you go ahead with it right now, then go ahead—and lie your soul away whenever necessary. But return to the questionnaire later, when you are alone, and tell the truth. It is important, for the success of this program, that you are fully aware of your own strengths and weaknesses.

Answer the questions in whatever order you like. Once you've finished, you can burn them, turn them into paper airplanes, or lock them up in a secret drawer.

Best of all, send them to me care of the publisher along with any extra details about yourself (e.g., age, where you live, etc.) you care to give. This will serve two functions. On the one hand, if you're anything like me, knowing that someone else wants to see them will make you answer the questions more fully and carefully. On the other hand, your answers will provide unique and fascinating material for a broad-ranging, international survey of women, sex, and orgasm, the like of which has never been done before. Of course, your answers will be treated in strictest confidence—in fact, you needn't send your name at all. And you can fictionalize the irrelevant, nonsexual details if you feel the need.

Enough of this delay. Get ready with your pen. Let yourself go!

INTRODUCTORY

1. Does the word "orgasm" embarrass you? Why?
2. Does the thought of other people knowing you have this book embarrass you? Which people and why?
3. Do you think orgasms are overrated?

MASTURBATION

4. How often do you masturbate? Does the frequency with which you masturbate vary? If never, why not?

5. Do you find masturbation enjoyable both physically and psychologically?

6. Do you have an orgasm every time you masturbate? Usually? Sometimes? Rarely? Give details.

7. What is the greatest number of orgasms you've had during one masturbation session? Do they vary in intensity? On the whole, how many do you need to feel really satisfied?

INTERCOURSE

8. How often (roughly speaking) do you have an orgasm during intercourse? Never? Rarely? Sometimes? Usually? Always? Think about this carefully. Don't overestimate: Remember, when I began, my reply to this would have been a solemn "never."

9. If never, do you feel that you have ever come close? Do you know what prevented you from getting there?

10. Have you ever felt desperate because there seemed to be *no reason* why you shouldn't have an orgasm?

11. Is it easier for you to have an orgasm during intercourse if you stimulate the clitoral area directly with your hand at the same time? Can you have an orgasm without added clitoral stimulation?

12. Do you ever feel physical discomfort during intercourse? Do you know why?

ORAL/MANUAL

13. Do you enjoy manual sex physically and psychologically?

14. Do you enjoy oral sex physically and psychologically?

15. Do you find it easy to have orgasms during manual sex? If not, why not?

16. Do you find it easy to have orgasms during oral sex? If not, why not?

17. Does the quality of your orgasm depend on what type of sex you have? How does orgasm from masturbation compare with orgasm from sex with your partner?

18. Do your orgasms vary in intensity? If so, can you think of any circumstances which influence the intensity?

19. Does the time of the month make any difference to your enjoyment of sex?

20. Are there any times when you don't mind about not having an orgasm, even if your partner does have one? When you *do* mind, how strongly do you mind?

21. Do you think your difficulty with orgasm affects your attitude to sex? Does it affect (insofar as you can tell) your attitude to men? To life in general?

22. Have you ever felt when you were unable to have an orgasm during sex that it was your "fault"? Why? Has your lover ever implied that it was your "fault"?

23. In your opinion, is it true that most women are less interested in sex than men? How about orgasm?

24. Do you think men dislike women who initiate sex? Should a woman be submissive during sex?

25. Do you think that women are more emotional about sex than men? How would you compare the average woman's sex drive with the average man's?

26. Are fantasies important to you during sex? What sort of fantasies?

27. Have you ever had an orgasm during your sleep—i.e., a nocturnal orgasm.

28. Do you ever feel self-conscious during sex? Why?

29. If you and your partner like different things during sex, how often do you have it your way?

30. Do you fake orgasms frequently? Sometimes? Rarely? Never? If you have ever faked your orgasm, why did you do it? If not, why not?

31. How easy do you think it is for your partner to tell if you've had a genuine orgasm or not? How easy do you think it would be for a person you'd been to bed with only once to tell?

32. Do you ever feel intimidated by the constant media preoccupation with sex? For example, that you may not be as sexually sophisticated or as skilled as other women?

33. Sex manuals often talk of sex and orgasm as profoundly beautiful and significant, one of the greatest experiences life has to offer. Do you ever feel that your experiences cannot match up to this ideal?

34. On the whole how useful have you found sex manuals to your lovemaking? Have you learned more from them than, say, talking to friends? When I say "learned," I mean learned things that you *enjoy,* not simply what you are "supposed" to enjoy.

35. Is there anything else you would like to add? Do you have any tips, however odd or silly, for women who have difficulty with orgasm? Any stories that are revealing or helpful?

CHAPTER SIX

Step 1: The Mirror

This program began the moment you picked up this book. The early chapters, apart from giving you information about myself and our—womankind's—difficulties with orgasm, were written to help you realize that you are not alone, and that there is an enormous amount you can do for yourself. You've already been asked to answer a questionnaire and write down your worries, fears, disappointments, and hopes for the future. You are starting to treat your difficulty with professionalism and determination. You are already on the path to success.

Now that you have finished the introductory part of this program, it is time to start training and begin the plan.

I have stressed the importance of feeling at ease with your own body. As this ease develops, so will your sense of relaxation about orgasm and your self-confidence.

So, let's begin with a splash. Lightheartedly.

Take an evening off alone, when you know you will not be disturbed. You must have at least two hours for this, preferably more. Turn on your answering machine and pour yourself a drink. Choose some music that really gives you pleasure. It might be gentle, soothing classical music. It might be a romantic love song. Or it might be a jazzy, exhilarating disco tune.

Now rig up a good-sized mirror. It needn't be a full-length one; it can be a wall mirror, a bathroom mirror, or whatever—just so long as you have a good view of your face and at least half—preferably all—of your body.

You will also need good lighting: not strong, uncompromising bulbs, but flattering, angled lighting, such as a photographer uses to get the best from his shots—after all, that's exactly how models get to look as good as they do in the pictures. If necessary, borrow some lamps from another room. Don't stint and compromise. If the lights still aren't right, buy a pink bulb or two.

Now you are going to fix your face, hair, and body exactly the way you like it. Begin with a long, relaxing, scented bath. Then sit down and make yourself look as delicious as you like. By that I do not mean how you would make yourself look if you were going out to an important dinner party. I mean how you—in all your dreams—would like yourself to look, regardless of other people. (I first used this step after I'd broken up with a man who had been particularly unpleasant in our parting argument. I went home, poured myself a strong cocktail, and flattered myself until I fell asleep.) Your ideal look may be sweet, demure, and romantic, or it may be outrageous and bold. Susan, for humorous example, has always had a secret longing to dress up as a barmaid in a Wild West film:

> **You know, one of those really curvy women who heaved their chests up into a merry widow. I bought one, but I've never dared wear it. One night I put it on, along with some fishnet tights. I noticed the tights had a great rip in them—then I thought, no, that's all part of it. I bunched together a load of petticoats and put on some high heels. I thought I looked great and was prancing around my apartment having a great old time. I ended up quite drunk as well—well, a *barmaid*, I *had* to . . . I wish I'd had a photographer there.**

I'd never have done that except in private. The next week, my best friend and I did it together. It was the best evening of the year.

Annie dresses in black:

All black. Then I powder my face so that it's ashen. It's really startling. I wish I had the nerve to go out like that.

In short, you are going to dress up as what you fantasize about being. If you want to pose as a scantily clad model, then go right ahead: to hell with your principled objections to girlie magazines—this is not for the titillation of some anonymous man, this is for *yourself*. Sometimes I like wearing high-heeled leather boots and a long, deep-blue velvet cloak that I bought a few years ago at an antique-clothes market, with a silver-topped cane and nothing else, and I imagine I'm going through the dockyards late at night watched by hungry longshoremen who haven't the nerve to approach. As I look at myself in the mirror, I try to give my stride just enough length to reveal my thighs.

Another friend of mine, an earnest New Ager who does admirable things like make her own sesame-seed bread and pick mushrooms in the autumn, pictures herself as a scandalous fur-clad socialite with silk stockings. She likes to talk out loud and dazzle the imaginary company. Once people open up about themselves, you learn the most curious secrets!

Roberta, who is distinctly large, explains that she likes

to come home, and just pose without trying to cover up. It's there that I can feel at ease with my size and don't have to be continually seeing magazines advertising the latest diet and all that nonsense. I like to stand with my shawl around my

93

waist, like one of those lovely island women you see in their reed skirts. They're always pretty ample, and not ashamed of it. I say to myself: "Bobby, this is what you've got. There's a lot of it, and you couldn't do with an inch less!"

Use whatever accessories you like—sexy panties, a shirt revealingly draped. Put on high heels to make your legs look alluring. You can pout, look over your shoulder, pose on a chair the way the *Playboy* models do—it's all for your own immodest satisfaction!

As you look in the mirror, don't think: "My God, I look sexy, I bet Harry/Sam/Steve or whoever would go for me." Instead you must make the fine mental adjustment to "God, I look good—period!" Gently shift your emphasis *away* from pleasing the man *toward* pleasing yourself.

As you stand there in front of the mirror, remove a garment or two. Let the shawl slip from your shoulders. Unhook a garter and roll your stocking top down. Undo the buttons on the front of your blouse. Gradually, little by little, reveal your body. Reveal it so that it pleases you at all stages.

I want you simply to enjoy watching yourself and your body in the mirror. Instead of your usual critical examination standing on the scales, pinching the inches here and there, and groaning about the cellulite on your hips, you are going to *pose* in the most alluring way you can. You need not remove all your clothes. Take off as many pieces as you feel comfortable with. Turn around and look at yourself from behind, over your own shoulder, with perhaps your shirt hitched up over one buttock. If you don't like the shape of your breasts, pose in such a way that they do please you.

While you are doing this, try rubbing a little body oil over yourself. You may or may not take to this: some women hate it (I'm one of them), but others find it a wonderful feeling, smoothing it over their breasts and the curve of their thighs.

If you have a camera with delayed-action shutter release (not at all uncommon nowadays, even on inexpensive cameras) take some photos of yourself. If not, simply try pointing the camera at the mirror. You won't get your face (because of the flash) but you'll probably get the rest of you. Best of all, do this exercise with a close friend and take photos of each other. If you feel nervous about what the film processor might think, use a Polaroid. Once developed, take out any you hate, get hold of a pair of vicious-looking scissors, and *ritually snip them to pieces*. Keep the rest where you can continue to look at them. They'll do wonders for your confidence.

The idea is simply to see yourself in the most flattering and attractive angle, and as somebody with *power*—the power to please yourself, to get what you want out of sex. It is no more than a frivolous exercise; but it is also the first step in gaining control over your own body.

And that's it.

Once you have indulged in your first celebration (it's most important that you don't neglect it), you are ready to progress to Step 2. Repeat this simple, undemanding, rather theatrical exercise whenever you want to.

CHAPTER SEVEN

Step 2: Masturbation

The foundation stone of your sexual progress is learning to achieve orgasm on your own. It is the easiest part, and it is also extremely pleasurable.

Masturbation is important to this program for two reasons:

(1) It trains your body to respond sexually. For obvious reasons, this is best done when you are alone and at your most relaxed. Once you have learned what your *basic* sexual needs are and how best to satisfy them, then you will be a long way towards your goal. You will then progress to experimenting with masturbation, learning a variety of ways of coming to orgasm in private. This is absolutely crucial, because

(2) Masturbation is a means of self-control, of exercising control over your own body. As I have already pointed out, control is a vital factor in your sexual fulfillment. By thoroughly familiarizing yourself with your own sexuality and experimenting with it, you learn control over it. At the end of this stage of the program, you will be able to masturbate successfully in many different ways. This is a skill you must acquire. It takes time and patience, but, once acquired, it will never leave you. You will be ready to continue your training in intercourse.

It is also worth noting that almost all professional sex

researchers and therapists recognize masturbation as a vital path to achieving orgasm during sex.

About Masturbation

Virtually all women who masturbate can do so to orgasm. Think about that: it's an amazing fact. Women who have never managed to have an orgasm with a partner can almost always have one on their own quite happily and quickly.

Even so, ignorance and guilt are *still* obstacles preventing women from masturbating. Ignorance is comparatively easy to overcome. Just read on! Guilt is more difficult. So, for the sake of those who find masturbation shameful, I want to spend a little time discussing the subject. I don't expect to help you overcome your feelings in so brief a space—from bitter experience I know that these feelings can run deep. I also know how infuriating it is when someone tries to solve your difficulties with a few trite phrases. But, as one who has herself experienced great inhibitions with masturbation, I do hope that I can help you to overcome those obstacles—by dint of patience, encouragement, and practice—showing that you too can learn as I have done.

Some women begin masturbating when they are children without even knowing what it is they are doing. Many stumble upon it later, by accident: they feel an urge between their legs, begin to rub themselves, and then, rather unexpectedly, reach orgasm.

My friend Laura discovered masturbation because she loved jigsaw puzzles:

Several years ago I was living in a miserable little apartment in Cleveland. I didn't have much money then, and instead of going out in the eve-

97

ning, I used to spend most of the time drowning my sorrows with 5,000-piece puzzles. None of the tables was big enough, so I had to spread them out on the floor. Since I always sat with my legs bent underneath, the heel of my foot pressed between my legs; and, as I reached out to get the piece I wanted—well, all I can say is that things started looking up. It used to give me a real thrill to do it when a friend came around, especially one of my roommate's numerous boyfriends!

Oddly enough, I recently came across a very similar method of masturbation, in Sai Kaku's *Life of an Amorous Woman,* but this time practiced several hundred years ago in Japan.

One day, as I was examining a fascinating depiction by Hishikawa of an erotic scene, I was stirred despite myself to the most intense excitement. I sought then to quench my amorous flames, now with my heel, now the middle finger of my hand. These were cold and insensible tools indeed for stilling my wanton lust, and soon I was overcome with desire for a more solid form of love.

Personally, I was quite old when I began masturbating —well into my twenties. I had never tried it, never wanted to try it, and hardly knew what it involved. I remember that around this time there was a great deal of fuss in the newspapers over a very advanced new sex-education film which showed a young woman—a schoolteacher, apparently—masturbating. I thought I knew the meaning of the word "masturbation," yet I had literally no idea what this woman could be doing to herself. The possibility of orgasm never entered my head. As I never saw the film, it was still a while before I found out. Sitting in a tree watching an extremely dull baseball game, I discovered with a rush of pleasure what all the publicity was about.

For several weeks after I made my discovery, I would make any excuse to go to bed early so as to enjoy myself. But every time I felt a pang of guilt. I worried that I was doing something wrong; not so much that it was wrong in the eyes of God—it was always my opinion that he would be little interested in my physical weaknesses, and concern himself more with my spiritual failings—but that it was wrong in the eyes of society and nature. It was such an intimate, self-centered sort of pleasure—all that concentration on your own satisfaction indicates something unseemly, rather like an obese glutton sitting alone with platefuls of caviar, Belgian chocolates, and vintage wine, and not sharing it with anybody. It had to be done in private, on the sly. I was constantly worried that someone would knock on the door, or peek through the curtains, or hear me breathing.

People rarely discuss masturbation openly and honestly. At best, the common reaction is giggling, sniggering, and blushing. At worst, the very word has a nasty ring to it—it not only sounds unpleasant, but actually derives from the Latin *manu-stuprare,* meaning "to defile with the hand." Added to which the slang term for a person who masturbates—jerkoff—is a particularly scathing term of abuse.

I know that when I walked down the street just after I had indulged, I felt that my guilt was written large all over me. If I happened to catch the eye of a passerby, I'd blush with shame, feeling like Mary McCarthy's heroine Libby in *The Group,* who

> **had a little secret; she sometimes made love to herself, on the bath mat, after having her tub. She always felt awful afterwards, sort of shaken and depleted and wondering what people would think if they could see her, especially when she took herself what she called "Over the Top."**

After a while, I forced myself to give it up. My goodness, what agony that was! I felt noble—occasionally. But then as soon as I began to dwell on my newfound virtue, the desire sprang up afresh.

We all know that sex talk can be embarrassing. But it puzzled me why masturbation should be a doubly shameful thing. After all, not only is it enjoyable, but it costs nothing, it harms nobody, and it is *safe*. Because we do not risk venereal disease from a partner, it should be viewed as a particularly *clean* form of pleasure; yet the atmosphere that surrounds it is one of murky nastiness.

Actually, I reckon it has a lot to do with men. After all, when men masturbate, they discharge semen. During sex with a partner, the semen is neatly "contained." In masturbation the wet, sticky mess is liable to spill in the most awkward places. No wonder masturbation is deemed "dirty."

Of course, here women have a great advantage over men: no mess, nothing to show. I've often roared with laughter over my friend Sam's tales of the difficulties that men have in relieving themselves.

Sometimes you simply have to do it, like it or not. But, believe me, it can be misery. First of all, an erection is no easy thing to conceal—it's terribly embarrassing when you're just stepping into a crowded train and bang, for no reason in particular, you get an enormous hard-on. There you are standing with your whatsit on a level with all those seated passengers, desperately trying to keep your newspaper in place. And there's no possibility of relieving yourself unobtrusively. In this respect, at least, I really envy women.

Masturbation still carries overtones of guilt and selfishness, maybe even pathos. In Victorian times, masturbation was considered the cause of everything from nosebleeds to insanity. Early in this century, the U.S. Patent Office even granted a patent for a masturbation alarm that rang in the parents' bedroom when the child's bed began moving in a suggestive way! And did you know that in 1898 an antimasturbatory food was invented which was supposed to take away all sexual desire: corn flakes!

Religion also tends to have a bad effect on women's tendency to masturbate, but despite what the minister might say, modern biblical scholars accept that there is no criticism of masturbation anywhere in the Bible. And what references there are, are to male masturbation, anyway. The real condemnation in the Bible is not of masturbation, but of wasting semen that might have been (on certain occasions) put to better use. Onan, for example, was killed by the Lord because "he spilled it on the ground" instead of impregnating his brother's wife Tamar, as God expected him to do. In short, he was condemned for practicing *coitus interruptus,* a primitive form of contraception. The fact that "onanism" is used today to mean "masturbation" merely reflects the biblical ignorance of the person who coined the term in the eighteenth century, rather than any disapproval on God's part.

For about fifteen years, since I sat watching the baseball game that fateful day, I felt ashamed of private sex. It was only in my early thirties that I started to feel the self-confidence to think the matter over slowly and analytically. *The Hite Report on Female Sexuality* was perhaps the greatest liberation. Here at last was a forum in which not just a few, but thousands of women were talking about subjects with complete honesty, free of the usual mockery and guilt. I discovered I was not in the least bit unusual in my private sexual needs; neither was I alone in having difficulty coming to terms with them. Over 80 percent of women in Hite's book admitted to masturbating, and the figure is even higher for men. Another person's expression of worries and reactions similar to your own can have a very therapeutic effect. Furthermore, masturbation is extremely good for you. *A woman's ability to have an orgasm during masturbation is widely regarded as one of the best ways of determining her sexual potential.* It is an indication of natural desires and sexual behavior; it is one of the ways in which your body learns about its sexuality and comes to terms with it; it is also one of the ways your body relieves itself of sexual tension that otherwise would have to find some less-pleasant outlet. Finally, as sexologists agree, it is a simple and highly effective means to help you to become fully orgasmic.

You'd be surprised how many times masturbation crops up in literature. The heroine in *The Story of O*

remembered seeing her friend Marion doing it. O had been only fifteen years old. Marion had sat in an armchair in a hotel room, with one leg flung over an arm and her head sagging to the other, caressing herself and moaning in front of O. She had once done it in her office and her boss had come in and caught her . . .

I remember one day in the library picking up a book that showed an old-fashioned advertisement for some complicated patent gadgetry involving leather straps and metal clasps designed to be worn at night by Victorian males to prevent nocturnal erections, masturbation, and wet dreams. Well, I thought, what in the world can be more *un*natural than that? I laughed out loud and suddenly felt a whole lot better.

Then I began to realize that animals do it—even out in the open. Standing around the primate cages (our distant ancestors, remember) at the zoo was an enlightening experience. I got so interested that I even looked it up in the library. In *The Sexual Connection,* that I finally summoned the courage to order from the request stacks, I read that

Female mammals in peak heat may resort to rubbing their sensitive genitalia rhythmically on the ground or on sharp projections, thus creating the stimulus of a penis jerking in and out. Female cats regularly resort to this kind of simulated intercourse. Female monkeys do it by tweaking their clitoris. Female talapoin monkeys finger themselves through their back legs, becoming more and more excited.

That same book goes on to talk about a bottle-nosed dolphin who lived off the southwest coast of England and used to sidle up to boats, "his massive pink penis rubbing against the hull." Once again, what could I do but hoot with laughter? Always a very liberating response.

Picking up some anthropology books, I learned that many tribes regard both male and female masturbation as vital to an individual's development. Amongst the Bala peoples of Africa, little girls masturbate first with their fingers and later with something called a "kankondenkonde" —a dildo made of manioc root.

More and more I became convinced that masturbation was a perfectly ordinary function, that virtually everybody does it, and that many more would happily do it if our culture weren't still emerging from the repressive sexual atmosphere of the last century. And this is certainly the view endorsed by almost every medic and therapist in the West. As for the East, they've known about these things far longer than we have. As one doctor friend told me, the only way that masturbation can be construed as harmful is when it causes guilt.

Now, whenever I think of masturbation, instead of imagining something sordid and greedy, I visualize those wonderful masterpieces by Goya: *Maja Clothed* and *Maja Naked,* or Titian's nudes. They really put me in the mood.

Unfortunately, there are still some women who cannot

get rid of superstitions. They worry that having an orgasm alone means they will be less able to do so with a man. Others find it depressing, lonely, empty, dirty, cheap.

That's old-fashioned talk. But, if you cannot rid yourself of it, think of it this way. In this program, masturbation is nothing more than a means to an end. Quite apart from being a perfectly innocent, safe, and satisfying pleasure, it's the route by which women can learn how to make the most of sex. Masturbation is the means to satisfying love-making with a partner—and when I say *satisfying* I mean satisfying for *both* of you. And, what's more, it's a great cure for insomnia.

How Do I Masturbate?

Of course, many of you will have been masturbating successfully for years and will have your own special method. You can skip this section and go to the next; "Improving Your Ability to Masturbate." Do *not* skip that section, however. It is pivotal to your success with this program.

For those who have never tried masturbation, let me suggest the following:

Complete relaxation is essential. Make sure you will not be disturbed. Disconnect the phone, close the curtains, shut the doors—do whatever is necessary to put yourself at ease and make you confident that you won't be interrupted. Since this is your first time, allow yourself at least an hour during which you know you can be alone. Some women climax very quickly; most women I've met who masturbate often can do so in less than five minutes, although they might continue again and again for a long time after. But when you are beginning, it is a good idea to allow yourself leeway; it helps you increase your relaxation, and you will probably find that like any other skills it takes a lot more concentration and effort to begin with than it will later on.

Put yourself to bed—alone, of course—and lie in a warm and comfortable position. If the thought of removing all your clothes makes you nervous, then leave some on. Above all, the most important thing is that you feel as much at ease as possible.

Open your legs. Begin by exploring your body very gently with your hands, up and down your torso, over your breasts, in whichever way feels most enjoyable. Now bring your hands down between your legs. Gently explore all around the area of your genitals, probing and rubbing, in whichever manner pleases you most. You will probably find that one area is more sensitive than another and by using your fingers to manipulate it you can produce a pleasant sensation that seems to extend vaguely into other parts of your body. It is not the same as the pleasurable relief one derives from rubbing or scratching some other part of your body; it is warmer, making you slightly breathless and perhaps want to tense your legs, and it is much more directly *pleasurable*. But don't worry. You'll know it when you feel it. It is quite unlike any other sensation. The more you play with your hands in that area, the more the sensation will increase. This sensation is not an orgasm, but it is the prelude to one. If you keep it up, sooner or later the orgasm will follow: a sudden, intense climax of the sensations that preceded. Some of you will climax in five or ten minutes; others—especially to begin with—may well have to work at it for twenty or thirty. You may have to try it for days or even weeks, but if you relax and do exactly what pleases you, you will succeed.

Your own hands are the most useful tool for masturbation: they are warm as well as uniquely sensitive. However, many women find that pressure from another object also produces satisfying sensations. When Nora began masturbating, she used to use a rolled-up sock which she pressed against herself. Susan always uses the arm of her teddy bear, which is soft and firm. The ways and circumstances in which women masturbate are legion. Some prefer a full and slow fantasy lasting an hour or more; others get straight to the point. Some get completely dressed up for the occasion; some look in the mirror while they do it, or rub their breasts. One woman I know stands in front of the mirror dressed only in a shirt and tie and places a vibrator sticking out between her thighs, like an erect male member. Then, by rubbing the vibrator she pretends to be a man masturbating. This gets her so worked up that she is able to climax almost without doing anything further. Another friend does it with her husband lying asleep beside her: "Don't laugh," she told me, "but I learned to keep in rhythm with his snores, so that he wouldn't wake up."

Perhaps the most dramatic masturbation scene is related in the Old French work of literature, *L'Escóle des Filles,* the story of

a king's daughter who had made for her a bronze statue of a man, painted flesh color, and furnished with a phallus of a more yielding material. This machine was erect and hollow, it had a red head and a small hole at the end, with two pendants in the shape of testicles, everything in close imitation of nature. When the damsel was inflamed by the presence of this figure, she approached the phallus and thrust it into her vulva, clasping the buttocks of the statue and drawing herself against it. When she was on the point of discharging she touched a certain spring which projected from the buttocks and the statue immediately squirted a warm and thickened liquor, white like pap, into the lady's vulva, thus satisfying her venereal desires.

106

Rubbing fur and feathers against breasts and inner thighs is another popular method, or sitting in a bathtub and directing the shower jet between the legs—even if it doesn't specifically lead to orgasm, it's useful preparation. Other women move actively against objects; for example, putting a pillow between their legs, or beneath them when lying down and using the effect of friction and pressure to lead them to climax. Some simply squeeze their thighs together. Most do a combination of things, depending on the circumstance and the degree of their desire. But the traditional way, with legs apart lying on the bed, seems to be the most popular—at least for novices.

Comparatively few women insert objects into their vaginas. This is for a straightforward reason: the pleasure center—the clitoris—is outside the vagina. Penetration into the vagina is not the primary stimulus to orgasm, although it may well serve to exaggerate the response induced through clitoral stimulation. I personally find the knowledge of there being a penislike object within oneself very arousing. Ginny has a special method:

I prefer to do it in the usual way, that is, lying down with my own hands. But just as I feel I'm about to climax, I push a vibrator into me. Having something to contract around is far more satisfying than doing it with an empty vagina. I used to need to do it three or four times before I was satisfied, but this way just the once is enough.

Finding a suitable object to insert is not easy. Try looking for one, and you'll begin to realize that the penis is really rather a well-designed object: it's not simply the shape, but the unique combination of firm yet soft, and warm as well. Objects that are too hard—like a hairbrush handle—are at best unsatisfying, and often painful. Carrots are clammy as well. Once, when I was in a hotel room in Bali, the waiter knocked on the door with a dish of exotic fruit. Feeling horny, I sized up the man—and decided his bananas looked more appetizing than he did. When he had shut the door, I unpeeled a not-too-ripe banana and used it to great effect. This, I later discovered, was a favorite with the harem ladies of the Orient, who rarely had sufficient access to a man to satisfy their needs, and therefore had to be inventive with bulbs, roots, and fruits—sometimes even with well-endowed statues.

While we're on the subject of artificial penises, some of you may decide to invest in a vibrator. They certainly have their uses, as Jessica found out:

> **They're the right size and shape—a lot better than most other things I can think of—but even so they're not perfect. A bit too hard and unyielding. After all, they're little more than a jazzed-up stick of plastic. I tend to buy a smallish size—for some reason, a vibrator always seems much larger and more "filling" than a real cock, so a big one can be uncomfortable.**

My own vibrator had an in-and-out thrusting movement which was pleasant. But buy a good-quality one: mine broke because the contractions from my orgasm proved too strong for the motor, and it seized up! If you are using a vibrator, try unrolling a condom over it. This helps the shaft slip into you more easily, and it creates a more realistic feel. If you don't go for that rather crude rubbery smell, try hunting out the new fruit-flavored condoms.

Nuns are traditionally supposed to use altar candles, although Apollinaire describes an episode with a young boy who hears his aunt confessing the following story to a priest:

> **"Once my sister said to me, 'Our maid uses up an awful lot of candles. She's obviously reading**

novels in bed, and one of these nights she'll end up setting the house on fire. You sleep near her, so you be careful!' That very evening, when I saw a light in the maid's room, here's what I did. I left the door open and tiptoed noiselessly into Kate's room. She was sitting on the floor with her back half-turned to me, and leaning towards her bed. In front of her was a chair with a mirror on it, and to the left and right of the mirror two candles were burning. Kate was in a nightgown and I distinctly observed in the mirror that she was holding something long and white and was manipulating this with both hands back and forth between her thighs, which were wide apart. She was sighing deeply and trembling all over. Suddenly I heard her cry: 'Oh, oh, aah! it feels so good!' . . . She explained to me she was doing it in memory of her lover, who had been conscripted into the army. . . . I left, but the spectacle had left such a mark on me that afterwards, Father, I couldn't help trying the same thing, and alas! I've often repeated it since."

Another important factor in masturbation is fantasy. So important, in fact, that I devote a whole chapter to it later on. Suffice to say here that working out your own particular fantasy can greatly increase your enjoyment.

Improving Your Ability to Masturbate

I have emphasized that learning to masturbate is extremely important for this plan. Learning to masturbate *with ease and flexibility* is the real clue to success. You must become extremely accomplished at masturbation; only then are you beginning to acquire control over your own sexual responses. Until you are a real *expert* at seeing to your own pleasure, you cannot be sure of having it with another person. Versatility is the keyword.

You are now at the stage where you are able to masturbate fairly easily. Having got this far in the program, I want to make an analogy. Think of yourself as a woman who has begun to learn a foreign language—Italian, for example. You have arrived in Naples, and after all your hours of perseverance with the Teach Yourself manual, you have mastered some phrases and expressions. You can manage basic things like ordering a meal in a restaurant or buying a ticket for the theater—providing people speak slowly. You have broken the ice, but now you must learn fluency—even when people speak at their normal speed, without the helpful gestures.

So it is with your sexual training. Like the language student, you must learn *fluency*. That is, you must learn to bring yourself to orgasm in a variety of situations. As the course progresses, you will see the wisdom of this advice more and more.

Those of you who have just begun to masturbate will, as I said above, probably find that to succeed requires concentration and effort. You must simply press on, masturbating regularly whenever you have the desire and opportunity. I have no hesitation in saying that you will find your ability improves quickly—provided, of course, that you are uninterrupted and in a comfortable setting. If you feel uneasy or guilty about devoting so much attention to your private sexual satisfaction, just remember that this is all part of a process; *it is a means to an end.* The end is to learn how to make your sex life with your partner more enjoyable *for both of you.*

How Do I Build Up My Skills?

There are two ways in which you build up your masturbation skills:

1) by gradually masturbating more frequently,

2) by doing it in a variety of different situations. This creates the sexual *versatility* that is so important to your progress.

To begin with, you will most likely find that after having achieved orgasm, it will be some time before you are ready to do it again. Gradually, as you develop, you will be able to do it more frequently, with less effort. When I first began, I could manage one orgasm a night at best, if I was lucky and if I concentrated hard. I'd masturbate as I settled down with a book. After a while I found that, with a half-hour break in between, I was ready for another orgasm to send me off to sleep. Now I am versatile enough to masturbate in virtually any position, several times in a row. Likewise with the *circumstances* of your masturbation: to begin with you will need "ideal conditions." Gradually, like the language student, you will grow accomplished in ways that were previously quite impossible.

Below, I outline fifteen different ways of masturbating that you can practice. In each case, it is not sufficient to do it just once and then move on. You must—*I simply cannot emphasize this enough*—grow adept. However, you need not do them all. You should aim to succeed with ten out of the fifteen. The important thing is that you feel at ease: never attempt any if the idea upsets you. But be as adventurous as you dare. If you can do the whole group, you're a star pupil!

These fifteen methods are divided into four classes. The classes are simply a way of grouping together types of masturbation that make use of different skills. If you can think of others, which exploit new positions and new circumstances, then by all means try them, too.

Of course, all women are different. Some of you may already be expert in some of the stages. The stages I have set out begin, roughly speaking, with the easier ways and progress to the more difficult and skillful. If you prefer, you may rearrange this part of the plan according to your ability.

I propose that you do each method at least three times before moving on to the next step of the program. *But don't stop then.* You must keep learning, keep exploring, keep training.

If some of the methods I suggest are really beyond you (doing it in a public place, for example), or you can't succeed however hard you try, don't worry. Versatility can be acquired in many ways.

The important thing in each section is to *try* them. Time and again I have seen the look of horror on a woman's face when I have suggested some of the exercises, only to find that when she actually tried them she enjoyed them. Sandra was typical:

> **When I saw I was supposed to masturbate in semipublic, I just collapsed. "You can't be serious. It's a joke." Rachel came straight back with: "Fine, laugh as much as you like. It's good for you. *But do it.* It's not so outrageous." So I did. And she's right. It's no big deal—and the exercises work, I promise you.**

If you don't reach orgasm, don't worry. Continue, relishing whatever pleasure you *do* give yourself.

Exercise 7.1 Lying down on the bed: on your back, using your hands. This is the basic skill, discussed above at length. Make sure, as with all the methods of class A, that there is no risk of your being disturbed, that you do not feel hurried, and that you can devote your full attention to the task. Do this first with your clothes off. Then do it with your clothes on, by slipping your fingers into your underpants and gaining direct contact. As a third alternative, try bringing yourself to orgasm simply by rubbing yourself through your underwear.

Exercise 7.2 Lying down on the bed: on your front or on your back (whichever you prefer) using an object. *Not* an object for insertion, but one for rubbing against, such as a rolled-up sock or pillow, or pulling a sheet back and forth between your legs, or simply moving against the mattress. You can rub something against *yourself* or you can rub *yourself* against something. As for all the methods of this class, do them both with your clothes on and with them off, direct and indirect contact.

Exercise 7.3 Sitting up in bed: arrange yourself comfortably, sitting at the head of the bed, with your back against the headboard or wall. Once again, use all the usual variations.

Exercise 7.4 Sitting in a chair: at first use a comfortable chair, perhaps with your legs splayed over the padded arms. Next try sitting in an ordinary, hard chair. Usual variations.

Exercise 7.5 Lying down on the bed: on your front, using your hands. You may find that pillows help you to get comfortable. If so, use them. This is important for building up your ability to have an orgasm in less-than-ideal conditions. Again, learn how to climax with clothes on and clothes off, with direct contact and indirect contact. (This is a difficult one.)

Exercise 7.6 In the bath: if you have a shower attachment, turn it on while sitting in a full bath, and direct the stream of warm water between your legs. You may not reach orgasm, but see how much pleasure you can give yourself from this method alone. After this, try masturbating yourself to orgasm with your hands, still in the bathtub.

Exercise 7.7 Standing up: my friend Sasha first masturbated standing up out of necessity. She was walking around an art museum and stopped in front of an extremely arousing painting—some voluptuous seventeenth-century woman in an intimate situation with a man. She simply had to satisfy herself, so she hurried down to the museum's ladies' room and locked herself in a cubicle. Wishing she were at home and not having to put up with such lousy circumstances, she lifted her skirt. Still standing and leaving her panties on, she inserted her fingers and began. It took a while for her to climax, but when she did

My God, I was nearly knocked backwards. Standing up, the pleasure travels all the way down both legs, like an electric charge seeking earth. A pretty good consolation for an otherwise not wildly comfortable position.

So there you are: if you've never done it standing up before, try it leaning against a wall. Progress to all the usual variations.

Exercise 7.8 Squatting down, kneeling: quite a difficult one. Try this both against a wall and in the middle of the room. Usual variations.

Exercise 7.9 Let your imagination run free: if you've got this far, you're really on the way. Now as well as variations of position, I suggest variations of speed. Try a slow session, long and drawn out lasting double or triple your usual time, all the while holding back your orgasm. This teaches you control. Now try to climax as quickly as possible. Try doing it twice in a row. See if you can do it twice within ten minutes. Try to do it as many times as possible, and keep a note of your record. Remember: it is part of the sexual pleasures of being a woman that not only can we have numerous orgasms in one afternoon, but that we can do it without fuss or mess. Learn to develop and exploit these advantages.

Exercise 7.10 Masturbation with a dildolike object inserted at the climax: for this you should masturbate in your usual manner, using only your hands, but have some sort of "dildo" handy—it can be a vibrator, a banana, a candle, whatever you feel happiest with. Then, just at the moment of orgasm, insert the dildo, so that you enjoy the unique sensation of climaxing around something.

Exercise 7.11 Masturbation using a "dildo" at all stages: this exercise speaks for itself. Basically, I want you to try to masturbate yourself using your chosen dildo-type object as a penis—that is, moving it in and out. I personally cannot climax this way, without some help from my hands, even though I *can* do so with a man—perhaps because the angle of the man's body provides some of the necessary clitoral friction. You may have more success.

Exercise 7.12 Masturbation in semipublic: the ideal place to begin this stage is the ladies' room at work, or possibly the ladies' room of a museum or of a train. Nobody can break into your cubicle, but you might have the thrill of hearing people coming and going next door. You must remember, also, that however discreet you are with your hand movements, your breathing may give you away. After all, you don't want to be cosily tucked away in the office toilet and be disturbed by your boss knocking on the door to ask if you have been taken ill and need some brandy.

Now progress to doing it under your desk at work or in the library. Don't faint at the very idea. Nobody will know you are doing it—it will be a totally private action. All you need to do is exert a little pressure in the right place. You can use a book or your handbag: be inventive. You can always stop if it gets too dangerous. You'll find it a great deal of fun, and surprisingly easy on days when you're feeling especially horny. I used to do it in the movies, where I could unzip my jeans unobserved. Best of all if it's a sexy film. Even if you can't actually bring yourself to orgasm at first—keep trying.

This is not simply a flippant exercise. It is an important part of the plan that you get accustomed to relaxing sufficiently to enjoy orgasm in situations that involve others. It is part of the process of breaking down that invisible barrier between you alone and you with somebody else.

CLASS C: MASTURBATION IN PUBLIC!

Exercise 7.13 For the really daring: if you can do this at will, then you're a star pupil. Of course nobody will know what you're doing. The trick is to exert some pressure where it matters, without seeming to be doing so. I've done it on the subway timed to the rhythm of the train. More than once I've taken my cue from Laura, and used my heel while kneeling on the floor talking about the state of the nation. But if you're at this stage, you don't need me to point out the possibilities. If you really can't face it, don't. The truly important thing is to manage the methods up to this point with ease.

CLASS D: IMPROVING YOUR TIMING

These exercises simply concentrate on your timing.

Exercise 7.14 How many times in a row can you masturbate? Use your favorite position. At first it won't be more than once or twice. Later you'll progress—I know one woman whose record was thirteen times in one session. I thought that was pretty good going, but I recently read of another woman who managed 134! Beat that!

Exercise 7.15 How quickly can you masturbate? At first you'll be slow. Later you'll succeed in under ten minutes; and when you're really good, you'll be able to come in a very short time indeed. This exercise depends a great deal on how horny you're feeling to begin with.

The Golden Rule is: KEEP IT UP. As you progress through the rest of the program you *must* continue to practice, improve, and vary your masturbation repertoire.

CHAPTER EIGHT

Step 3: Intimacy Without Orgasm

By thoroughly mastering Step 2, you've made excellent progress. You will have greatly increased your control and understanding of your own sexuality. This constitutes a major advance towards your goal—don't let go of it! The lessons learned in Step 2 should be regularly rehearsed so that they give the best support for your progress through the remaining steps. Keep practicing masturbation in the old positions and circumstances and build on your skills by continuing to invent new ones.

Step 3 provides the link between having an orgasm on your own and having one with the aid of a penis. How does it do this? Quite simply by insisting that you don't bother about orgasm at all. Just as in Step 1, I want you to concentrate only on the feeling of nonorgasmic pleasure you can derive from sexual activity.

The advantage of this stage is that while it is sometimes difficult to initiate intimacy without orgasm, once it becomes a regular feature of your relationship, he won't want to give it up.

Sexual Relaxation

Don't we all remember the following scene? It's been a tiring day. You feel worn out and run down. Your boss has snapped at you, the supermarket has run out of a vital ingredient for dinner tonight, and to crown it all the phone rings just as you step into the shower. Your partner is due any minute. You are looking forward to a quiet evening of affectionate intimacy and understanding.

For a while things go fine. You embrace. You sit down to a tempting meal. He compliments you on the food. You bring on the dessert. The wine is helping you relax, but you're still a little edgy. You both move to the sofa, he puts his arms around you, nuzzles your neck, and lightly strokes the neckline of your dress. Very pleasant.

But all too soon those little gestures of affectionate physical contact become *foreplay*. You wanted to have emotional comfort and the security of physical closeness, yet it quickly becomes a matter of sex. And sex, of course, concerns orgasm.

The evening may end in one of several ways: either you get mad and have a fight; or you tense up, he doesn't notice, you go to bed, he has a whacking great orgasm and you feel foul; or you both tense up, you have sex, and neither of you enjoys it.

I have great sympathy. Maddening though my first husband could be, he was gentle in bed. After we split up, it was a shock to find out that this quality is rather rare, and that too many men seemed to be the "quick unzip, fumble and shove" type. I, who was wanting a warm, sympathetic relationship, felt that genuine intimacy was impossible. As far as my lovers were concerned there seemed only two types of closeness: nice, consoling talks about what to buy for supper, and a good screw. Nothing in between. This disheartening period of my life made me realize that however enjoyable you find sex there are times when the *inevitability* of it is distressing—times when one wants sexual understanding and appreciation without the passion and demands for penetration and climax.

So for this step I want you to establish intimate situations with your partner in which, before you even begin anything, there is no question of penetration and orgasm.

These situations can be of two types: either occurring during special times set aside by mutual consent, or as a result of incidental encounters between the two of you whenever mood and occasion warrant them.

There are three great advantages to these situations. First, by eliminating even the possibility of orgasm, they encourage mental relaxation for you and help to put you at your ease about your ability to have an orgasm. Learning to relax during sexual encounters is a crucial part of learning how to have or improve your ability to have an orgasm. Second, such situations tend to be more gentle, slow, and appreciative than intercourse, and this will help you to grow increasingly at ease with both your sexuality and his. Finally, they help develop a sense of control and sexual self-esteem, because *you* are employing the man for *your* purposes.

Setting Aside a Special Time

If you have an understanding partner, it is worth asking him outright for such a session. Arrange a period of about thirty minutes to an hour when you can lie down together on the bed undisturbed. At first do this when you are both dressed. Explore each other's bodies, pass your hands under each other's clothes, but do not concentrate on the genital region. Caress, touch, massage, kiss, rub, stroke, play, snuggle up, murmur sweet nothings, hug, entwine, fondle—do it continuously or do it intermittently while you talk about other things. Be physically intimate however you like, but do not progress to penetration or to orgasm for either of you.

Try to establish this sort of involvement as something usual in your relationship. After a few such encounters, start taking off each other's clothes. In order to ensure that you don't go too far, it's a good idea to begin such sessions just before an important engagement like a party, meeting, or picking up the children from school. Obviously, it's not something you want to do to the exclusion of full sex altogether, but it is a form of restrained contact that you should try to establish as common. Do it as often as you feel comfortable.

Even if, after a few minutes, you find that you would like to progress to intercourse, *don't.* You must be strict with both yourself and with him. If you feel that he may be able to bring you to orgasm this time without intercourse, or that you would like to try, or he seems to be getting it into his head that he'll make you climax, STOP. Thoughts about orgasm during these sessions are not only to be avoided, they are forbidden. These are purely times of relaxed intimacy.

The main difficulty with planned encounters is not so much *your* desire as *his.* Men are not used to such things; they tend to make the mistake of thinking that penetration (followed by their orgasm) is the goal of any sexual circumstance. Even if your partner does not, or you manage to enlighten him and free him from his prejudice, *you* may continue to worry that *he's* still wanting to get it on. Or you may feel the very fact that the situation lays so much emphasis on lack of orgasm that orgasm continues to be a disturbing issue.

There are a number of ways you can deal with this problem. Since the important thing about this step is that *you* do not feel that you are expected to have an orgasm, you can make him climax before you begin the exercise. That over with, go on as before. Not only does he owe you the attention you demand, more importantly your worries about satisfying his desire have been removed. Alternatively you can make it clear that if he does this step with you as required, you'll satisfy his needs later in the day. The better he does it now, the greater his attention and expertise, the nicer his reward. Bargains are annoying in sex; but, realistically speaking they can be useful. As Ovid remarked, "Bribes, believe me, buy both gods and men."

Finally, even if you have successfully arranged and agreed upon sessions, don't skip the following—unplanned encounters can be extremely arousing.

Unplanned Encounters

If you do not have a sympathetic partner, then you may have to rely on your own ingenuity to create situations where you can have intimacy without orgasm. It probably won't be easy to set up special sessions. If it is, then have them whenever you can. But in either case, you should also take advantage of situations which have not been specially planned; with a little subterfuge you can arrange them fairly frequently.

Chris tells her story:

> **I didn't feel I could ask Alan for arranged sessions. At first I was quite stumped as to what to do —then I thought of the television. I waited till I knew there was a film he was really eager to see, then set to work. All the time he was engrossed in *Death on the Nile*, I had my hands around his prick, and I made sure he had his in my panties. It's all a question of getting the balance right: he must like doing the two things equally. A detective film's the best because he can't get too carried away or he misses the plot.**

The best way, as before, is to begin arousing him just before you have to do something important. If you're both about to go to a party in the evening, wait till he's showered and shaved before you start to feel around. It needn't last long, but it must be understood that if things progress too far, you'll miss the event. For this reason, a dinner-party engagement is obviously better than an ordinary cocktail party, as there's not so much scope for being late. If possible, continue to give and receive a little more sexual attention during the party: under the table in the semidarkness. But again, there should be no prospect of orgasm. Or take advantage of the darkness in a movie or theater, or on a train at night.

Ideally, you are ready to progress to the next stage when you have managed to introduce these nonorgasmic situations as a familiar and accepted part of your normal sex life. But you may move on sooner, once you have learned to accept them yourself as something reasonable and enjoyable without guilt or tension.

As an added bonus, I might point out that I've found such unplanned encounters *unfailingly* popular with men, and the end result is usually greater willingness to do what *you* want. For this reason, I think you'll find that these escapades—especially those that take place outside of the home—will become a permanent feature of your relationship.

CHAPTER NINE

Step 4: Masturbation With a Penis

Now that you are thoroughly familiar with masturbation, it is time to progress to Step 4. For this stage, you *will* need a partner. Either (as we discussed before) a willing and compliant partner, or a partner who remains in blissful ignorance of the fact that you are in the midst of a training program.

The idea is to develop your newfound versatility, to use it as a stepping-stone to obtaining orgasm *in coitus*. Put simply, in this chapter you will learn—in four stages of increasing penile involvement—to masturbate with a penis.

Step 4 is the pivotal stage in breaking through that invisible barrier, because in it you are getting accustomed to the idea of another person, while still retaining essential control.

As with all stages in this program, it is important that you are thoroughly comfortable and relaxed. Therefore, as before, spend a little thought in setting the scene first. Read through Chapter 5, "Preparing for Orgasm." Decide what you will wear during the evening, and later in bed. Adjust the lighting in your bedroom so that you are quite comfortable with it. If you feel comfortable, you will be relaxed.

The Starfish Position

Some years ago I was invited to a book-launch party at a friend's house. I can't remember what the book was—a first novel probably, because there was a young man hanging about looking humorless and artificially bitter—but there was a lot to drink and the fun went on until quite late. Somehow I ended up with a very suave individual—and that night, thanks to a great deal of inventiveness on my part, the Starfish Position was born.

This is a sexual position that I have found to be ideal for the exercises in this step. I would like you to practice it—as far as you can—alone at first. When you are thoroughly familiar with the idea of it, you can join with your partner.

Begin by making the bed comfortable.

Now lie on your back, with your partner to your right. He lies on his *left side*. Then you lift your right leg up and slip his right leg beneath it and over the top of your left, so that his thigh crosses between your legs with his penis able to slip into you just beneath. It sounds hideously complicated in print, so I've included a diagram of it—in practice it's as easy as pie.

The Starfish Position has many advantages for the woman on this program:

1. You are lying on your back in your *familiar masturbatory position,* so that you feel quite comfortable.

2. It is an extremely relaxing position, physically, because you are not having to support yourself or your partner. It is also versatile: try it out and you will see that while retaining the essential position, all kinds of slight variations are possible.

3. It is mentally relaxing and allows you plenty of freedom to concentrate on your own needs. The only essential point of contact with your partner is the genital region. Because he is lying off to one side, he need not gaze into your face, which frees you from the obligation to "look" a certain way—beautiful, enticing, loving or obviously aroused. *Don't underestimate the distracting power of this kind of thing.* Furthermore, you do not have the "diversion" of kissing, and the other usual attentions of sex—of course these are all an integral part of making love, but at this stage of your learning they can disrupt the task in hand. On the other hand, if you do wish to kiss and fondle, it is quite possible to do so by simply maneuvering your torsos closer together.

4. It is the *most private* position, allowing you great independence and freedom from embarrassment. If you're shy about your body, you can pull the bedclothes up around you.

5. It allows you *free access* to your own genitalia—you may rub yourself without impediment and *probably without your partner knowing that you are doing so.* This depends on precisely how you arrange his leg across yours.

6. His leg serves as a means of providing pressure *where* *you want it.* It is easy to adjust the position slightly, here and there, without very much disruption.

7. It is difficult for the man to insist on his pace. If he does try to speed up too much, exert pressure from your legs to slow him down. If you want to speed him up, try moving your hips.

8. Last but not least, the Starfish is an excellent way of getting sex from a sleepy or drunk partner who looks like collapsing. His active involvement is minimal, and the position is remarkably comfortable.

In short, the Starfish Position gives you the means to be entirely in control of the situation, and of yourself. I found it was ideal for the progression from masturbation to intercourse. In fact, after I had recommended it to a number of women, I found that there were even more unexpected advantages. Susan explains:

> **I use it most in the mornings. You wake up, feeling sleepy and lazy, you haven't brushed your teeth, the remains of last night's mascara may well be creeping where it shouldn't, but you're as horny as a unicorn. . . . Neither of you has the energy to climb on top. You just sidle up to each other, and it's as easy as pie. After all, you don't always feel like kissing first thing in the morning!**

I personally think it's perfect for the morning after the night before, when you may have a hangover. If you decide that the guy you met last night doesn't look so good in the daylight, you can still get him to please you without all the intimacy.

Nancy was having trouble with her husband. Not because she couldn't climax, but because she just felt *bored* with sex. I suggested she try this position for a bit of variety. Three weeks later she wrote to me:

> **The Starfish is great, and I don't just mean for the reasons you gave me. I got my husband to try it, simply as a new position to give a bit of pep to our lovemaking. What you didn't tell me is that the type of pressure exerted on my pussy is unique. A sort of gentle *nudging*. Not insistent at all, and so mild that I hardly noticed it at first . . . Never mind his penis going in and out like a piston, it's the soft bumping against my pussy that makes me come. We do it all the time now.**

All in all, to date I have not come across another position which provides so many of the private advantages of masturbation, but also allows for maximum stimulation of both partners *in coitus*.

However, it is not essential that you use the Starfish for the exercises in Step 3. I *recommend* that you do so, but I don't insist. What I do insist on is that you try it. Don't dismiss it out of hand. It's far too valuable for that.

Stage One: Exciting Yourself with His Penis

The first stage is to pursue your normal masturbation, but with a small amount of penile involvement. You are going to practice stimulating your clitoris and the area around it with the head of his penis. Just think of it as another example of masturbating with an object, as discussed in the last chapter. Except, in the place of a sock or a teddy bear, you're now using a penis.

The following instructions are given on the assumption that you are both in the Starfish Position. If for any reason you are not, you must be inventive in adapting yourself to the circumstances.

Instead of inserting his penis right into you, have him

rest it just inside the lips of your vagina. Then reach down between your own legs and gently grasp the shaft of the penis. Rub the head of it softly back and forth around your clitoris and the entrance to your vagina. You will find this a very delicious feeling, for the head of the penis is the softest, gentlest part. *Do not* attempt penetration. And don't even think about orgasm; just lie back and enjoy the pleasurable sensations this manipulation produces.

After you have been doing this for a while, bring your own hands into play and try to bring yourself to orgasm in the usual masturbatory way that is familiar to you. But even if your own hands are doing most of the work, don't lose hold of his penis. If you find that you cannot keep hold of it, or it is too distracting for you to do both—don't worry. It doesn't matter in the least. Simply continue and practice this step until you are able to bring yourself to orgasm *with the help of the penis*. However long it takes, continue until you have achieved this.

While you are exciting yourself with his penis, try to think of it as no more than an extension of your solitary masturbation sessions. As far as possible forget about him. If this sounds sacrilegious, all I can say is that this is a means to enable you to love and appreciate him tenfold. For the moment you must think of yourself.

And what is he doing all this while? Encourage him to lie back, close his eyes and relax altogether. Perhaps ply him with a drink beforehand. If he gets restless, moisten your hand and at the same time as you are pleasuring yourself, contrive to rub the shaft of the penis itself. This should ensure his enjoyment, especially as he is having to do none of the work. If this technique is new to your partner, you may well simply have to be inventive in how you initiate it. Jessica's husband was a very traditional guy, with reservations about anything new. She cured him of that by taking him to a blue movie; and later, when he was feeling mellow, suggested they try some of the positions they'd just been watching. Which, of course, led on to trying the positions *she* wanted. In fact it's usually enough just to make it quite clear that you enjoy it. If not, I find that, contrary to the popular saying, flattery gets you *everywhere*. Try something like "Your penis is so attractive, but I never get to really *feel* the head."

This stage has a special benefit for you because as the shaft of the penis is not employed, there is much less risk of the man ejaculating before you are ready. The very knowledge of this should reassure you, as we all know how off-putting it is when we feel that your partner is about to come too soon.

A very sleepy man is useful in this respect. If he comes home and collapses on the bed, take advantage of the situation. Get undressed, climb into bed with him, and remove his pants quietly. Now massage his penis until it is sufficiently erect to be of some use to you. With a little ingenuity, you should be able to maneuver yourself into position. Now lie back and have fun.

Jackie quickly became an expert.

> **The first time I tried this method, it was as good as masturbating; only I got an extra kick because as well as using a real penis *I* was the one fully in control. . . . The trouble was, I got to like it so much that I had to think of ways of getting Pete immobile. Before then I used to get really angry when he got drunk and fell on the bed. Nowadays I'm always plying him with drinks, and when we go to parties together I usually offer to drive home, so he need have no inhibitions. . . . Once we get home I slide into bed beside him, open my legs, and rub myself with his prick.**

Louise finds that this method works well on those occasions when she's suffering from insomnia and he's not. "Very few men will object to being awakened in the night for this sort of treatment," she insists, as long as you don't choose a night when he's got to get up early the next morning.

If you find you cannot climax, it is probably because the penis—being attached to a hunk of man—does not have quite the same flexibility as your usual masturbatory tool. (Hubby is not so obliging as Teddy.) Never mind. Transfer the penis to your other hand and masturbate in the usual way. Do it just as you have been practicing. It's now that your program of masturbation practice comes in really useful. You must start learning to achieve orgasm with the *help* of his penis. It doesn't matter if his penis does not do much of the work—just masturbate with you as you are used to doing. But make sure the p where nearby.

The important thing is that gradually you ing from pure masturbation into a sex-with-p tion. And, because you are learning, practi menting each stage as you go, you are teachi skill that you will not lose.

Continue until you are adept at this stage

Stage Two: Having an Orgasm with a Penis

The next stage is to introduce a little more penile involvement. You will bring yourself to orgasm, either as above or in your normal masturbatory way; and, as you climax, *insert your partner's penis into your vagina*. This is a parallel to Exercise 7.10 in the chapter on masturbation. Get yourself and your partner all set up, as before. As you rub yourself, make sure the penis is nearby. The moment you feel yourself go beyond the limit—that wonderful uphill surge towards orgasm—maneuver yourself onto his penis as far as you can. Even just a little will do; it needn't go in all the way. As you come, savor the sensations of your vagina contracting around it.

Congratulations! This is one more vital step in breaking down that invisible barrier between orgasm alone and orgasm with a man. If you can establish a situation of penis-related orgasm, followed by his penetration, then you are well on the way to full acceptance of him. But it's not enough to do it once. You must practice until it is no longer a hit-or-miss affair, but something you *know* you can do.

Remember, as always, it is essential that you do not neglect your private masturbatory program. If you have a setback with this stage, never mind. Return to Step 2 and *practice, practice, practice*. It will come out right in the end.

If Step 4 is occupying all your nights (although there's no need for this—as I said earlier, you should ensure that the plan fits into your usual sex life in the most convenient, least stressful way, not that it takes over), continue practicing Step 2 during the day. You must continue to improve and explore. With each new stage, you must make sure that your learning is backed up by appropriate skills in private masturbation.

Now that you are so far along, and you are beginning to become an advanced pupil, you should continue to masturbate with an object for insertion.

Stage Three: Masturbating with an Immobile Penis

Now is the time to make a significant advance. You are going to encourage the man to insert his penis gently *all the way in*. Let him lie very still, while you gradually masturbate to orgasm in whatever way you find most effective. This will probably be rubbing yourself just above the clitoris, as other types of access will be restricted by his penis.

Of all the stages of Step 4, this is the most important, and it is worth spending some time to perfect it. In fact some women (those with very uncooperative partners) have found that it is the only stage out of Step 4 that they need to do. I personally find it the most enjoyable, and once you've initiated it with a man he usually falls for it too. As Gina pointed out:

It's a very easy way for him to prolong sex before he ejaculates, so he doesn't have to feel guilty about being a trigger-happy male. He can do it in any way he likes without having to worry about giving me enough clitoral stimulation. It's wonderful! Much more intimate.

Of course, the Starfish Position is ideal because it leaves you freedom to move your hands. On the other hand, if your partner is on top of you, in the Missionary Position, it is still relatively easy to reach down. Obviously, you will have to encourage him to stay still.

Simply continue to masturbate yourself in whatever way you like, until you climax—however long it takes you. It is an *extremely* pleasurable feeling.

Thomas likes to give "a helping hand." He says he finds it really sexy to reach down, sometimes holding my hand as I'm doing it and following the movements. I think it can be quite helpful, too, not only because it means that you're both playing an active role but because it makes your partner's involvement greater—breaking down the barrier and all that. I'm slower when he helps, because I still feel a bit embarrassed, but I'm much easier about it than I used to be.

Stage Four: Masturbating with a Moving Penis

Now that you have succeeded in climaxing with his penis immobile inside you, encourage him to have intercourse with you gently *while you masturbate*. It is a sort of double act: he moves slowly in and out while you rub yourself.

Once again you may find it helpful to forget that you are with a partner. Relax, close your eyes, and think that you are alone, practising one of the masturbation exercises of Step 2. The importance of Step 4 is that it appears sufficiently close to Step 2 (masturbation) to seem but a small progression, and therefore a very possible one.

You may wish to stop him now and again—either to prevent his reaching orgasm too soon, or to catch up yourself. If you have difficulty, try a different position. At this stage the important thing about positions is that they give easy access and are comfortable. Later on, when you are more accomplished, you will think of positions as exciting ways to expand your sex life.

Thelma, who helped me to do some research for Chapter 16, offered the following advice:

At first the problem was that Ray always came too soon. But I quickly realized that I *enjoyed* this. We begin by my rubbing myself while he moves in and out. After he comes, he just stays there in me. I go on rubbing myself until I come—which I always do very quickly. It's a halfway house between this stage and the previous stage, but a good one. Often, I think, you'll find that the mere fact that you don't have to worry at all about his timing anymore can greatly help you with your own.

If, despite trying a variety of positions, you still have difficulty, don't worry. It takes time. It will get better. Hite reports that of women who do climax easily, most require direct clitoral stimulation. Keep on with the plan and you will get past this stage as well. Clitoral stimulation is something both of you can easily work on to improve, as the next steps explain. But for the moment recognize that you have come a long way.

You are well on the road to success.

A Word of Advice

I am well aware that the four separate stages of Step 4 may seem confusing at first. Trying to put physical actions into words always appears to add complications. In fact, they are very simple. When you are familiar with the program and have read it through once or twice, the steps will clarify themselves.

As I have already said, in a sense Step 4 is the crucial part of the whole program because it brings together two situations: sex without a penis and sex with a penis. For this reason, it will probably take longer than the other steps. Practice each stage fully until you are thoroughly familiar with them and they are no longer hit-or-miss affairs.

Ideally, you should aim to accomplish the four stages as I have set them out. But only if you can do so easily. If your partner is uncooperative, it's far more important that you take advantage of natural situations as they present themselves. Just don't give in too easily!

Therefore, if you have the opportunity for Stage 4 don't pass it up just because you haven't accomplished Stage 3. Be flexible. To perfect each stage—so that you are *certain* that you can achieve it—is more important than the order of the stages. And, if your options for this step are really limited, confine yourself to Stage 3.

And remember, just as with the other steps, once you have completed this one, *don't forget about it.* Keep making sure that you continue now and then to bring yourself to climax in the ways suggested here.

How Do I Get My Partner to Cooperate in Step 4?

This, of course, is the million-dollar question. So let's divide the answer into six possible categories:

1. Request
2. Suggestion
3. Guile
4. Bribery or bargaining
5. Threats
6. Give up and find yourself a new man

1. Requesting is straightforward. If you have a good relationship, sexual openness can only benefit you both. The only debatable point is do you reveal *why* you want to do it this way, or do you simply say you like it—period. That's up to you. My advice: if you feel uncertain keep your plans to yourself for now. You can always reveal your intentions later. I think it's better to feel quite comfortable about your progress in the program before you bring him in, if you have any suspicions that his involvement might not always be helpful.

2. By suggestion, I mean lots of "mmmmms" and "aaaaahhs" when you "happen" to find yourself in the position you want. So he puts two and two together and thinks he's discovered a way to be a great lover: before you know it, he's suggesting it himself.

3. By guile I mean such wiles as manipulating a drunk or sleepy partner.

4. Bribery or bargaining involves a trade—you agree to do such and such if he agrees to the position you want. As I've already mentioned, this strategy is not ideal, but it is definitely not to be sneezed at for tricky situations. Handled with a bit of subtlety, it can be made into a personal joke between you.

5. By threats, I mean threats to walk out on him/go home to mother/run off with the next-door neighbor, etc. This may sound alarming, but if he so doggedly refuses to help with what gives you special pleasure, then you're justified. Besides, you may find that if you really stand your ground he'll give in, especially if you've never tested him that far before.

6. Option 6 is the most drastic of all, but it might actually be your best bet. If agreeing about something so fundamental to a relationship as sex is impossible, ask yourself what you *do* have going for you as a couple. Quite frankly, if he's not prepared to be a little accommodating to your needs, then you don't have a great future together. Sounds brutal? Ask yourself: Would he keep *me* on if I didn't give *him* what he wants? If the answer is no, *don't hesitate to set the same standards for yourself.*

CHAPTER TEN

Step 5: Intercourse

Now you are going to attempt to have an orgasm with you partner's penis inside you, but *without* masturbating yourself.

In theory, this is a big step. In practice, it's a small and manageable progression. First, by continual exercise and learning, you have been gradually narrowing the gap between this and the last step. Second, by virtue of having had to train your body and its sexuality up to this point, you have become much more understanding of your needs, and much more in control of your responses.

Remember, at this stage you are still not expecting orgasm to happen immediately. Just as you practiced and practiced Steps 2, 3 and 4, so you must thoroughly practice Step 5 until you succeed. And, as always, you must support your program by continually repeating and improving on your earlier successes of the last two steps.

Once again, you must prepare carefully. Take out your pen and paper and think hard. What inhibiting factors are there in your lovemaking? Be ruthless: write them *all* down and think about how to correct them. Are you still making little concessions to *his* pleasure at the expense of your own comfort?

It's not easy to identify inhibiting factors. Sometimes they're so subconscious that we can't spot them at all, yet they spoil our pleasure. With practice your self-awareness will increase. And when you do come across something that bothers you, put a stop to it. Or try striking a balance, even if you have to invent something he does that annoys you. *Selfishness* is all-important—at least for the time being —and that is an attitude many women find difficult to exercise in the bedroom.

Lori, for example, was making good progress in the program, but she was conscious of a nagging anxiety. After careful thought, she realized that she always felt slightly self-conscious with the light on.

It wasn't a significant thing, really. I mean I wasn't messed up about it. My figure's not bad, but I have stretch marks all round my stomach and thighs. Mark's told me loads of times that he doesn't mind, and the crazy thing is I even believe him. But they went on bothering me. I *knew* I wasn't 100 percent relaxed. The problem was, that Mark said he hated making love in the dark. Sometimes I simply insisted we turn the light off, but it made me feel mean, and therefore I couldn't relax then either. So I evolved a plan where I simply made love clothed—either partially or fully. I bought one of those sexy one-piece garments made of black Lycra stretchy stuff that unbuttons at the crotch. Now, if Mark wants the light on, I wear that. He unbuttons the buttons, and of course I *have* to keep it on—that's part of the pleasure. So we're both satisfied. He seemed to find that a real turn-on. It gave me a lot of confidence.

Light is a very common anxiety—and not only because we worry about our bodies. I once made the mistake of faking a really strong orgasm with a boyfriend when he was feeling low about his work, just to give him a boost. He came home one sunny afternoon and was moping about the apartment. I felt sorry for him and inveigled him into bed. His lovemaking was no great shakes at the best of times, but I would have earned an Oscar for my performance. My artifice did wonders for his morale (he was promoted a month later), but nearly destroyed mine, because it gave him a disconcerting desire to watch my face so he could see how much satisfaction he'd given me. After that he started insisting that we make love with the light on. In those days I hadn't learned to be inventive. It killed my desire stone cold.

Suzy was worried about the noises she made during sex:

I couldn't help it; if I was enjoying the sex, I'd make a noise—groans and moans. I was so embarrassed about it. For one thing, we lived in a prefab bungalow, and the walls were really thin. Our next-door neighbor used to give me some looks. I also worried that Pete would think me disgusting and animallike, but I couldn't stop. I put the radio on, but that never worked because quite often half my mind would be on what the DJ was saying. Once in desperation I even tried chewing gum, but Pete objected (can't say I blame him). Then one day he put his hand in my mouth, and instead of making noises, I sort of sucked and bit on that. I began to feel his fingers probing around my tongue and lips and pushing in and out—he was too excited to notice until after. We do that quite often now. Otherwise I use my own hand, or the edge of a pillow, and I try to make sure I have him in positions which make this gesture less obvious.

While on the subject of noise, let me say that the *Kama Sutra* takes love noises very seriously and lists eight classes of sound that women utter during sexual pleasure: hin, thundering, cooing, weeping, phut, phat, sut, and plat. So next time, instead of feeling self-conscious, try to work out which category yours falls into.

Which Position?

Once you are quite certain about details such as lighting, clothing, etc., it is time to consider which sexual position you are going to use for Step 5. Here are just a few comments on the suitability of the sexual positions for the plan. I have deliberately included only the standard ones (with, of course, the exception of the Starfish) for the simple reason that these work best for orgasm. It is another outrageous sex myth that bizarre and exotic positions equal explosive sex. They may do for someone highly experienced in orgasm, and they probably pep up a routine-bound sex life. But for a woman wanting to improve her orgasm skills, they can be fatal. Besides, you'd have to be double-jointed to manage some of them. A curiously large number of the ancient Oriental guides to sophisticated lovemaking were written or painted with a complete disregard for human anatomy. Unless you can devise a position that for some reason particularly suits you, my advice is to stick to the basics.

The Missionary Position

The Missionary Position has long been out of fashion. "Boring," "old-fashioned," "redolent of male dominance" are just some of the descriptions used to denigrate this old favorite. Personally, I'm a great believer in it, at least for the early learning stages of Step 5. It is extremely comfortable for the woman, who (unless the man is very large indeed) can lie back without the need to support herself.

141

And it is comfortably close to the familiar masturbatory position you have been practicing. You need have few worries about your figure, as you will be largely covered by your partner.

Also, it is not simply the *insertion* of the penis that is pleasurable, but the clitoral stimulation. In this position the angle between the man's body and his penis is such that his pelvis can rub against your genital region where it is most effective. Only in rare cases—such as Joyce's—is this undesirable:

> **It's all in, out, in, out, and not enough shake-it-all-about with Steve. All the concentration, in other words, is on my vagina, and the result is that not enough gets to my clitoris. I wish he'd slow down a little and not plunge quite so much, but spend more time moving his hips over me and putting pressure on my clitoris.**

Another slight disadvantage is that your partner controls the rhythm and pace.

If you are in the Missionary Position and find it difficult to climax, try this: using either both hands or just one, clasp your partner around the buttocks as if it were you who is causing him to move in and out. First, you will be modifying his rhythm and pace to suit yourself. But, more importantly, it gives an excellent *illusion* that you are in control. The fact of your seeming to use him as a tool puts you back in the familiar and reassuring position of masturbation—that is, you controlling yourself, rather than someone else controlling you. Again and again this tip has helped women who are having trouble climaxing.

Man raised   If your partner, instead of simply lying on top of you, pushes his body up above you slightly by resting on his elbows or (if he's got the strength and inclination) on his outstretched arms, this will put greater pressure on the clitoral region. This may require a bit of experiment to get it right because too much pressure can be painful on the skin, both for you and for him. But once you succeed, you'll soon realize the benefits.

Man on top with legs apart   Instead of his legs between yours, try it the other way around, with you keeping your legs together and he opening his. As with "man raised," this is a useful variant because it provides a good deal of friction on the area around the clitoris.

Woman on Top

Many sex therapists suggest that this position is helpful for women who find it difficult to climax. I don't necessarily agree—it depends very much on your circumstances. Being on top gives the woman a certain amount of control: she does the rubbing, sets the pace, and stops when she feels like it. And because *rhythm* is a crucial feature in learning to climax, this is important.

If by being on top you can really give yourself a sense of control, marvelous. But, as this position is something of a male fantasy, too often it ends with the woman as being manipulated by a lazy man to his own preferences. Don't let this happen. If necessary, make an exaggerated play of dominance and control by pinning your lover's arms above his head, so that he *has* to submit. For Judy, this is what gives her sex a certain thrill:

I don't think I'd get any pleasure out of sex if I thought I was "submitting." I want him to know who's boss. I like to get on top, sink myself onto him, grind away for a few delectable minutes, then stop and deliberately watch him beg for more. Then I put my fists on his chest and lift up and down slowly, pumping him, so that his chest gets white with the pressure I'm putting on, but he doesn't dare move in case I stop moving. Sometimes I slap him. He tries to slap me back, but I grab his arms and force them down. Also I can make him suck my tits, which sends shivers down my spine—like aah!

On the other hand, there are certain disadvantages to the woman-on-top position. Thrusting up and down on top of a man can be very tiring indeed—moving more against gravity than a man on top would be. This is particularly true if, instead of lying on the man, the woman remains upright—as that infamous turn-of-the-century writer and lothario Frank Harris explains here:

She got up smiling and straddled kneeling across me, and put my cock in her pussy and sank down on me with a deep sigh. She tried to move up and down on my organ and at once came up too high and had to use her hand to put my Tommy in again; then she sank down on it as far as possible. "I can sink down all right," she cried, smiling at the double meaning, "but I cannot rise so well!"

Sitting on the man has the added disadvantage of diminishing clitoral contact. This can be counteracted if he uses his hands, but otherwise it's only by lying on top and making sure of sufficient clitoral friction that you can get the necessary amount.

The woman on top may have the added distraction of

having to support herself on her arms. And many women feel they must go to great lengths not to seem too heavy and "unladylike." The position can be actively uncomfortable in certain situations: for example, if the man is very skinny and the woman has long legs. In this case, placing pillows beneath his buttocks usually remedies the situation.

Above all, if you are self-conscious about your breasts, don't attempt it. However much *he* appreciates your assets, if *you* feel awkward about them, then don't choose a position which puts them in the limelight. "I used to feel that I was the lone contestant in a topless-bathing-suit contest," remarked one woman. "It made me nervous as hell." It's little anxieties like this that can spoil your chance of orgasm. Later, when you are more accomplished, these details will no longer be so important.

The Starfish Position

The many advantages of this position have been discussed in Chapter 9, so I shall not repeat them here. I can only add that both of you have pretty equal control; neither one of you is "dominant." If you sense that your partner is close to climaxing, you can pull out or stop. Also, it is the most private of the positions, and best if you feel sensitive or nervous about yourself.

Side by Side

The Roman poet Ovid, who wrote copiously on the art of love, found this position a great favorite:

There are a thousand modes of love; a simple one and least fatiguing is when the woman lies upon her right side, half-inclined.

Though not an easy position to achieve, this has the advantage that it avoids the heavy macho thrusting sometimes associated with the Missionary. It has another major advantage: because there is constant likelihood that the penis will slip out, you can ensure a very slow, careful pace. If your partner is a fiery stallion who won't slow down, try this one. There is, however, a reverse side to the coin: unlike women, men sometimes come much more quickly if they're having sex in an unusual position, so you'll have to break him in. Furthermore, if he has to concentrate about keeping his penis in, this isn't much help for rhythm and your concentration.

Man Enters from Behind

In my experience women vary greatly in their opinions about this position. The most common response is "I like it, but it's hard to climax this way"—because there is very little contact with the clitoris. In fact I know several women who have learned to climax readily in a variety of positions, but never in this one. Others, like Loretta, find it highly enjoyable:

> **I like the slight anonymity of this position. You can really feel the man, but you also feel unencumbered. I love Rob dearly, but sometimes I need the freedom of nobody in front of my face, watching me, bearing down on me. I do it with me kneeling and him kneeling behind me.**

Nora has another slant:

> **What I like about it is it's a great means to make love in odd situations, without all the bother of getting undressed and into bed. I'll give you an example.**

Jack and I were recently staying with friends in the country. It was a hot summer's day, they'd made a barbecue, and we were all milling about feeling relaxed. Their garden is huge—lots of ponds, trees, and bushes. I got fed up with talking, so I went for a walk. I'd just knelt down to look at some flowers when Jack came up behind me. He'd seen me slip away and followed. He lifted my skirt and began stroking between my legs. He didn't even bother to take my panties off (I was worried someone might surprise us) but just pulled them aside and did it to me, while I carried on picking flowers. Definitely one of the best fucks I've ever had. I could see the rest of the party through the hedge.

This position has all the obvious advantages of privacy, but it's not so good on control. You can, however, reach behind and hold his hips if you need to. It has the obvious disadvantage of making your ass the focal point, although it's worth pointing out that in a kneeling position all asses —unlike breasts—look pretty much alike, so this shouldn't disturb you!

You might find with appropriate masturbatory practice that this position becomes more satisfying, particularly if you put a pillow beneath you to enhance the friction. Some women, I know, can have an orgasm this way, although I've never managed it myself.

My Partner's Penis is Too Small!

I wonder just how many thousand times each year despairing women utter this exclamation. Perhaps understandably, many women who are unable to climax feel that their lack of success must be due to the size of their partner's organ. I have to admit I'm tempted to answer, "Yes, only with a great whopper can a woman be truly satisfied," simply to reduce some egos a little—certain men seem absolutely obsessed with huge penises. That might make them a little less critical of women's sexual parts. However, the general consensus seems to be that size makes little difference to a woman's ability to climax. So next time you're confronted with a modest little weenie, don't despair. The vagina is very elastic and therefore accommodates itself nicely to organs large and small.

This *doesn't* mean, however, that individual women don't have distinct preferences. I, for one, make no apologies for saying that I prefer a good-sized article—circumcised if possible. It may not make you have a better orgasm, but it gives you a nice full feeling. On the other hand, some women can feel affectionately protective towards a small penis. Men have the advantage that, if they go for big-breasted women, they can see what they're after before they commit themselves. Not so for women if they happen to prefer a large penis—unless you're a nudist. And even then, a limp penis gives little indication of the size it will eventually grow to.

But one thing that reading a lot of erotic literature will tell you—it's *men,* not women, who are obsessed with enormous cocks. If you're not getting satisfied, it's far more likely to be *how* your partner is using his penis than how big it is. Besides, a too-big one is downright uncomfortable.

The subject of different-sized organs leads me on to another point. That is, that several women I've met succeeded in having an orgasm with a lover, where they had consistently failed with their husband (or regular partner). Since the organs in question were all pretty much the same size (and, in two cases, the lovers' were smaller), this is good evidence that it's the use a penis is put to rather than its dimensions that counts.

In one case, the relationship with the lover ended, and the woman felt uncomfortably guilty afterwards. I tried to encourage her to regard this lapse not as the end of the world, but as the beginning of a new life with her husband —a life with successful sex. Since her experience with her lover proved that she could climax, why not think of it as something positive for her husband, too? I urged her *not* to confess: oh, how rarely are those confessions justified— most of the time they serve to make the guilty feel less guilty, while the innocent partner suffers. Instead, she put her attention into repeating the orgasm with her husband: a far smaller step than she originally thought. Remember, orgasms don't belong to your partner, they belong to *you*. And, if you have lapsed, what you learn with another man you can offer to your permanent partner. The chances are that your sex life will improve so much that you won't want to do it again with someone else.

Two Vital Ingredients of Successful Sex

The two vital ingredients of successful sex for women who have trouble climaxing are often overlooked or taken for granted: namely *rhythm* and *concentration*. I have said again and again that in the early stages of learning to have an orgasm, it is simply not enough to "lie back and relax." Until you are really proficient in achieving orgasm, you must put a little thought and effort into it.

Rhythm: The Snakes-and-Ladders Principle

The man's failure to maintain a consistent and acceptable rhythm is one of the chief causes of women's failure to climax. Of all the women I have spoken to about difficulty with orgasm, all agree that a consistent rhythm in the lead up to orgasm is crucial. If the rhythm is broken, then the gradual ascent to orgasm is also broken. Many of you will have discovered the use of rhythm while masturbating: there are days when you feels so horny that any pressure makes you come, but often as not to reach a climax you need to establish a steady *rhythm*.

Men are much the same, although in general less sensitive to changes: when you rub his penis with your hand, you establish a rhythm he likes. The trouble is, in *coitus*, when he's doing the thrusting, it's *his* rhythm and not necessarily yours. Susan takes up the point:

> **I've been in situations where I'm wild with desire. He tries all sorts of crazy things—does it hard, then soft, then very slowly—you name it. I've been so worked up I could scream. But if I want to actually *come* I have to get him to establish a consistent rhythm, a pace if you like, for at least five or ten minutes beforehand.**

In fact Susan was so interested that she called it the Snakes-and-Ladders principle.

> **I think of it like this: orgasm is to be found at the top of a long ladder. Each rung of the ladder is equally spaced, and each rung represents a thrust of his penis—a steady rhythm. I can get to the top of the ladder [orgasm] only by going up each rung one at a time. You *must* have that even rhythm for the lead up. If he breaks the rhythm, he jumps *you* onto a snake—and you go all the way down again. The funny thing is, if he does break the rhythm, I can still find it terribly sexy but I know I won't climax from it. Then you're torn between urging him on and begging him to go back to the original.**

Of course I am not saying that this particular need for a consistent "ladder rhythm' will apply to all women. Some of you may reach orgasm more readily from varied movements. But I have found that, in the great majority of women still learning to be proficient in orgasm, this is the case. The more accomplished you become, the less the "ladder rhythm" will matter.

Exercise 10.1 In order to fully understand rhythm, I want you to try the following. Begin masturbating *at a period when you don't feel particularly sexy*. As I mentioned above, when you feel very horny, you will have an orgasm readily, so the exercise will not help you with your difficulties. But if you have to work hard for your orgasm during masturbation, the chances are you'll have to find a rhythm. Work yourself up until you are close to climaxing —then stop and alter the rhythm. Do the same thing again, but this time lose the rhythm altogether and simply rub yourself randomly. You'll soon begin to see the importance of rhythm—and, more importantly, to gauge the one that suits *you*. Then, when you go back to sex with your partner, be similarly conscious of which will help you best.

And, just to show how important tempo can be, let me quote from Dr. Sofie Lazarsfeld's *Woman's Experience of the Male:*

> **We are reminded of the popular custom in Thuringia. There a couple will not marry until the boy and girl have sawn through a log together. If the rhythm of their movements agrees, the marriage takes place; otherwise the association is broken off.**

The essential partner to rhythm in achieving orgasm is *concentration.*

Concentration

Believe it or not, concentration and relaxation are companions—not opposites. We are all aware of how many climaxes fail because women get distracted by worrying about the children, or the neighbors banging on the wall, or the thought of being late for work. One woman gave me the following wonderful description of misery:

> **You can love any man in the world, but you can't make love to a man with a mobile phone. It just doesn't work. You've got him all relaxed and your hands are gliding into each other's pants when "ring, ring." Okay, so business is business. The world can't wait just because you're dying for a screw. That settled, you strip off his trousers and he goes down on his knees and unzips yours and begins . . . "ring, ring." Hell, you think, the world can't be *that* desperate; but it is, and you wait, and then he drags you to the floor and fits in nicely and gently and begins to move real slow.**
>
> **"Ring, ring."**
>
> **And so it goes on. Forget it. You might as well fuck a telephone booth.**

These are obvious distractions. But are you aware of just how distracting *local* elements can be? Elements that you'd always thought of as part and parcel of your love-making. The need to return his kisses, to keep fondling his penis, to answer his sweet nothings, to indicate your responsiveness when he fondles you. Of course these things *are* important; people don't do it merely because of need, but because they wants to return kisses, to fondle and exchange murmurs of devotion and delight. Sex is emotional, not a cold race for orgasm. Furthermore, these pleasant "distractions" help to create the mood, to make us feel aroused. All this is true, but the fact remains that for the woman inexperienced in coital orgasm, these "distractions" can be disruptive.

To return to the foreign-language analogy—it's work for a United Nations interpreter, listening and translating *at the same time*, not a job for a fairly new Teach Yourself student, who still needs a bit of practice. When you first start to learn a language or to have an orgasm, you have to think very hard and concentrate on what you're doing. Later, when you're fluent, it comes more readily, often without thinking at all. I'm not saying that you should strip away these "distractions" altogether, but I am saying that while you are training yourself, you should sometimes try to suspend them. You'll be able to return them tenfold if, later, you don't have the worry of orgasm to bother you.

The next time you make love, I want you to relax and, as far as possible, *forget all about your surroundings*. If necessary, even try to forget about *him*. Close your eyes and concentrate on one thing: what he is doing to you, the movement of his buttocks, his penis sliding in and out. Or choose a favorite fantasy and concentrate on that. Ruth's worked well, but she also had reservations about it:

> **I like to think I'm on a small island, lying on the beach taming one of the natives between my thighs. But I wonder if it would be better if I concentrated on the fact that I'm really on the floor with my boyfriend Harry? Surely fantasy detracts from concentration and therefore from orgasm?**

Fantasy does not detract from orgasm if used correctly; it is an extremely important *aspect of concentration*. The fantasy acts as a stimulating focus for your concentration. The thing that matters now is *your sexual needs*, not the natives, or your boyfriend. Therefore use whichever *works*.

At this stage, don't worry about pleasing him: if you are

busy nuzzling his ear, or showing what a skillful lover you are by tickling his balls and sucking on his tongue, chances are that your concentration is draining away. Besides, the last thing you want just now is to help him any closer to *his* orgasm.

Julie also had reservations about concentrating too much on her own pleasure:

I have a fairly new boyfriend, and I feel I have to show him some attention and appreciation while we make love, or he'll think me unfeeling. And I couldn't possibly *tell* him what to do.

Of course you must show some attention and appreciation in a new relationship. The idea is simply not to let this get in the way of your own training. The trick is to make telling him *what* to do part and parcel of telling him that you like what he is doing. For a start, we've seen that men dislike unresponsive women. But there are two ways of being responsive. You can either say baldly, "I love what you're doing," or you can *imply* by encouraging him to continue with a certain thing: "Mmmmm, do this, no—like this, yes, mmmm. Please go on." The second—if you think carefully about it—is a far more seductive way of saying that you like his attentions. In fact, the more deeply involved you are in enjoying his attentions—and therefore the more distracted in praising them—the more profound is your appreciation. As long as you are loving and attentive some of the time, you need have no fear that during that crucial lead up to orgasm you are quiet and concentrated. And the thought of mutual pleasure should be far more satisfying to him than a couple of lost last-minute kisses.

Exercise 10.2 Here is a tip I have found extremely helpful. One of the women who had used this program suggested the following:

For some reason—I can't explain why—when I'm very worked up, I clench my vagina tightly. If I keep that up for quite a few minutes, it really gives me a big boost towards orgasm.

This may remind you of the Kegel exercises I discussed in Chapter 5 (which, by the way, you should be still practicing). The vaginal muscles developed by those exercises—the P-C or pubococcygeal muscles—are the same ones you should try tensing in this exercise.

Tensing your muscles is a well-known way of increasing arousal. You may find that contracting other muscles, such as your stomach, legs, feet, and hands, makes you feel closer to orgasm. Conversely, for men, an ancient technique of helping to delay orgasm is relaxing all the muscles, especially in the legs and buttocks.

The Disembodied Woman

Discussing concentration leads naturally on to a phenomenon I have called the Disembodied Woman. It is an aspect of sex that is rarely—if ever—recognized in sex manuals. Yet it can be crucial to your success.

When you have sex with your partner, many things come into play. Not only is he thrusting his penis in and out of you, he may also be stimulating your breasts, nuzzling your earlobes, etc. The point is that these things can detract from your orgasm *even when they increase your overall desire*.

Obviously if you don't enjoy his stimulating your breasts, it risks detracting from your ability to climax. But, for many women, even when it *heightens* their overall excitement, it can still lead them down the wrong path—the path *away* from orgasm. The reason is because it replaces that badly-needed concentration on orgasm with a more diffuse sensual pleasure. Now this more diffuse pleasure is all very well, but if you're feeling a little nervous about orgasm, it can tip the balance in your disfavor. As Sally explains, it's almost as if for some women (some of the time, at least) there are

> **two parts to me. On the one hand, there's the orgasm. I may want to have one very much, or I mightn't mind too badly, but whatever my desire for it I must either go full out for it alone or give it up. I've got to get the timing right and the rhythm and so on. I've got to think only about the feeling in my groin. It's like coming up to a hurdle in the steeplechase: you've got to make sure you jump from the right foot at the right time with the right stride and so on. On the other hand, there are the general body pleasures. I can just lie back and enjoy the idea of sex, or the feel of his hand playing over me, or the intimacy of his kissing and affections—but if I do that I'm limiting my chances of coming. As if my friends who had come to watch me jump the hurdle began an interesting conversation amongst themselves as I ran towards it.**

Now, you may well not be this sort of woman. If you are, you must learn to distinguish those aspects of your lovemaking that contribute directly to orgasm, and those that, however pleasant in themselves, can prove distractions. I have little hesitation in saying that, once you become more adept at it, these distinctions will matter very much less—if at all.

Try the following:

Exercise 10.3 Start making love with your partner. Begin with the usual methods that get you aroused. These may include stroking your thighs, kissing your breasts, biting your neck—whatever. But, as you become extremely aroused, get your partner to stop these attentions and concentrate only on the actual act of penetration or of clitoral stimulation. Do you feel yourself getting closer to orgasm, or farther away?

A Word About Lubrication

All the sex manuals tell you that when women get sexually excited, their vaginas become naturally lubricated. As one put it, lubrication is the equivalent of the erection: a physical manifestation of sexual arousal. What they usually omit to say is that not all women do this, and that that is quite normal, too. However excited I am feeling, I rarely have enough lubrication when we begin.

For a long time, I hid this, ashamed of yet another "failure." After all, the horny woman with her "dripping cunt" is the crude byword of sexual arousal. In fact it is quite usual for a woman not to get lubricated—from nervousness, change in hormones, or simply because she's made that way.

All you have to do is use some other sort of lubrication. KY Jelly—available at the drugstore—is a colorless lubricant which you really need to apply before you begin. But for those women who need only a little warming up before they get wet, I personally think there is nothing better than saliva: it does the job well, and it's readily available. No getting up to go to the bathroom, and no bad taste if you go on to oral sex. Apply a large amount to your first two fingers and smear it up *inside* and around the entrance to your vagina. This has the great advantage that it can be done surreptitiously while lying down before he puts his penis in. Alternatively, the man can provide the lubrication on his own penis. For Barbara, the act of lubricating is an important part of lovemaking.

My favorite moment is when David straddles me. I always prop my pillows up so I can see him lick his hands, then slowly take his own dick and rub the saliva all over it. There's something very sexy about a guy rubbing his own dick. And something slightly threatening, in the nicest way possible, about seeing him preparing himself to fuck you.

Sexual Timing: His Versus Yours

One of the greatest problems a woman has to contend with is that she will almost certainly take longer to reach orgasm than the man. "Surely one of Nature's great practical jokes," said one male friend, "only not a very funny one. Men have orgasms quickly and then it's all over, while women want to do it slowly, and usually more than once."

Mind you, the hasty lover is in distinguished company, if this limerick by Norman Douglas is anything to go by:

> There was a young lady of Thun,
> Who was blocked by the Man in the Moon,
> "Well, it has been great fun,"
> She remarked when he'd done,
> "But I'm sorry you came quite so soon."

Man in the Moon or no, a good lover should be able to control his orgasm; but then a good lover is not always to hand. Remember that, ideally, you should *both* be learning at the same time. *You* are learning to have an orgasm, while *he* is learning *not* to have his too soon. (You might remind him that a man known to have staying power is *always* in demand.)

On the whole, young men are more prone to ejaculating too soon—but they have the great advantage that they can get another erection again very quickly. And, as Julie found out, some young men can do even better than that:

He was spending the summer vacation in a farmhouse I owned, studying, before going back to graduate school. He was really diligent, but nice, polite, and not bad-looking. He invited me up to his room for supper once, and one thing led to another, and I seduced him before we got to the dessert. He was really nervous (which got me going something terrible) and began making excuses, saying things like he didn't have a condom, but I told him to be quiet. I could tell he wanted me. I got him quickly onto the bed (the only time I ever regretted giving my tenant a cheap mattress!) and we did it for about an hour, nonstop, and he didn't come once. I was crushed. I thought: I made a mistake. He didn't like me, he did it only because I owned the place. I felt ugly and unattractive. Two hours later, I found out he'd ejaculated twice and still gone on—but had been shy and controlled enough to prevent my noticing, because he thought he'd been too quick. We're still together.

The major problem with the woman taking a long time is that it causes anxiety, which hinders orgasm. This was constantly happening to me in the early stages. I could have done it reasonably soon if only I hadn't been worrying that I was taking too long. That's a vicious circle.

The most common means to get around this kind of problem is by having a lot of foreplay. I'd teach my partner how to rub me gently and then make him do it until I was really aroused. But this carries a drawback: even when I had a nice guy who said he didn't mind and would wait, particularly since he liked it lasting a long time, I felt guilty that he was having to please me and so was prevented from pleasing himself. That's another vicious circle. In time, you can get used to this and overcome the feeling of tension. But it's often a good idea to have a couple of occasions when he really is slowed down. So, if necessary, you must revert to any subterfuge that will put you at ease—as Esther does:

If I know I'm going to want it in the evening, I give him a blow job during the day. Just after he gets back from work. This slows him down later in the evening and makes him feel he owes me something, too.

Alternatively, if you've done it before going to sleep, wake him up again in the night. Remember also that tired and tipsy men do it more slowly. So many women tend to write off a man who looks drunk or exhausted. This is a wicked waste. Instead, as I've suggested before, be inventive in using these occasions. They can be wonderfully helpful in defusing a potential argument, or in avoiding that threatening, macho style of sex.

As a very last resort, ask a Fairy Godmother to turn you both into minks. Those darling little animals have been known to spend as much as eight hours in intercourse. It gives a whole new meaning to why women are supposed to yearn for a mink coat.

Making Use of a Limp Penis

You may be lucky and have a man who is willing—and able—to go on. But if the worst comes to the worst, don't despair. Although we have all been taught to think of an erect penis as necessary for a woman's satisfaction, this is not true at all. If your man ejaculates, it is not a disaster. Encourage him to leave his penis in position—which, sleepy and satisfied, he may be very happy to do. Simply continue to rub yourself as you have learned to do in Step 4. Some penises remain hard for a long time afterwards; others go limp very quickly. Whichever is the case you can use it to your advantage. Sandra takes up the theme:

I was full of the usual prejudices when I met Peter: a big, stiff cock was what was needed to satisfy a woman; and, as I had never had an orgasm, when I first saw Peter's my hopes soared. I had fucked a dozen men and had always had a sense of being close to climaxing, but never actually getting there. One day we started fucking in the middle of the afternoon. I'd been looking forward to a long, slow session, and I was furious when he came after just ten minutes. My first thought was to go to the bathroom and masturbate—my usual way of getting satisfaction. But he fell asleep, and somehow I hadn't the heart to just push him off. That was my liberation.

I began to rub myself, with his cock still inside me. I found that with him half-asleep I could really relax and enjoy it. After a while, his cock started getting a bit limp, but for some reason it felt not less satisfying, but more. It was as if it was

less of a threat, less aggressive, more soft and gentle and responsive. I don't think I'd ever enjoyed sex so much up until that moment—suddenly I found I was having a strong orgasm around his penis.

That was a turning point for me. I realized I could do it with a man. Up until then I'd had a sort of mental block, thinking I'd never be able to. The next day I encouraged him to do the same. When he wanted to roll off me I said, "No, no, please stay there. I like to feel you." I practiced every day—and three weeks later I had my first orgasm with him actually fucking me. I know it would never have happened but for that first time. He doesn't know that it was his limp prick that started me off—perhaps one day I'll tell him. He's quite macho about that sort of thing. I'd like to see his face!

Sandra made use of a penis that had become limp inside her. It is also possible to get pleasure from one that is not hard at all. If your partner is unable to get an erection, don't reject him. With a little ingenuity (and his consent, of course) you can manipulate even a limp penis inside you. It'll probably have to be the Missionary Position; then, once it's in, he makes gentle, rather minimal thrusting movements with his hips. Obviously it's not the same as sex with a zonking great erection—in many ways it's more pleasant: less threatening, and there is more concentration on your clitoral area.

I strongly suggest that you give it a try. But make sure your attitude is that this is something pleasant *in itself*, not a second best because he can't get a hard-on. That way you are doing his confidence a great deal of good and, almost certainly, helping him to overcome his erection problems.

How to Deal with Premature Ejaculation

Women whose partners suffer from premature ejaculation —that is, not just sloppy lovemaking but genuine inability to prevent themselves coming almost before you've begun —have both advantages and disadvantages.

The disadvantages are obvious: little or no penetration. Like difficulty with orgasm for women, premature ejaculation is the most common male sexual complaint. Both can be readily cured by training.

The advantage of a premature ejaculator for the woman on this program is not simply that he owes you plenty of attention—but that *he knows he owes it to you.* Premature ejaculation can be very distressing for the man who suffers from it, so it goes without saying that you must be kind. But then, because you understand sexual difficulties, you probably *will* be kind. Mutual sympathy for each other's problems can greatly strengthen a relationship. You may even find that you'd both like to try going to a sex therapist. It is in this area that they have the most success. But, if you do, don't give up this program; just adapt it to your circumstances. Outside help can be extremely useful, but it rarely beats self-training. So, even though premature ejaculation will delay your training for this step, don't worry—be inventive, not defeatist.

Make sure there is foreplay *and* afterplay. Teach him how to use his hands and mouth. Concentrate on Side Steps A (manual) and B (oral). If you can learn to climax under these circumstances, the chances are you will find it a small step to climaxing with a penis once his premature ejaculation is cured.

And, just to show that not all women want a man to spin it out, let me quote you another Norman Douglas limerick:

There was a young lady of Kew,
Who said, as the curate withdrew:
"I prefer the dear vicar;
He's longer and thicker;
Besides, he comes quicker than you."

CHAPTER ELEVEN

Step 6: Success and How to Build on It

Congratulations! By now you've probably had your first *trained* orgasm with your lover. The hard work is behind you. Now it is only a matter of practice and expanding your abilities.

Keep Improving

Before I had my first orgasm, I used to think that women were divided into two categories: those who could have orgasms and those who could not. That when you'd done it once, there would be no more problems and you would do it happily ever after. If only! The truth is very much more complex than that, as those readers who began this book having experienced only occasional orgasms will know. Now you must build on your ability gradually.

So here it is in capitals, the Golden Rule:

KEEP PRACTICING AT ALL LEVELS

And this means:

1. Keep improving your masturbation techniques.
2. Keep finding times to have sex where there is no question of it ending in orgasm.
3. Keep having sex and orgasm occasionally without penetration.

Your first *self-trained* orgasm is a sexual milestone. For those who have never done it before it represents positive proof that things can get better. You will never look back. What you are going to aim for now is an orgasm *each time you want one,* with the minimum of effort—and eventually several orgasms if you and your partner feel like it. From now on they will gradually get more and more frequent. More importantly, they will cease to be a hit-or-miss affair. Even on the days when you don't come, you will understand why it didn't happen and what went wrong.

What About When I Don't Climax?

Unless you are a very remarkable woman indeed, there will always be the occasional day when you don't climax: because you're feeling anxious, or painful, or simply tired, or you may have had too much to drink—there are all sorts of reasons. Don't worry about these days. With practice and repetition of the exercises, they will become fewer. Besides, I can pretty much guarantee that once you know you *can* do it, you will no longer be distressed when you don't. The whole subject of orgasm, which assumed such gigantic proportions when you couldn't do it, now seems just one pleasant aspect of life.

In the early days of your success, however, you may still feel impatient to climax and be disappointed when you don't. On these occasions, instead of sighing in despair, *take action*. Get out your pen and paper and analyze what went wrong. Some of the possible causes of failure are:

1. Local circumstances wrong—light on, felt nervous, people walking about outside the bedroom door, etc.
2. Outside causes—drank too much, felt too sleepy, etc.
3. Lousy lover—perhaps he came too soon, or neglected to give you any attention.
4. I simply didn't like my partner.

All this is still part of the process of gaining control and mastery over your own body and lovemaking. You will get more and more adept at knowing what circumstances upset your skill, and you will learn either to cope with them or to avoid them altogether.

How to Measure Your Success

It's always helpful to chart your successful achievements. The language student will be taking exams—you have other means. I measured my success at orgasm in three ways:

1. By *how often* I could do it. At first, as you know, I couldn't do it at all. Gradually training brought it up to approximately one orgasm every three times I made love. Now I do so every time I want to, sometimes two or three times a night.

2. By *how readily* I could do it, regardless of nonideal circumstances. For example, I used to find orgasm impossible if I'd been drinking, or if I felt tense after a hard day at the office. Now these factors make very little difference.

3. By my *versatility*—different positions, different places in the house, etc. This really is the fun part. As you build up

167

your repertoire, you will become more adventurous. You will learn to do it standing up, or out in the open. The more versatile you are, the more your confidence will grow, and that, in turn, will help your ability to reach orgasm.

Obviously, the rate of your progress will depend to some extent upon the quality of your lover—even more so in the early stages. If necessary sit him down and train him, too. *All* men need instruction in sex, and very few get it. Most importantly, get him to read Chapter 18 of this book, which has been written especially for him. If you want to keep the rest of the book secret, photocopy those pages and tell him a friend at work passed it on to you.

The Intensity of Your Orgasm

Just as in masturbation, you will find that the intensity of your orgasms with a partner varies a great deal. Some days they may be strong, other days weak. I've never found any real reason why some orgasms explode while others just fizzle, although a friend of mine made the following curious connection:

> **I've noticed that if I'm *really* horny—you know, aching for it—my orgasm is a great relief but not necessarily top quality. Yet, several times when I haven't been thinking of sex at all, and Jeff's come along and persuaded me, it takes a while to get me going, but when I do climax, it's incredibly intense.**

Other women, like Melanie, claim that it depends on their state of mind, physical comfort, or even the sexual position they adopt:

If I had to think of a pattern I suppose it's that the best orgasms are the most easygoing ones, when I'm not thinking to myself, "Oh, God, when will I come?" and so on. It depends on position, too, of course. Oral sex, particularly the way Mark does it—I don't know where he learned it from, but I hope it was a book and not another woman—just collapses me. Missionary is usually never quite so strong.

Just keep up the good work, and the good results will follow.

Masters and Johnson concluded from their researches that the most intense orgasms came not from intercourse with a man, but from masturbation. You won't be surprised to learn, academics being what they are, that other researchers disagree. What do *you* think? You are now in a position to answer that question yourself.

Simultaneous Orgasm

Now here's a subject that causes a lot of squabbling. Many writers talk of the beauty of simultaneous orgasm with your partner. Personally, I think it's greatly overrated. It is, of course, a standard requirement of lovers in romantic fiction. Perhaps the most ludicrous description I've come across is "twin internal explosions." D.H. Lawrence's famous erotic novel *Lady Chatterley's Lover* also expresses the ideal of climaxing together, and the likes of Frank Harris would not be complete without a good mutual orgasm:

"Let me," I cried, and, in a moment, I was on her, working my organ up and down on her clitoris, the porch, so to speak, of Love's temple. A little

> later she herself sucked the head into her hot, dry pussy and then closed her legs as if in pain to stop me going further; but I began to rub my sex up and down on her tickler, letting it slide right in every now and then, till she panted and her love-juice came and my weapon sheathed itself in her naturally. I soon began the very slow and gentle in-and-out movements which increased her excitement steadily while giving her more and more pleasure, till I came and immediately she lifted my chest up from her breasts with both hands and showed me her glowing face. "Stop, boy," she gasped, "please, my heart's fluttering so! I came too, you know, just with you," and indeed I felt her trembling all over convulsively.

All very dandy to read about, but is it what we should be aiming for?

I don't think so. Simultaneous orgasm is nice (all orgasms are nice), but it's not necessarily the high point of good sex. The fuss made over it is largely because film directors, pulp-fiction writers, and some sexually distressed geniuses have adolescent fantasies about the subject.

I view simultaneous orgasm with great caution. It's relatively easy for a man to choose the moment when he ejaculates—at least if he puts his mind to it—but it's extremely difficult for most women to do so. And who gets the blame when it doesn't happen? You guessed it.

In fact, simultaneous orgasm has some serious drawbacks. First—from the point of view of women on this plan —worrying about timing is the last thing you need. You'd do far better to establish with your partner that you have *no* intention of trying to come at the same time he does. I take great care to make sure my partner understands this at the beginning of any new relationship. If he wants us to come together, then *he* must time his orgasm, not I mine—

it's much easier for him than it is for me. Another disadvantage of simultaneous orgasm is that if you work too hard to have it, then you'll often find your own climax to be diminished as a result.

But perhaps most importantly, to my mind, it's a serious impediment to one of the greatest pleasures of all—savoring your partner's orgasm—because you're far too busy being carried away by your own. And, what's more, you also risk losing much of the pleasure of your partner's exciting *buildup* to orgasm, because you are too preoccupied with getting your own to come on cue.

For Sally, the greatest drawback of simultaneous orgasm is that

> **it doesn't allow the enormous pleasure of having Mike go on after I've climaxed. If I come first, then there's nothing sexier than to feel his penis moving inside of me in time to my contractions and then a little later to watch him gasp with the same pleasure that I've just enjoyed.**

To expand on Sally's comment briefly, many women have stated that one of the most enjoyable sensations is to let the man continue thrusting after they have climaxed. Leslie writes:

> **I very rarely climax twice, but after I've had my orgasm I feel wonderfully liberated. I no longer have the anxiety of making sure I come before he does, and my orgasm leaves me feeling terribly responsive. Those five or so minutes between my orgasm and his are the best. And there's always the hope that you *might* do it twice, after all.**

So my advice is: *don't* view simultaneous orgasm as something to aim for. If it happens, let it happen naturally.

Multiple Orgasm

Multiple orgasms are, famously, an almost exclusively female talent. Even with men who can come more than once in a row, there's usually a limp period after the first ejaculation. Naturally, this inequality has given rise to a lot of extravagant fantasy and prejudice. Some men have dreams about satisfying the insatiable woman (Frank Harris, once again, and dozens of other writers of similar "confessions"). Others—the Roman satirist Juvenal was a particularly bad case—prefer simply to grouse about women being naturally insane with lust. In both cases, of course, such attitudes say more about the men who hold them than the women they have in mind. Sometimes you'll even come across stories in which the woman has all her orgasms during the time that the man is having his one.

"When I was a boy," a friend wrote to me recently,

I used to dread the idea of going to bed with a woman. Absolutely awful. I thought all you had to do was touch one in the wrong place and she'd start going off like a jackhammer. And I'd heard that women liked to claw your back and scream at the top of their voices during sex. I couldn't figure out why anyone would want to go through with it.

Outside of the usual nonsense, there's been a lot of serious interest in women's ability to have more than one orgasm, but not many conclusions. True multiple orgasms—that is, several orgasms with no or hardly any break in between—are a luxury and very rare. I've certainly never had them. "Sequential" is one orgasm after another with pauses to cool down in between. Sequential orgasms are much more common and certainly within the reach of many women. I've already stated that in masturbation you can quickly improve your personal best. The same is true of orgasms with a partner, except that progress is a little slower.

Some women find they feel too sensitive to be touched after the first orgasm, but those who boldly continue often report subsequent orgasms increasing in intensity.

The biggest barrier to more than one orgasm per session is often the attitudes of the women themselves, who feel "greedy," "unnatural," or "a nymphomaniac" for having more than their partner. If this is your problem, try looking at it this way: if men and women ought to have an equal amount of sexual pleasure, without one or the other being "greedy," let's calculate it over a lifetime. That way you've got an awful lot of catching up to do.

Solo Orgasm

Now here's some advice that is seldom put forward. What I call "solo orgasm" is when one partner brings the other to a climax, without taking anything in return. Rosalind explains:

> **I was sitting at my desk at home, going through the bills one Saturday afternoon. Bob came in. He took hold of me and led me to the bedroom. On the bed he stripped off my skirt, and panties and threw open my legs. Then, for half an hour, he just concentrated on giving me oral sex. I protested a bit at first—but, what the devil, it felt great!**
>
> **He kept on at me with his tongue till I came—**

twice, as a matter of fact, which is unusual. Then he simply stood up and walked off, leaving me collapsed on the bed and the bills still unpaid. . . . I thought I was seeing things at first—I mean, men normally want something in return. But he said no, he'd take his pleasure later. It's something we do quite often now; we both find it extraordinarily sexy.

Solo orgasm is, of course, particularly helpful for the woman on this program because she has no distractions whatsoever. We are all familiar with the old scenario of the man who demands or begs for a "blow job" or "a bit of manual relief"—and damned irritating it can be. But if you can engineer a situation where you *both* do it to each other, at different times, that's great. It's easy enough for you to sidle up to him—but you'll need a sensitive and understanding partner to do the same back.

Get into the habit of solo sex. Mutual pleasure is great, too, but selfishness is a delight once in a while.

The Unpalatable Male

I want now to take a look at some of the more intangible problems you may be faced with.

Fear of the penis, and all it represents, is a common one —more common than you may think. However much we feel aroused, there is no doubt that a naked man, with a 7-inch erect penis, can be threatening. As Julie points out:

It's not so much that it looks large because I like the idea of a big one, but that it looks so terribly uncompromising. Once you see it you can't help thinking "good-bye, tenderness, hello, beast."

174

Some days I don't mind so much, but it can seem such an unemotional thing.

This sort of abstract anxiety is at the heart of a lot of female sexual dissatisfaction. For Pat it was plain old distaste:

Such a big red horrible-looking object. I can't remember where it was, but I remember reading as a child in some dirty book (it might have been a copy of de Sade that my father kept in the liquor cabinet) about the penis's purple head and red balls. A cock was always painted in the most lurid colors. I was quite curious about it at the time, although my brother's example proved a little disappointing. But later, when I saw one properly while crammed in the back of a car after a date with a college boy, I almost felt sick. I mean all those veins and that sort of "throbbing" look. It looked like a growth—a tumor, maybe. So ugly.

Both of these responses—fear and distaste—are well known. Some women feel them frequently or all the time; most feel them occasionally to varying degrees. These feelings are not to be dismissed. Recognize and acknowledge them, then take steps. Below is a short list of suggestions I've received from women: some of them are more light-hearted than others, but I'm assured they all work.

1. Explore him all over while he's lying down, after you've made love: it's important that you grow familiar with his body in circumstances that aren't about to become purely sexual. If you can arrange it with him, lay off full sex for a while and instead spend the time exploring each other's bodies and talking to each other about how you feel. If need be, get him to masturbate just before in private, so that when you are together his penis is not erect and there's no suggestion that sex is to follow. After a few sessions like this, get him to masturbate in your presence and then play gently but undemandingly with each other afterwards. By progressing in this manner, slowly becoming more familiar with the penis as a nonaggressive, sensitive object of pleasure, you will gradually build up confidence and lower your fear or distaste.

2. Let his penis go limp inside you: after he's ejaculated, make him stay put until you feel it slip right out of you. The importance of this suggestion is in allowing you to appreciate both the strengths and weaknesses of the penis and the male sex drive.

3. Watch his penis grow small after sex: hold it gently after ejaculation and withdrawal. The more you familiarize yourself with the whole process, the better your understanding and the less your unease. I find that just after ejaculation, when it is half-up and half-down, the penis is at its best.

4. Hold the erect penis in your hand. Moisten the head and rub it gently around your mouth, just as if you were applying lipstick. This is a lovely exercise because the head is the softest, gentlest part.

5. If he's a great big stud of a man whom you met at the party the night before, *catch him in his underpants and socks.* That'll bring him down to size.

6. Think of as many words for "penis" as you can. Some of them are so delightful or ridiculous—Gregory Pecker, for example—that you end up feeling quite affectionate towards the dear little thing.

7. Say the word "penis" itself ten times: you'll realize what a comic word it is. Keep saying it and you'll soon be laughing out loud. The woman who recommended this invented a wonderful, silly game that had her and her friends all rolling in the aisles. She found some popular songs and substituted "penis" for one of the main words of the song, which they then all sang aloud, with much wine flowing. The favorite was "How Much is That Penis in the Window?"

CHAPTER TWELVE

Side Step A: Manual Sex

The great advantage of the man's arousing the woman by manual sex is that it can be done almost anywhere: in the movies, driving a car, at a party, standing in line—the possibilities are endless, and the variations infinite. One friend of mine used to get his girlfriend to climax during the rush hour on the train, while the two of them were standing, strap-hanging, pressed closely together. It can be done with your clothes on or off, in private or in public, with penetration (of your partner's fingers) or without, as foreplay or afterplay. . . .

So why does manual sex come as a side step in the program, rather than as a logical progression from masturbation?

The answer is partly because many people still regard manual sex as not quite respectable, and partly because men are notoriously bad at using their hands.

It's not entirely men's fault. Manual sex on a woman is a very difficult thing to do well. On a man it is relatively easy —the penis is a large and well-defined organ, which needs a certain amount of fairly vigorous, unimaginative attention. There are extra tricks that a woman can learn—sex manuals are always going on about them—but the great majority of men seem perfectly happy with the basic rub-a-dub-dub.

A woman, however, has a very delicate, sophisticated sexual area. What's more, women vary from individual to individual in what they find most stimulating. As one female friend of mine put it, "I'm damned glad I don't have to make love to another woman. I wouldn't have the first clue about how to arouse her, or where to fiddle!" The anonymous *A Protest by the Medical Profession* contains the following verse:

There's the vulva, the vagina and the jolly perineum;
There's the hymen which is sometimes found in brides;
There's the uterus, the clitoris, the ovum and the oviducts, The ovaries and Lord knows what besides.

It's no surprise, then, that men, whose sexual experience with their hands is normally limited to masturbation, are usually a little ham-handed when it comes to satisfying a woman's needs manually.

The trouble is not enough men have the tact—or the courage—to ask which technique their partner likes. Too many either consider it a slight to their manhood to hesitate and show ignorance, or fear that the woman will mock him as being inadequate. This seems to me one of the great tragedies of relations between the sexes. Because, for most women, the idea of a man who bothers to ask what she likes is a dream come true, not a cause for mockery. However, until communication between men and women improves, this miserable misunderstanding will continue. Let me simply repeat—for the benefit of any stray male reader—*there is no reason why men should feel shy or inadequate in admitting that they don't know their way about down there.* Julie, usually rather a reticent woman, becomes quite outspoken and lyrical on the subject.

I always say that there are two aspects to a good lover—his hands and his questions. If he uses his hands sensitively, exploring and investigating,

never crude but always responsive, then he's got the makings of a prince of pleasure. He should ask questions with his hands as well as his mouth. His hands should notice what gestures are effective, what rhythm most pleasing, and his mouth should be ready to ask verbally if the sexual signs are too difficult for him to interpret.

It is, in short, ignorance and lack of communication which often makes manual sex more difficult for women than it ought to be. That is why I've put it in as a side step. Personally, I only succeeded after progressing through steps 1–4, largely because my partner at the time—a nice guy, I'm still in touch with him—had hands that reminded me of a trouser press. Other women, however, have succeeded at an earlier stage of the program. It's up to you when you try it. And remember, whatever the level of your lover, with a little bit of ingenuity you can usually improve the situation a good deal.

Manual Sex with Clothes On

Begin your manual-sex program with your clothes on. I want you and your lover to try to do each exercise successfully three times before you can really feel you have mastered it. You may either stick to the same exercise until you achieve this, or you may alternate with another exercise. Do not, however, attempt more than two different exercises at any one time. After you have moved on, you should still repeat the previous exercises periodically.

The concentration will be on you, so you must decide whether or not to see to your partner's needs beforehand or afterwards (assuming you do so at all, that is). Men who haven't yet been satisfied sometimes get impatient for their turn, which will inhibit you. On the other hand, some women prefer to satisfy their lover afterwards because they have a partner who, once satisfied, tends to lose interest altogether. Only you can decide.

A very good friend of mine found herself in a situation similar to that described by Erica Jong in *Fear of Flying* (quoted in Chapter 15). She was crossing Europe by train, but in a completely full carriage. As none of the passengers had paid for a sleeper, when night fell, a guard brought around blankets which everybody snuggled into, sitting upright. Somehow my friend found herself pleasantly and secretly beneath the blanket exchanging manual sex with the young man sitting next to her. "Heavenly," she concluded. "I never even learned his name."

Exercise 12.1 To begin, arrange situations in which your lover arouses you with your clothes on, when it's acknowledged by both of you *before you begin* that you're not aiming for full orgasm. Arrange the situation so that it enforces this restraint (reread Step 3 for advice).

Do this exercise in circumstances you find most relaxing and suitable, but don't do it in the bedroom. I want you to avoid the undesirable orgasm-as-goal situation.

Exercise 12.2 As above, but vary the circumstances. Wear different clothes. Do it at different times, in unusual settings. But, once more, avoid the bedroom. If you are sitting in the movies, there is no danger that he is going to try to go too far. A little gentle rubbing while watching the film can be very constructive. You can relax completely because *nothing depends on it*. All in all try to make it a normal part of your relationship that he gives you manual stimulation now and then when you're out together for whatever purpose.

Reread Step 2 on masturbation for a further discussion of the possibilities. Masturbation and manual sex have numerous similarities and you can model your progression here on your masturbation progression.

By all means give him occasional attention and encouragement while he's doing it (some kisses, stroking his penis) but no more than that. This is *your* time, and you must feel free to concentrate.

Exercise 12.3 As above, but now leave the outcome—orgasm or no orgasm—open. Don't say "This time I'll come" —just allow for the possibility of it. Give yourself a little more time. As before, try to avoid the bedroom, but make extra sure that you're not going to worry about the amount of time you're taking, or the fact that all the attention is on you.

If you find that you do not climax, don't fuss. You have plenty of time, and there are other things you can be getting on with in the program meanwhile. Keep practicing. You will succeed.

Pass on to the next exercise only when you feel comfortable with your response to this one.

Exercise 12.4 This exercise is not strictly speaking manual, but it's definitely sexy. Lie in bed naked beneath the bedclothes. Now have your partner, also naked (at least on his lower half) lie on top of you. You open your legs and he presses his penis against you, as if in the Missionary Position. The crucial difference is that, of course, the bedclothes are between you. But the effect is similar to that of manual sex. See if you can reach orgasm this way.

Manual Sex with Clothes Off

There are various scenarios for disaster when it comes to a man trying to stimulate a woman by manual sex. Most of us know them from bitter experience:

The man who sticks his finger in all the way and nothing else. A familiar species. A young man, quite likely a student. I seem to recall he's usually a bit acned, eager, and uses that revolting phrase "finger-fucking." Perhaps not to you, but probably to his pals. He shoves it in and out a bit—basically he thinks a woman's vagina is just an inside-out penis: you rub his on the outside, he does yours on the inside. This is the technique of the complete novice: the man who has never read about women's sexual organs, and certainly never bothered, or had the chance to ask a woman about them. By virtue of his being "male," he thinks that knowing what to do to a woman is an "instinct."

The man who concentrates on the one spot to the exclusion of all else. This character has done some reading, or he's overheard a conversation in a bar. Perhaps someone has whispered to him that the clitoris is "the seat of a woman's desire," nudge, nudge, wink, wink: Well, all I can say is you're a lucky woman if he's got the *wrong* spot. Because, as we all know, the clitoris is an immensely delicate organ that needs the most gentle handling. There's a park that, ever since I climbed into it over the railings one night with an early boyfriend, makes me wince when I pass it. Because underneath the chestnut tree, he demonstrated his agonizing skill!

The man who is like a bull in a china shop. The particular specimen I had dealings with was a builder, used to rubbing his hands over piles of bricks, I suppose. . . . This tends to be another failing that results from men not appreciating that males and females have very different sexual organs and sensitivities. So, once again, it's car-polishing time.

No doubt you can think of a number of other types. So for the exercises that follow, if your lover has certain manual faults spend some time educating him to be otherwise.

Exercise 12.5 Direct manual sex (as opposed to the indirect of the first three exercises) is much the easiest when you do not have your clothes on. Don't—to begin with—let him do it to you underneath your clothes. This restricts his movement and makes it harder to apply the proper pressure in the right places. So take your bottoms off and lie in bed.

Manual sex as performed in bed has, of course, two classic functions: as foreplay to stimulate you and prepare you for full sexual intercourse. And as "afterplay" if the man ejaculates too soon. Make use of this. If you need or want to, bring him to climax first. Then let him concentrate on you.

The first few times you may want to establish beforehand that orgasm is not the goal—all you want to do is enjoy the sensations and become familiar with them. If orgasm follows, then all well and good, but the important thing, as ever, is not to worry about it and upset your sense of ease.

Apart from the immediate pleasure it gives, manual sex serves an important role in this program: it gets you accustomed, gradually, to a sexual situation where *somebody else* is in physical control. Because of this, it is worth experimenting with it. It is also important that you do not neglect the gains made by your training. Make sure that you maintain and improve on your ability and try to establish it as an acceptable part of your normal sex life and an alternative to intercourse, rather than merely as something to happen either before or after.

If you still have trouble enjoying yourself with manual sex, set up a situation on the bed at home that is as close as possible to your own familiar masturbation sessions. Now, as he caresses you, lie back and imagine you're masturbating alone. If necessary, use your own hands as well as his.

CHAPTER THIRTEEN

Side Step B: Oral Sex

Like manual sex, oral sex can be introduced into your program at any time after Step 2. When you decide to do it will depend on the quality of your lover, the type of relationship you have with him, and also on the degree of confidence you have in yourself. If you have completed Step 2, then you are making wonderful progress and are well on the way to your goal. But you may still feel that oral sex is something of an exotic option, and that you'd prefer to consolidate your gains in the traditional way before attempting it. This is your decision. It is important that you do it when *you* feel ready.

I think oral sex can be wonderful. But not everybody agrees. This is the other reason that I have made it a side step in the program. It is not crucial to your progress. It is a bonus if you do it, but if you don't it in no way detracts from the huge gold star studded with rubies and diamonds you get for completing the main program. I advise you to attempt it; but if, despite my arguments in its favor, you still think it somewhat beyond the pale, don't worry. If, on the other hand, you have no worries about it and are eager to learn how to make it serve you to best advantage, then you can skip what follows and go directly to the next section, "Stage One."

Oral sex—"cunnilingus" when the man does it to the

woman, "fellatio" when it's the other way around—engenders strong feelings. I was in my twenties when Dr. David Reuben's book, *Everything You Always Wanted to Know about Sex (But Were Afraid to Ask)*, hit the headlines. The following piece of extravagant nonsense clammed me up for years:

By simultaneous cunnilingus and fellatio every possible sense is brought to a fever pitch and a mutual orgasm occurs rapidly unless the couple switches to a penis-vagina position. The most presumably undersexed man or woman will be brought to an explosive orgasm by using this technique, providing they are willing to do it.

If I could have my way, I'd send the author to the lions' den, and throw in some vipers for good measure. Oral sex can be extremely satisfying, but for few couples is it so glib and easy as Dr. Reuben describes. It is simply absurd (and somewhat savoring of cheap pornography) to suggest that mutual orgasm will occur because of it.

"Simultaneous cunnilingus and fellatio" consists in the man and woman lying top to toe with each other—either side by side, or one on top and one underneath—and simultaneously stimulating the genitals. (Because of the position it is also often known as "69.") But it can be extremely uncomfortable for the woman, and should *never* be tried by the beginner. The guaranteed "explosive orgasm," rapid or otherwise, is one of the most outrageously wicked promises I have ever heard. But it took me nearly two decades to find out.

Of all the many sexual myths, the idea that even the most "undersexed" women will succumb to oral sex is one of the worst. First, it's simply not true. Second, it assumes that one man's method of cunnilingus is as good as another's, which is nonsense. Men's ability and skills vary wildly. Finally, it makes the woman for whom orgasm has never been easy (such as myself at the time of reading that book) so terrified that she is going to fail even where the most frigid have supposedly succeeded, that she freezes up completely. Stephen Vizinczey's novel *In Praise of Older Women* is the story of Adras Vadja, a young man, and his sexual encounters with—guess what?—older women. In it, Vadja's thoughts about his mistress's dislike of cunnilingus is a tribute to his sexual sensitivity on precisely this point.

> **There would be very few sexual problems if they could all be ascribed to inhibitions, yet at first I took it for granted that Paola refused to consent to any unfamiliar love-play out of modesty. However, her violent resistance showed not shyness but fear. It leaped through the blue of her eyes and hung over her long white body—the fear of false hopes and deeper defeats.**

Paola, having failed to have an orgasm in a more "normal" way, fears yet another failure.

At the other extreme from Dr. Reuben are those who consider oral sex dirty or perverted. Many women feel uncomfortable receiving oral sex—even the most liberated have confessed to their closest friends that they cannot relax while it is happening.

There are many reasons for these feelings, ranging from the obvious physical fact that a woman's genitals involve a hole and various funny extra parts that need regular washing, to the more subtle influence of a puritanical upbringing or the trauma of an earlier sexual encounter. None of these is to be dismissed lightly. If, whatever the cause, you feel uncomfortable with the *idea* of cunnilingus, then you will feel uncomfortable during the *act* of it. This is why the self-analysis of Stage One, below, is so important, even though it involves no physical contact.

Stage One

It is of paramount importance that you get your ideas, hopes, and fears about oral sex into perspective. Doing so constitutes the first part of this side step. It is *not* the short route to success. You must train yourself here as you have trained elsewhere. But, given a good lover and proper training of your own sexuality, it can be one of the delights of making love. The tongue is a gentle, soft, and versatile part of a man's body; I have often felt that there is no better use for it. If you feel that there is something fundamentally dirty about the process, or fear that your partner feels that there is, then you can always make a point of washing just beforehand, and making sure that he has noticed the fact. You might find it helpful to take a shower or bath together and wash each other during it.

And here I'd like to introduce a piece of good news: most men like doing oral sex. Virtually all the men I've asked about it agree that it's extremely sexy. If you don't believe me, just take a look at *Hite* on men.

In my case, a lot of my reservations about oral sex had to do with disastrous early cunnilingus. My partners might have enjoyed doing it, but they weren't much good. Let's face it, most sexually active women have some pretty dismal oral-sex scenarios to relate—grim or comic, depending on which way you look at it. I hardly know a woman who hasn't had a good giggle with her friends over men's oral catastrophies.

Here are a few typical scenarios, some of them abominably reminiscent of the manual-sex disasters of the previous chapter:

1. Down he goes, very purposeful and direct. He has read that the clitoris is the seat of sexual feeling; and, having found, it he's not going to let his concentration be diverted. He's made the mistake of assuming that the clitoris is just like a penis. That's a painful mistake: it is much more sensitive. A good lover will spend much more time around the clitoris, stimulating it indirectly. Not so, oral sexer number one: Just keep this up, he thinks, mistaking your writhes of agony for intense pleasure, and you'll be having an orgasm in no time.

2. This man's been told he has a long tongue, and he also thinks that the vagina is the seat of all passion. He sticks his tongue in and out, simulating a penis, pausing every ten times or so because his mouth is tired. You, of course, feel little. His stubble scrapes on you.

3. The man of method. He's cultivated a Latin appearance —open-necked shirt, medallion, foreign sports car, possibly even funny-colored sheets (black maybe). He thinks of oral sex as just one of the many courses on the sexual menu, somewhere between the foreplay starter and the coital main course. All you can think of while he's busy down there is that you've got dessert, cheese, and coffee still to go—with increasing foreboding you wonder what they will consist of.

4. Rather a sporty type, this one. He doesn't really want to do it (although he doesn't mind if you do it to him) but he feels he must, or he's responding to your complaints. This man is rather fastidious. The penis, he thinks, is a straightforward thing—little more than a large finger really. Who ever minded sucking a finger? But all that funny stuff on a woman is a different story. Okay, so it doesn't squirt a mess all over the place when it climaxes, but still, it can't be said to be a thing of great beauty, can it?

5. At last a civilized man! Everything is going well. You've settled down, gotten yourself comfortable, and begun to concentrate on the delicious feeling spreading through your body. He's not rough or painful; he's moving his tongue around nicely and taking care to find your rhythm —and then he ruins it all by looking up and meeting your eye. Oh, the embarrassment of it! You don't know him very well, so there's no intimacy there. You'd just begun to let go when he starts staring past your breasts (which are too small), over your double chin, up your nose and into your eyes. What a time to be caught unawares. My sister's boyfriend even used to wink!

If your worries about oral sex are more deep-seated—not confined to unsuitable partners—then it will pay to examine them carefully. If you still feel ill at ease, leave this chapter for now. You can always come back later, after you've made further progress in the main body of the program.

Stage Two

As with all other parts of the program, make sure that you are feeling comfortable and relaxed. If necessary, make a display of the fact that you have just washed yourself thoroughly before beginning: this is important not so much for his sake, but because it will put *you* at ease about *his* reservations. Naturally if you have any discharge or an unpleasant smell, don't do oral sex, and don't let yourself be pressured into it. Your lover may have a fetish about dirty panties (don't laugh, some men do), but unless you share his delight, it's best to steer clear. In fact, there are men who love oral sex even with a menstruating woman. I know I could never feel at ease in such a situation, however much he reassured me. Remember: *nothing* must spoil your sense of ease.

In general, the first few times it is best to do oral sex with as much anonymity as possible. A dark room can be immensely comforting. If you like, get him to do it while you are still largely clothed, or hiding beneath the bedcovers. The first time Laura ever managed to climax with oral sex was with the lights out and with the added sense of privacy from pulling the quilt over herself from the hips up, even over her face.

> **That way I wasn't in any doubt that Mark couldn't see all those parts I knew could have been smaller and thinner and a better shape. I mean, I hate all this dieting nonsense, but I'm just as much a victim of it as anybody else. I just can't get down to it [oral sex] without feeling uncomfortable and tensing up so much that he might as well be licking a lamppost. But that night I just covered my top up completely, while leaving my legs free so that I could move them about easily. . . . It was such a silly position—and yet I *did* relax totally. I just let myself go. Mark's never been difficult about time. We just kept on, and I didn't have to look at him or see his movements to make me worry that he might be getting tired or bored, I just lay back and thought about *me!***

However, to begin with, *don't think about having an orgasm.* This will come later. The important thing is to introduce yourself to the sensations of oral sex and to teach yourself to feel at ease with it. If you feel awkward or embarrassed, pour yourself a drink. Alcohol slightly inhibits the physical ability to climax, but the relaxing effect will counteract this. Besides, to begin with you shouldn't be worrying about actually climaxing. A warm bath also helps to loosen you up, and makes you smell nice. Only when you begin to feel relaxed with the fact of oral sex should you start to think about concentrating on orgasm.

Paola (in *In Praise of Older Women*), whose refusal to even contemplate the idea of oral sex is uncompromising, finally has her first orgasm during cunnilingus because Vadja has approached her when at her most relaxed and least inhibited:

Late one Saturday morning, I was awakened by the heat. The sun was shining into my eyes through the curved windowpanes and gauzy white curtains, and the temperature in the room must have been at least ninety degrees. During the night we had kicked off the blanket and the top sheet, and Paola was lying on her back with her legs drawn up, breathing without a sound. We never look so much at the mercy of our bodies, in the grip of our unconscious cells, as when we are asleep. With a loud heartbeat, I made up my mind that this time I would make or break us. Slowly I separated her limbs: a thief parting branches to steal his way into a garden and rest his head. Though her body remained motionless, by then Paola must have been awake, but pretended not to be; she remained in that dreamy state in which we try to escape responsibility for whatever happens, by disclaiming both victory and defeat beforehand. It may have been ten minutes or half an hour later (time had dissolved into a smell of pine) that Paola's belly began to contract and let up and, shaking, she finally delivered up her joy, that offspring not even transient lovers can do without. When her cup ran over she drew me up by my arms and I could at last enter her with a clear conscience.

"You look smug," were her first words when she focused her critical blue eyes again.

If your lover is the sort who feels no sex is good without orgasm, and you are uncomfortable or preoccupied with this feeling of his, then fake it. But tell yourself right at the beginning that you are going to fake it, and not halfway through, after you've begun to panic about not having a real one.

The other familiar problem with oral sex has been discussed above, namely the quality of your lover. But bear in mind that the man who knows "how to do it" is simply the man who gives you pleasure. A little gentle guidance from you might be in order.

At all costs avoid "69" at this early stage—as I'm sure Julie would agree:

> **When I was in my teens, "69" was all the rage. The boys at school used to whisper about it. I was so naïve that one day I asked the math teacher what it was. He was a very young man, a substitute teacher who was there only for a week or two. He blushed and pretended he hadn't heard. It was an omen, however, because after I'd left school and gone to college I met up with him by accident in a café. We got on really well and before long were sleeping together. One day he said did I remember that time when I'd asked him about "69." Yes, I said, and then a little while later he arranged the position. My God, what a disappointment! I mean, by then I'd got to think of it as automatic orgasm, a real bang, but it was just damned awkward. At first he went on top of me. He was bony, and his prick nearly choked me. Then I went on top of him and I worried that I'd flatten him. Then we tried it side by side but his neck got tired and he kept rolling away. . . .**

Let Julie's story be a lesson. Believe me, no woman is going to learn to have an orgasm while she is grappling upside-down with a man's penis. You might as well go right back to square one.

Stage Three

Only once you have accommodated yourself to the idea of having a man down there should you start to concentrate on the possibility of orgasm. The interesting thing about oral sex is that when you *do* succeed, it can be extremely intense—more intensely pleasurable than anything else.

Perhaps the most alluring description of oral sex comes from Katherine, who after many years of inability to climax in this way, now believes she's found the ultimate pleasure:

> **I lie naked on my back while Freddy gives me oral sex. He makes it last a long time. He's naked too. Then, just as I feel myself beginning to climax—that wonderful point of no return—he moves up and pushes his penis into me. That way I get the full pleasure of orgasm with him inside me, and he usually climaxes just afterwards. It needs some pretty clever timing, though!**

SUPERTIP

If your partner is busy giving you some very enjoyable oral sex, but you are still conscious of that "invisible barrier" stopping you from actually climaxing, try this. Using your own hand, manipulate yourself around the area of your pubic hair, almost as if you were masturbating. It's too high up to exert much pressure on the clitoris—and besides, he will be responsible for that—but once again the *illusion of control,* the illusion of being in your own familiar masturbatory position, is often sufficient to overcome that invisible barrier and bring you to orgasm.

I have found this tip quite invaluable.

PART THREE

CHAPTER FOURTEEN

To Fake or Not to Fake?

Counterfeit the sweet bliss with lying sounds. . . . Only, when you pretend, see that you are not caught, win assurance by your movements and even by your eyes. Let your words and panting breath make clear your pleasure.

———**Ovid,** *The Art of Love*

There is no doubt about it: for me, faking was a significant step in my success.

Do I hear cries of protest? Faking entails deceit and distrust and that sort of thing? I do hope so. There is nothing so encouraging as a big chorus of outdated moral disapproval. For although faking remains one of the last real sexual taboos, thousands of women do it every day. The fact is that there are very good reasons for faking your orgasm, especially during your learning period. Faking can *help* you to achieve orgasm.

Why Do Women Fake?

Let's face it; nobody *wants* to have to fake an orgasm. Why then do we do it?

There are many reasons. By far the most common is that we fear to display our so-called "inadequacy" in not

being able to climax. We are afraid of being labeled *frigid.*
There are many variations on this particular fear. Here is
just a small sample of comments I have come across:

> I always felt that because I couldn't come I wasn't
> a proper woman. I mean, imagine a man who
> couldn't ejaculate. I certainly wasn't going to ad-
> vertise that, so I started faking.

> I simply couldn't stand the snotty look when I told
> them I hadn't come. As if they were getting sec-
> ond-class goods. It's so much *simpler* to fake it.

> I tried not to, because I always felt it was the
> wrong thing to do. My therapist impressed upon
> me that the idea was to build up a loving relation-
> ship, and that faking introduced deceit. So next
> week I didn't bother to fake, but Mark got really
> angry because he said I wasn't trying hard
> enough. I suppose that dumb psychiatrist must
> have really gone to my head, because then I con-
> fessed to Mark that I'd never had an orgasm. Wow!
> Did the shit fly! He said he felt that he was dating
> an iceberg, and left me a few days later. I changed
> my shrink.

> You're caught: if you don't fake they think there's
> something wrong with you, and if you do fake
> some asshole starts sounding off about it being
> dishonest and underhanded. The only thing is to
> tell the jerk to fuck off, and keep faking.

> I think I could have accepted a man who got angry
> when he found out. I mean, then I'd have known
> he was a bastard and that would make things sim-
> pler. Even an indifferent man would be okay, in
> fact, he would be best of all, because I could just

get on with it myself. But it was Ben's endless little attentions that got on my nerves. Always worrying about me and looking at me with pitiful eyes as if I had three arms or something.

For me it's very simple. When my husband keeps pumping away at me, in and out, my vagina gets sore. It's okay for the first ten minutes, but I just don't have that much lubrication. If I didn't fake, I wouldn't be able to walk the next day!

Often when I had sex with my boyfriend, he'd compare me unfavorably with his previous girlfriend. If I wasn't writhing in ecstasies, he used to tell me how hot she was. That upset me more than if he'd gone on about how beautiful she was. I felt really jealous. So I started faking so as not to be outdone.

Why do I fake? Oh, that's easy. I fake because I don't like doing it with my husband. Faking gets it over as quickly as possible.

What a dismal situation!

Another important reason why women fake their orgasms is the fear of upsetting their partner. Many men anxiously insist that the woman must have satisfaction—either because they are genuinely concerned, or in order to satisfy their vanity and prove they are a "good lover." It is one of the little ironies of our sexually liberated era of equality that men have come to demand that their partner have an orgasm *just as they do*. Or, in the words of Catherine Stimpson, an eminent feminist writer:

Men tried to invent a new, friendly, eager female sexuality in what has been called the sexual

revolution of the sixties. But after that experimental decade, the feminist movement emerged to challenge men's motives, insisting that the command to be sexually warm was as oppressive as the earlier command to be cold and pure. The pressures that gave rise to those inventions remain.

This is part of the reason that women like Harriet fake—in order to get a little peace:

Sometimes I get really angry that he can have an orgasm and I can't. But if you are with a man who feels that he ought to give you a chance, it can be very tiring. He might mean well—but to lie there while he keeps rubbing away at you, all the time expecting you to collapse into ecstasies, well it's hard work. It's also awkward—if he's been trying for ages and you still can't, there comes a point where it's very embarrassing to admit defeat and stop. I reckon it's simpler for everybody to fake it. He's satisfied, and you're as satisfied as you'll ever be.

Some women I've met even fake orgasms to be polite.

If I've been for a nice evening out, to a chic restaurant, maybe to a show, I figure it's rude and ungrateful not to indicate that you enjoy the sex that goes with it. Marilyn Monroe used to fake so as not to offend her partner, so why not me? You know what men's egos are like—and if you like the guy, why not? It costs you nothing.

I think if men knew just how *often* women fake they'd be astonished. I can recall several occasions when men I've known have let slip details of their partner's "great" sexual responses—when only the day before the woman in question has been congratulating herself on her skill in faking.

I've also known of one or two men to shake their heads over a woman's faking, with sympathetic and understanding comments like "She shouldn't feel she has to." But when their partner doesn't come, then, by God, don't these same men make a pained atmosphere, if not get actively angry? It's a sad fact that when it comes to sex, reality and ideals are a long way apart.

But faking orgasm in a relationship is not always intended as a major deception. Sometimes it begins as a temporary measure, as in Marie's case:

> **When Larry and I first met I didn't want to disappoint him. I loved him a lot, he turned me on, and I was sure it was only a matter of days before I had an explosive orgasm. The trouble was, the days turned into weeks, then months. The orgasm never happened. How could I tell him I'd been pretending all along? I had to keep it up. Now I feel resentful.**

In short, faking is a consequence—not a cause—of sexual difficulty. It is not so much a form of deceit, as one of defense. It does not exaggerate poor communication or sexual unease, it is only a response to them. In fact, with careful handling, it can, on the contrary, be the means to a far more open, honest, and satisfying sexual atmosphere.

I have already explained how, in my own case, when I was younger, it simply never occurred to me to fake orgasm. I was too naïve. I wish I had known, it would have saved me a lot of embarrassment, heartache, and guilt. It was only when I set about devising this program for myself that I realized faking could help me. I began faking orgasms quite deliberately. I decided it would be the first stage in my long haul—by buying me time to concentrate on myself.

And it worked!

How Can Faking Help Me?

I have all along emphasized the importance of a sense of *control* over your own body. By faking an orgasm, you are taking the pressure off yourself, ridding yourself of anxiety. In such cases, contrary to what so many well-meaning people say, faking can *help* to stabilize a relationship. It requires a form of deceit, to be sure, and we would all prefer to do without it. But it is no use talking of ideals when the reality itself isn't there. If having to announce your lack of orgasm makes you tense and worried, or causes friction between you and your partner, then it's often worth a little deceit to avoid what can be a major unpleasantness.

So do not frown on faking. It can be an invaluable aid to your progress, and it need not upset a loving and caring relationship. In fact, it can do a lot to help breed stability and understanding. Once I knew that I didn't have to worry so much about the humiliation of admitting to my partner I was *not* going to climax, I was free to concentrate on my enjoyment during sex. Instead of constantly getting in a tizzy about the fact that in ten minutes' time my boyfriend would be over and done and probably starting to ask me difficult questions—and looking hurt when I gave him truthful answers—I could relax. And relaxation, as you will have gathered by now, is an essential part of this program. Furthermore, if the man feels you will *eventually* reach orgasm (i.e., your faked orgasm), he'll usually be prepared to go on a great deal longer than if he feels it's all for "nothing."

Naturally, I don't mean to say that you should fake whenever you feel the slightest desire to, or whenever you know you won't be able to have a genuine orgasm. I certainly don't think you should fake to be polite, or to pander to your man's vanity. If and when you fake, you fake *because it is helping you towards a more satisfying sex life.* On those occasions when you feel that the pressure on you to have an orgasm detracts from your pleasure and concentration, then faking may be the answer. These occasions are personal. I cannot dictate under what conditions your need becomes great enough: that is for you to decide. All I can do is say that you should not feel it is necessarily wrong or harmful to fake an orgasm. On the contrary, it may be the only way you can get that sense of ease which is so important to your progress.

Ann is assistant manager in a local insurance office:

Faking did help me, there's no doubt about it. My husband is a really nice guy, but when we first met he didn't give much attention to my needs in bed —this was twenty years ago, remember. We had a pretty average sex life I should think, though I never got aroused enough to have an orgasm. But we muddled along, and I was distracted by my career. After we'd been married for several years, Harry picked up a sex manual. That got him thinking about what he'd rather taken for granted before—my satisfaction. He began asking me if I climaxed, and because I loved him, I didn't want to lie. When I kept saying no, he felt he ought to put more effort into our lovemaking. That was okay, but it made me nervous, him always asking me, "How was it for you, dear?"—I mean it's a bit of a joke question.

It got to really bother me in the end—but how could I say "shut up" when he was trying to be decent? I remember one evening I'd had a hell of

a day out shopping and I came home and got into the bathtub. I took a drink in there with me, and I must have dozed off because when he came home I was still there in the bath. Watching him undressing while I lay there, I suddenly wanted him.

We got into bed, and I was thinking, "Yes, I bet I could do it this time—I feel so good." Well, Harry got on top of me and started away. We were doing really well, and then he spoiled it all by saying, "You really must have an orgasm tonight, darling, I'm determined to keep going till you do." Privately I'd been thinking just the same—but as soon as he said it, I sort of froze. I knew immediately, with him watching for it, that I couldn't. At work they say that if you're presented with a deadline, your adrenaline rises and you really get going. Well, sure as shooting, that's not true of sex. I let him go on for a while, and then I thought, "Oh, hell, I'll fake it"—and I did. He was thrilled to pieces.

After that I faked it most times we fucked. I'd felt really angry that first time, for having to. But after a while I realized that I'd bought time for myself. I'd get him to keep going for as long as possible, which he was more happy to do now that he felt there was something tangible at the end of it. And now that he "knew" I had no trouble climaxing, he left me alone more. Finally I could relax. And then I did do it: I climaxed. After that it got better and better. I'm certain I would never have been able to without that faking.

But there's more to it than that. Not only can faking put you at ease, so that you may enjoy your sex as much as possible without fretting constantly about whether you will or will not come at the end of it; but by making good use of your ease, you can *develop* and *train* your sexuality so that you will learn how to have an orgasm. For many, faking is the path to nonfaking!

Some men are not concerned whether a woman has climaxed or not, in which case this will not be your problem. If you know this characterizes your partner, then it might be worth trying to get *out* of the habit of faking (if you are already in it) or not getting into the habit in the first place. Faking is useful only if you feel awkward about admitting to not climaxing. There's no point in faking if you feel perfectly at ease with him about your inability.

I certainly do not think you ought to fake an orgasm to help his ego, or to be polite. But if faking an orgasm will allow you to be yourself, then I believe it is justified. You will be free of the anxiety of his asking constantly, "Have you come yet?" You will be free to concentrate on your own method of learning.

Surely He'll Know if I'm Faking

That's what I used to think, but I was wrong.

The positive news (at least in terms of faking) is that most men are lamentably ignorant about whether or not a woman has come. In my experience those so-called Lotharios with vast experience are often the worst. It tends to be men who have been in stable long-term relationships who are the most sensitive and the most acute.

But instead of taking my word for it, let men speak for themselves:

> **This business of knowing when a girl comes is pretty vague and shadowy. It's open to a lot of misunderstanding, as well as out-and-out fraud. I would have to admit that I'm often not sure at all.**

The subtlety of some women's orgasms can be deceiving. I usually try to tell by the partner's movements, a change of pace, quickening of breath, moaning, contractions, grip, affection, kisses, etc., but usually I am not sure.

I can never tell for sure . . . I am always in doubt . . . right now, since each woman seems to be different, it seems thoroughly baffling to me.

These are all from *The Hite Report on Male Sexuality*. Hite concludes: "Most men experienced a great deal of insecurity and confusion over knowing when—or whether—a woman had had an orgasm."

How Do I Fake an Orgasm?

If you *do* decide that faking is justified, it is very important that you do it convincingly. Bear in mind that it *can* damage a relationship if he finds out and feels you've wantonly misled him.

If you haven't faked until now, it will make him very suspicious to find you suddenly having orgasms to order. But think about it carefully: if you haven't faked until now, perhaps there's no need for you to start. Only if you feel it really would help you is it worth doing—*don't* start doing it just because you'd like to give him a little present now and then. It's *you* who need the little presents, not him.

If, having thought about it, you decide that faking is indeed the lesser of two evils, then introduce it gradually. Naturally, you'll have to be consistent. Fake it once, then leave it a few times. Then fake again, and so on.

Now you can't easily fool a sexologist in the laboratory

with all his measuring equipment, but you can fool your partner any day. Remember, when you fake, the following points are important:

1. Your breathing—probably *the most* important indicator. Don't ring up one of those sex lines to find out how they do it, because they're grossly exaggerated. Any man who thinks that's your average orgasm sounds as if he has unsavory hobbies. You'll notice during masturbation that your breathing changes quite a bit during the lead-up to orgasm and during orgasm itself. Notice that it is not simply a heavy panting which erupts at orgasm and then vanishes. Almost as soon as you begin to masturbate it will change. Gradually it gets heavier and quickens quite a bit towards your climax, then takes a minute or two to die away. Avoid making it too rhythmic; vary the pace every now and then. During orgasms some women make a lot of noise, some become very quiet just beforehand, and then start gasping during it. And most women vary from day to day. There is no one way. All women are different.

Exercise 14.1 To be done *before* you begin faking. Get hold of a tape recorder. Switch it on to *record,* making sure the microphone is close to your face. Now lie down and begin a masturbation session. Then replay the tape and listen carefully to your breathing—you'll be surprised at how much it changes, without your being aware of it.

Exercise 14.2 Again tape-record yourself masturbating. Then play it back and listen carefully. Now tape-record yourself faking an orgasm. Can you tell the difference?

2. Vaginal contractions. Although some men say they can feel these, most admit they cannot. (In fact, Hite specifically asked this question, and reported all negative replies.) This is good news for fakers. All the same, it's not a bad idea to rhythmically tense and untense your vagina a bit (you can do it three or four times at about one a second) at the moment of orgasm, just as you have noticed in your masturbation sessions.

Exercise 14.3 Masturbate yourself to orgasm. Just as you begin to climax, insert one or two fingers into your vagina. This will allow you to gauge the degree of the contractions.

Exercise 14.4 This exercise is nothing more than the Kegel exercises mentioned in Chapter 6—that is, clenching and unclenching your vaginal muscles. It can be done at any time of the day or night, without anyone else being any the wiser. Like all muscles, the more you use those in your vagina, the greater their tone will develop.

3. Erect nipples. Dr. David Reuben really did the dirty on women when he wrote:

> **Erection of the nipples always follows orgasm in the female. In spite of heaving hips, lunging pelvis, passionate groans—no nipple erection, no orgasm. It is an accurate mammary lie detector—for those who insist on the truth.**

We've had trouble with Dr Reuben's little sillinesses before. And, just as his nonsense about oral sex clammed me up for years when it came to cunnilingus, so this little gem was one of the reasons I never dared to fake—and so prolonged my misery in the face of men who resented my "frigidity."

There is, in fact, no need to be intimidated by this "biological fact." Like that age-old and very misleading test for virginity—the bloody sheet—erect nipples are *not* a reliable guide to orgasm. Believe me, I was so obsessed with Dr. Reuben's announcement that I've studied it in detail.

I'll begin by quoting the most famous sexologists of

them all, Masters and Johnson: "There is no specific breast reaction to the experience of orgasm." Those of you who are likely to show nipple erection at orgasm are also likely to show nipple erection when you are first sexually aroused.

If that's not good enough for you, the strength of the erection varies greatly not only from woman to woman, but from orgasm to orgasm. And if there are *some* days when nipple erection is minimal, then there's no reason why that shouldn't happen *every* day, is there? Also, remember that temperature plays a part in how nipples behave. On a cold day, they will be erect regardless of orgasm. If you really want to impress him with the quality of your (faked) orgasm, have him make love to you in the snow!

Also if the woman is lying on her back, gravity often ensures that any nipple erection is absorbed by the posture of the breasts, and can easily go undetected. Lastly, it is quite possible to engineer your position—or your clothing—so that he has no access to your nipples.

Exercise 14.5 Masturbate yourself to orgasm while standing up, in a *warm* room. This position will show you the *maximum* erection your nipples are likely to achieve through orgasm. (If the room is cold, you won't be certain which is the orgasm and which the cold.)

Exercise 14.6 Now masturbate yourself to orgasm lying down in a warm room. Again see how your nipples respond. The chances are they will be far less noticeably erect than when you were standing up.

4. When faking, bear in mind also that the quality of any individual orgasm varies greatly. I've had orgasms (real ones, that is) that have had me panting and moaning in a most theatrical manner. And then, the next day, I've had others that, even though intensely felt, I have enjoyed quietly and passively. Be inventive. Vary it—fake some nights, but not others. Incidentally, in the list above I have not mentioned the so-called "sex flush" that some women experience, simply because it doesn't necessarily accompany orgasm. Some women have it *some of the time,* and others don't. So don't give it a thought.

Exercise 14.7 For the really brave: to hell with the Sewing Circle, get some close friends together and form an Orgasm Faking Circle. Try this one: each of you tape yourself masturbating alone. Now get together and play them back, so that you get a really good idea of just how much women vary. Once the initial embarrassment has worn off, you'll have tremendous fun. Just remember the fake-orgasm scene in *When Harry Met Sally.*

If your man has never heard you climax before, he will have nothing to compare it with. But remember, it is still worth taking trouble to fake accurately, because quite soon you really *will* be having real orgasms—and you don't want him to think that you're faking then! So remember:

THE GOLDEN RULE
*In general it is always best to underplay it
than overplay it.*

If, when you do start climaxing, you find your responses are significantly more intense than those you've been faking, you can quite truthfully say to your partner something along the lines of "It's got so much more pleasurable lately, darling." Don't do too much of that heaving hips, lunging pelvis, passionate-groans stuff. Use your ingenuity: tell him to stop once or twice, and wait, thereby suggesting that you have almost had your orgasm and want to delay it for a while. Later, when you've completed your training, you may find yourself doing this anyway.

Don't fake too soon in your lovemaking session, or he'll ejaculate and you'll be left with nothing. Spin it out.

Remember: it is *not possible* to "prove" that a woman has or hasn't had an orgasm—unless, of course, you're down there with a flashlight and some pretty fancy equipment.

And last, an invaluable piece of advice: time your faked climax to coincide with his own—he will be in no position to judge you!

Questions and Answers

Because faking is a controversial subject I've included here a selection of some common questions, together with my responses:

I've read your list of faking advice, but it's scared me. How can I possibly remember all that?

A very good question, since the whole point of faking is to make you free from anxieties, not filled with new ones. That list covers all there is to know about faking orgasm. It's a connoisseur's list, if you like. All you really need to remember are the following very basic points:

1) your breathing;
2) don't overplay by heaving about, or underplay by lying dead still and then suddenly exploding.

Basically, as long as you are familiar with the chapter on masturbation, you'll know what's typical of you. In general, the more emotionally involved you are with your partner, the more you'll want to get it right.

What shall I do if he finds out I've been faking?

It depends what you mean by "finds out." If he *suspects* you, but you have made up your mind that it is the right thing for you to do, then simply stick to your guns and insist that you were not. He cannot prove it. On the other hand, if the manner of his approach is sympathetic, you may feel that now you would like to come clean.

If, for some reason, you feel he really has found out (read your diary confessions, for example), the important thing to remember is *keep your cool.* Don't look guilty or act guilty. Remember; nobody wants to have to fake. If you've been faking, it's for a very good reason. And, believe it or not, it's far more upsetting for *him* if you get all flustered and admit you've been "dishonest." Although in our initial hurt and anger we want to have the satisfaction of blaming someone, in the cold light of day it's easier to accept that there was a good reason for one's partner's "deceit."

So keep cool and talk quite matter-of-factly about it. Say, "Yes, you're quite right. I *have* been faking." Explain the reasons. Tell him that he's touchy about his ego and that this puts unpleasant pressures on you. Tell him you can't do it, and that his hopes for you doing it only makes it worse. If he makes a great big issue out of being hurt and upset, it's high time you reminded him that it's *you* who need the sympathetic understanding, not him.

I love my husband, and I can't get over feeling guilty about faking. What can I do?

Then don't fake. It's an *option*—it's not compulsory. That's why it's not part of the main program. But if you do feel there are reasons for faking, then you must simply concentrate on the fact that by faking you are paving the way ultimately to greater success. Think of it as a temporary measure only, a means to an end.

You say that failing to have an orgasm is nothing to be ashamed of, yet you recommend faking. Isn't that inconsistent?

I hope I have made it clear in the early chapters that being unable to climax is nothing to be ashamed of. If anybody is at "fault"—and often nobody is to blame—it is our partners. In an ideal world, faking wouldn't be necessary. I have introduced faking *because it can be a means to buy time and peace for yourself.* It is a temporary measure to help you along to total success, not simply a way of escaping the embarrassment of admitting "failure."

I cannot repeat this too often: *the only reason you should be faking is as part of a plan to help yourself.* If you are in any doubt about faking, ask yourself the question: "How is this helping *me?*"

CHAPTER FIFTEEN

FANTASY

PHEBE: Good shepard, tell this youth what 'tis to love.
SILVIUS: It is to be all made of fantasy . . .
———Shakespeare, *As You Like It*

I am a great believer in sexual fantasy. It has helped me immeasurably in learning to achieve orgasm. It continues to help me. However good my sex life, fantasy adds that extra touch of color.

Nobody should be ashamed of a bit of sexual inventiveness. In all cultures people who employ their imaginations are highly valued: storytellers, novelists, poets, filmmakers. Using our imagination in bed is just as wonderful, with even more direct results. Fantasy—particularly when carefully combined with reality—can be a crucial feature of satisfying sex. To quote one famous sex therapist, Helen Singer Kaplan: "Sex is friction and fantasy."

Men Only?

Sexual fantasy is more commonly associated with men than with women. The reason is, to my mind, clear and dully familiar—long years of cultural restrictions upon female sexual behavior have created deep-seated feelings of guilt or shame in thinking about sex. In a recent discussion, three women admitted that they would feel quite

214

unsettled if they allowed themselves to indulge in a wild fantasy about being ravished by a sheik: it's the sort of behavior that is still associated with unseemly and unnerving lust rather than respectable womanhood. (A fourth woman agreed that a sheik fantasy would unsettle her, but only because she normally goes for blue-eyed blonds.) Most men, however, because they are *expected* to behave in an aggressively sexual way, are quite happy to imagine *being* a forceful sheik ravishing a woman—even though when the climax is over, they might feel a little guilty and even blush pleasantly. (I always enjoy a blushing man.)

In the early days of psychoanalysis, sexual fantasy was treated as a form of sexual deviation. Dreary old Freud saw it as undesirable escapism, a repressive blocking of the sexual instinct that could lead to psychosis or neurosis (and thus, presumably, back to being treated by Dr. Freud). Even forty years ago it was assumed that for most women sex was the means to what they really enjoyed: romantic slush and motherhood. Their fantasies were supposed to be correspondingly limp. But today it is recognized that female sexual imaginings are as powerful and lusty as any male offering. Best of all, there are scores of reports to show that sexual fantasy has a very positive effect both on individuals and on relationships. Recent studies have concluded that the frequency of sexual fantasy was an excellent indication of a person's sexual health and success with orgasm. Another researcher went so far as to conclude: "Sexual fantasies help many married women to achieve sexual arousal and/or orgasm during sexual intercourse."

Interestingly (make of it what you will), it seems that in males, the younger they are the more they fantasize; whereas in females, fantasy is rare among young girls, but much more common among older women.

What Do People Fantasize About, and Why?

Some common female fantasies include sex with a man with a huge penis, with an innocent young boy, before an audience, with another woman, as a prostitute, with animals, with domination, with a friend or associate, with a group, or, just to make sure nobody's left out, with a stranger.

Jean is very forthright about her sexual fantasies:

> I literally couldn't have an orgasm at all without fantasy. And I don't regret that. Fantasy's great. It lets you really make everything you can out of sex. While I'm being fucked, I think of all sorts of filthy things. Sometimes I whisper them to Philip, and I can feel him begin to shake at the thought of the scene. . . .
>
> One of my favorites is that I'm a warden in a prisoner-of-war camp, Second World War. I walk into the room, and all the men are there looking unshaven, ragged, lean, and grubby. Then there's me, all clean and sleek, and wearing a really tight dress with my breasts half-showing. I walk down the lines, where the men are standing by their bunks. Somehow (I wonder why!) all the men that I actually notice are really nice-looking—tall, noble. Being officers, they are all very self-controlled, so the whole scene is very tense. I walk up and down looking furiously at them, a whip in my hand. I approach one man, my eyes bright with scorn and contempt. He, very anxious not to flinch, says nothing. I obviously inspect him, poking him here and there with my whip. Then my

hand goes to his trousers. I unzip his fly. Still he stands there. I order a box to be brought. Everyone thinks I'm going to indulge in some sort of torture. I order him to stand on the box. That means his fly is on a level with my face. I undo his trousers. I can feel him shaking. I take out his prick, which is in that lovely stage between limp and stiff—half-hard, really big and flopping in a sort of arc—he's fighting to control it, see. I take it in my hands. I place it in my mouth, suck on it, harder and harder until the moment he ejaculates, when I pull it out of my mouth and watch the semen squirt all over me. Still I show no emotion at all.

The majority of people fantasize in order to help themselves become more sexually aroused—an astonishingly high 46 percent of women, and 38 percent of men in one survey (Sue). Nearly a quarter of the women said that they fantasized to increase their partner's attractiveness, whereas 10 percent of the men and 15 percent of the women weren't sure why they did it at all! The great beauty of fantasy is that you are creating situations that are liberatingly impersonal and conveniently imprecise. Perhaps most important of all, *you* have complete control.

Even so, of the many female fantasies I have listened to I was struck by how many involved the *woman* being in control of the situation with the man in varying degrees of helplessness. Erica's fantasy is another good example:

I'm a thief—that's right, a female cat burglar. The house I've got my eye on is a big mansion, with landscaped grounds and naked statues. In the middle of the night I steal in through one of the upstairs windows. I'm in a black outfit, very tight-fitting with a black mask. I'm also carrying a large *screw*driver. (Well, what else?) I'm creeping qui-

etly around, filling my sack, when I hear a noise. The person in the bed has woken up. By the light of a small bedside lamp I see it's a man. *Of course* he's good-looking—mid-thirties, slender, dark—and terrified.

Slowly and with the tip of the screwdriver I roll the bedclothes back. With one hand I reach for his pajamas. As soon as he sees my hand, he realizes I'm a woman. I undo the button. My fingers brush against his prick. For a long time I play with his prick, part teasing him, part threatening. Then I force him to lie back. I straddle him. I unzip my pants in a special place, without taking them off. Pinning him down, I move up and down on him, up and down, slowly slowly, then faster and faster. I satisfy myself totally. Maybe I allow him to orgasm—maybe I leave him gasping for relief—it depends how I feel. Now the dawn is coming up. I peel off his pajama bottoms, drop them into my sack with the antiques, and slip out of the window.

Another noticeable feature of many such imagined situations is their *impersonal* nature: highly erotic, but no messing about with love and romance. Great stuff for fantasy—especially since nowadays the risk of AIDS makes such encounters in real life very risky. In her wonderful novel *Fear of Flying*, Erica Jong describes one scenario of what she calls the "zipless fuck," an ideal type of copulation in which passion itself and not the person of your lover is the issue. Her fantasy takes place in a second-class compartment on a "grimy European train." An attractive young widow in mourning is sitting there, along with four rather unpleasant characters. At one of the stations a sixth person enters, a "tall languid-looking soldier, unshaven, but with a beautiful mop of hair, a cleft chin, and somewhat devilish, lazy eyes . . . basically a gorgeous hunk of flesh." He sits down flirtatiously next to the widow. After a while he slips his fingers under her thigh. She shows no reaction. The four unsavories get off at a station. The man grows bolder, but still nothing is said. The train then enters a tunnel "and in the semi-darkness the symbolism is consummated" and the young widow gets off at the next town.

Zipless, you see, *not* because European men have button-flies rather than zipper-flies, and not because the participants are so devastatingly attractive, but because the incident has all the swift compression of a dream and is seemingly free of all remorse and guilt; because there is no talk of her late husband or his fiancée; because there is no rationalizing; because there is no talk at *all*. The zipless fuck is absolutely pure. It is free of ulterior motives. . . . And it is rarer than the unicorn. And I have never had one.

Fantasies are rarely well focused. It is more a matter of skipping here and there, picking up bits of mood and sensation, repeating parts you like, avoiding those you don't, playing not only the role of yourself, but also to some extent the role of the other characters. Unless my fantasy is a daydream and engulfs me entirely, then I don't ever have my whole mind on it—some portion of my concentration remains with the facts.

A huge number of women fantasize about people they normally know in nonsexual situations. I always look forward to hearing Laura's latest, which invariably focuses on her doctor. It's particularly entertaining because I know her doctor, too, and I cannot quite envisage him in the sort of situations she does. I see him as a rather dry, graying, middle-aged man; she sees him as a mysterious stranger, suppressing his sexual energies:

I've got a midday appointment for something quite innocuous. Something wrong with my hand, say, and by some sort of not quite clear reason, I have to take my top off and I can see him breathing more heavily but keeping up a deliciously professional air. . . . In the end, of course, he breaks down and pins me against the wall. The interesting thing about it is that I'm half-concentrating on the way he feels and half on the way I do. The real me is fantasizing about a sort of imaginary combination of the two characters.

Should I Feel Guilty?

There is one aspect of fantasy that used to make me suffer agonies of guilt, and that was my constant desire to fantasize about being raped, or forcibly made love to.

While it worked wonders for my ability to have an orgasm, the rest of the day I felt dreadful. I was under no illusion that such a situation in reality would be anything other than terrifying and hateful. To indulge as amusement in a situation that has in reality ruined women's lives seemed outrageous. It came as a surprise and a relief to learn that some form of "rape" situation is one of the commonest of all female fantasies. Writes Nancy Friday about women's fantasies in *Men in Love:*

the single greatest theme that emerged was that of "weak" women being sexually dominated, "forced" by male strength to do this deliciously awful thing, made to perform that marvelously forbidden act, guiltlessly "raped" again and again.

As has been proved many times, the point of the fantasy is never to replicate the horror of real rape but to overcome inhibitions by imagining that sex is compulsory.

In my fantasy, of course, I could also exaggerate certain things I found pleasurable without having to feel worried that I was too demanding or perverted. That's why when I write about "rape" fantasies, I put the word in quotes. Unlike rape, the whole point of the fantasy is that *you* lead the situation in the direction you want it to go, but under the pretense of having it forced on you. You choose your partner, the location, the way he approaches you, etc. In short, in an imagined "rape," *you* are in control, whereas a real rape is a situation of complete lack of control: the two are not only dissimilar, they are complete opposites. (It is interesting, by the way, that women tend to get appreciably more aroused from fantasizing than they do simply by watching an erotic film. I put this down, again, to the pleasure of being in control of the direction and details of the fantasy, even if not in control within the scenario.)

Recently a couple of researchers (Bond and Mosher) conducted a study specifically to help dispel the myth that women are secretly willing victims of rape. Using what they term "guided imagery"—that is, tape recordings of specially constructed scenarios—they presented two types of scenarios to a group of female volunteers. The first was "an erotic fantasy of 'rape,'" during which the women got aroused and reported "interest, enjoyment, and pleasure." As the researchers conclude: in this imagined "rape" "the woman is *in control* because she enticed and permitted the man to "rape" her for her own erotic purposes" (my italics).

It was a very different situation with the second scenario —a realistic scene of rape. The women reported "disgust, fear, anger, pain, shame and depression"—feelings very similar to those reported by rape victims themselves. So much so, in fact, that the article contained an ethical consideration of how to proceed in future with such tests.

221

In my own case, I think my forced-sex fantasies have as much to do with shame as guilt. Just as the idea of one's parents indulging in sex can be embarrassing and slightly distasteful, so I—and many women I've spoken to—feel something like that about themselves. One woman I know actually has nightmares about seeing herself in the mirror having sex, and wakes up hot with embarrassment—"as if I'd just walked down Main Street on a Saturday afternoon completely naked." So it's no surprise to learn that this woman's fantasies all center around forced sex, which is liberatingly impersonal. Her marriage is perfectly happy; yet, when she makes love with her husband she asks him never to use her name. It's a bizarre position for him, as he confided:

Men who keep mistresses go through agonies in case they blurt out the wrong name in a moment of passion. I go through agonies in case I blurt out the *right* name!

Surveys have shown that nowadays very few women indeed feel guilty about the fact of fantasizing. What they do sometimes feel guilty about is indulging in fantasies involving sexual intercourse with someone other than their partner. While it is sometimes kinder not to make these known to him (unless by mutual agreement), it really is a waste of energy to feel guilty, because the very nature of fantasy means that your mind is in an ideal situation, able to mold events exactly how you want them. You are able to imagine the pleasurable involvement in a scene that in the messy, uncoordinated real world would most probably be quite unpalatable. Fantasy is not infidelity, because the chances are a real-life encounter with the object of your fantasy would prove very different from your imaginings, as Dorothy's experience while working in an office in New York demonstrates:

222

I used to work for a big firm of accountants. I was one of three personal secretaries that dealt with my boss. I think we all were attracted to him—he was tall, quite powerfully built, with glossy dark hair just going gray at the sides. He managed to be distinguished and rakish at the same time.

After a few weeks working there, I began to fantasize about making love with him: I usually imagined us on the boardroom floor, in full daylight, with my shorthand pad in one hand . . .

Then one day I had to stay late because I was going out to the theater afterwards, and I had an hour or so to kill. I got out my makeup and things and spread them about. I was sure everyone had gone home. I stripped off my shirt and was sitting on my desk in my skirt. Suddenly the door opened and—you guessed it—he came in. I thought he'd get embarrassed and go away, but he didn't. He just stopped still and stared at me. Then he came over and without speaking, he began kissing me. At first this was quite exciting. He took my hand and guided it inside his open fly. "Take it, take it," he kept saying. He'd shut his eyes and was sitting there blankly, while I was rubbing his dick for him.

For just one moment I thought "Creep." But that thought quickly passed and we carried on.

Finally he rolled my skirt up around my waist and started playing with my pussy. He did it very badly, though he obviously thought he was cool. I was lying on the desk and he undid the top button of his trousers and they fell around his feet. He opened my legs and brought his dick up and pushed it inside me. At first I was torn between thinking "My God, fantastic—I'm finally doing it with him" and a nagging sense of distaste. It wasn't the way I'd envisaged it. I had my legs over his shoulders and he was standing there, puffing away. What he didn't know was that reflected in the glass doorway I could see his back view—a bare ass, skinny legs, and trousers round his ankles. He looked—well, a creep. No doubt about it this time. The whole thing was a bit squalid. I thought, "I don't even like this man, and here I am lying on a table with him jerking off inside me."

What really made me mad was that when he came he took his dick out of me and pumped his semen all over the blouse I was supposed to wear to the theater. Well, that's what comes of having fantasies—not much similarity! I threw the blouse away.

Another very striking example of the difference between reality and fantasy is provided by Kathy. She's been with Ed for seven years, and admits that she is sexually very jealous over him: "The thought of Ed even looking at another woman gets my teeth gnashing," she admits. Yet Kathy has a regular, favorite fantasy that she employs whenever she has sex with him. It helps her to reach orgasm:

Quite simply, it's Ed with another woman. For some bizarre reason, I find it incredibly sexy. All the while he's fucking me I transpose each little detail so that it's as if he's doing the same to her— only I'm watching through the keyhole. When I'm slow to climax, I just replay the part where he parts her legs, pulls her panties down, and enters her.

Obviously there are odd occasions when, either through too much to drink, bad lighting, or because we trod on our spectacles the day before, we find ourselves in bed with the *wrong man*, and then fantasy provides very necessary escapism. Janie was invited to a ball, where she was introduced to an impeccably mannered European count, who kissed her hand and waltzed her around the room. The lure of blue blood proved irresistible:

He took me back to his house in a taxi. I was so bowled over by the chandeliers, the Louis Quinze furniture, the Limoges china, that I didn't notice him unlacing his corsets. A cigar-smelling, pot-bellied male sidled into bed with me. I had no option but to fantasize as hard as possible about *anything* that would take my mind off him. A just punishment for being a snob!

On the whole, however, fantasies are valuable because they *enhance* moods and sensations that are actually taking place.

Even during sex with your preferred man, there are ways and ways of fantasizing. Lying back, forgetting about him and thinking through your favorite story like a day-dream is a waste: a waste of your partner, a waste of a good fantasy, and a waste of companionship. For the purposes of orgasm, the best type of fantasy is what I have called "blended fantasy." I know it sounds more like a recipe than anything else, but perhaps in a way it is—a recipe for orgasm. This is when you successfully combine fantasy and reality. Instead of imagining a completely foreign scenario, concentrate on interweaving the real and the imaginary, by making sure that every movement your partner makes fits in beautifully with what you're imagining. The ultimate sophistication of this "blended" fantasy is for you and your partner to indulge in mutual fantasies in which you *both* play a part.

Pornography, Erotic Literature, or Romance?

Close to the subject of fantasy is that of sexually stimulating literature. There has been for a long time a debate as to whether women are sexually aroused by romantic stories, or by the more explicit stuff. This "more explicit stuff" can be divided into pornography and erotic literature. Feminist Andrea Dworkin, whom I have only ever heard speak on television, and even then burst out in applause at the end of her lecture though there was no one but the cat to hear me—defines pornography in terms of sexually explicit material depicting violence against, or the subordination of, women. She believes—I think quite rightly—that it should be made illegal. Erotic material, on the other hand, can be just as hard-core, but it is without the enforced female sexual inequality and hence not so damaging to women nor so provoking to violence and domination for men.

Kinsey was one of those researchers who believed that women experience little or no sexual arousal when confronted with sexually explicit material, but require a romantic context. I've always been suspicious of this, partly because I've been turned on by explicitly erotic material, but also because the idea of women liking only "romance" is yet another way of patronizing them, keeping them in an inferior position as the weaker, less physical, more gullible sex; in short, suspiciously in tune with the sexual sentiments of the 1950s, the decade in which Kinsey did his work.

I'm glad to say that Kinsey is now regarded as out of date—especially where his conclusions about women are concerned. In fact, on this level, there's some suspicion that he was a bit of a fudger of results although no one quite likes to say so. More recently a researcher named Jakobovits challenged Kinsey's results and found that, on the contrary, there was very little difference between men and women in this respect: they both got aroused by erotic literature. Later studies have tended to support Jakobovits's conclusion that the crucial element which affects the level of arousal is the explicitness of the sexual material rather than the presence or absence of romance.

Of course, this romance/explicitness debate is difficult to prove either way. The big bar to conclusive results in women is—as I've said elsewhere—the fact that it is very difficult to monitor accurately female sexual arousal. We don't have erections to show unequivocally that we are feeling horny. The fact that female attitudes to sex scenes are changing—and coming towards a preference for more explicitness—is reflected in those stalwarts of women's romantic fiction, Harlequin. Nowadays the following type of scene is typical (and I should add that while this one is in itself sexually arousing, within the context of the plot it is very much more so):

He was already undressing her, his fingers deft on the buttons of her dress . . .

"Touch me, Beatrice."

She wanted to resist, to tell him that she wasn't ready, but she was overwhelmed by the sudden rush of emotion sweeping over her as his hands swept back up over her body to ease down the fabric covering her breasts.

"You can't know how much I've ached to do this," he told her softly, "and this."

He bent his head and she felt his lips gently caressing her breasts . . . He made a deep sound in his throat and moved his body deliberately against her, until the delicate friction made her cry out . . . His mouth left hers and she knew he was looking down into her unguarded face as he

deliberately aroused her . . . His voice shook and so did his body, the fierce thrust of it within her own suddenly wildly out of control. She clung to him, hearing him moan her name, feeling the sudden quickening of her own flesh as it responded to his male need.

Tiny quivers of sensation built up inside her, a quivery shivery tension that wouldn't let her go, that drove her to incite him to take her with him to that place where the boundaries of flesh and mortality exploded in a vast shimmering ball of sensation.

(Frances Roding, *Some Sort of Spell*)

Obviously not a piece to please radical feminists, but it does make clear that the situation is changing with the times—that is, that the more economic, intellectual, and sexual independence women achieve, the more likely they are to feel freely aroused by literature. Because the point here is not simply that the modern woman indulges in extramarital sex, but that that sex is evocatively described rather than simply reported.

So if you need to "get into the mood" before going to bed—or even before masturbating—then read a few pages of an erotic book. When I was still learning to have an orgasm, I often used to give myself a head start by reading a sexy book while my partner was preparing for bed. In fact, those early partners were positively hurried into the shower. (I daresay they all now have hideous complexes about being smelly.) There is no doubt in my mind that erotic literature can be extremely helpful in this program.

Exercise 15.1 This is really an exercise in timing and control. Find yourself an erotic book. Hold the book in one hand, and as you read, masturbate yourself with your other hand. I want you to learn to *time* your climax with the most erotic moment of the book. This may seem a frivolous exercise, but it will stand you in good stead. Repeat it as often as possible—if you like, combine it with exercises in Chapter 7.

Dirty Books or Literature?

"Masturbate myself to orgasm with an erotic story!" you may be thinking. "That's the sort of thing dirty old men in raincoats do."

Well, perhaps they do it, too. All I can say is, as an exercise and a way of sexual pleasure, it's a perfectly clean, useful, interesting, and delightful thing to do. The books you read can be the sort of scruffy thing you pick up from an adult bookstore, or they can be some of the more liberated works of great fiction that sober, white-haired academics daily analyze and comment on. They both have sex and sexiness in them aplenty—if you know where to look for it.

In the bibliography I have included a list of possible books you might like to try. Most of them are ones you can get in perfectly respectable bookstores, and nobody will think you're anything but a broad-minded and serious reader when you buy them. When you get home you can skip all the nonerotic parts and get to the nitty-gritty or savour their genius slowly—whatever you like. I personally think that the context of the erotic part is all-important, being fifty-five times more sexy if you've had to wait thirty pages for it. If you're not that patient, read the sober parts during the day and keep the hotter stuff for bedtime.

If you (like me) are also partial to the cruder stuff, then you can try the local sex shop. I used to go there quite often (some have a convenient back door for those who are a little shy), even though I had very mixed feelings about such places. Clearly a great deal of what they sell is highly degrading to women; but equally clearly some of what they sell I find highly erotic. The readily available videos tend to be just plain silly. I remember one in which two girls seduced the milkman, amid much squealing and giggling: you could clearly see that they were only pretending to ravish him, and at one moment a flaccid little penis hove into view. (There also exist sex stores specifically for women, such as Eve's Garden.)

On the other hand I've also seen some highly explicit videos (mostly imported from abroad) which leave you in no doubt at all that sex is taking place. I'm always torn between the arousing sight of couples actually coupling, and disturbing thoughts about what the female participants are *really* feeling. Dawn found an excellent antidote: gay videos. She assures me that if you want to see some really good-looking guys, with positively *enormous* equipment (I can vouch for the fact that the heterosexual penises are almost always disappointing), try getting hold of one of these. Though the more explicit ones may not be quite your cup of tea, the milder ones often show attractive males masturbating. And there are no uncomfortable worries about what the women are having to endure.

Nowadays, I have to admit, my feminist loyalties keep me away from the sex shop; but then nowadays, when I am so much more practised at orgasm, I don't need that extra stimulation. Quite apart from ideological issues, the danger of sex shops is that you don't know whom you'll meet there. My friend (who lives in a small town) never quite felt the same about her chiropodist after catching him gazing at a foot-fetish magazine. She bravely continued to consult him because, as she pointed out, "I ought to have guessed. I mean who else would *choose* to spend their lives with other people's feet? As long as he doesn't get *carried away,* I think of it as rather flattering."

Mail order is another option—you find advertisements

in all kinds of newspapers and journals. That way you've only got to worry that the postman is reliable.

Literature can, of course, be erotic either explicitly or by implication. Jane Austen's *Pride and Prejudice* is not only one of the world's great classics, but probably one of the most genteel novels ever written. Yet the sexual tension between the two main characters, Elizabeth Bennett and Mr Darcy, is dynamite. This strikes me as a book that hovers delicately between "romantic" and "erotic"—it is far too forceful for the former, and a little too restrained for the latter. I don't believe there's a woman alive who having read *Pride and Prejudice* hasn't fantasized about meeting Mr. Darcy in the woods. Rose's favorite is Thomas Hardy's *Far from the Madding Crowd:*

> **I fantasize about being Bathsheba [the heroine] and having three totally dissimilar men in love with me. The dashing Sergeant Troy swishing his sword in the moonlight; the passionate, repressed Farmer Boldwood, and then that wildly sexy union with the shepherd Gabriel Oak at the end. It may not sound particularly erotic—and there's nothing sexually *explicit*—but when you've got so involved with the characters, you can't help sharing in their passions. I find it much more sexy than the movies.**

Another one of my favorite "classics" is the eighteenth-century literary masterpiece, John Cleland's *Fanny Hill.* It is the story of an innocent young girl's adventures in a brothel, written in the most improbably novelettish fashion you can imagine.

> **. . . his breeches, before loosen'd, now gave up their contents to view, and shew'd in front the enemy I had to engage with, stiffly bearing up the port of its head unhooded, and glowing red. Then**

I plainly saw what I had to trust to: it was one of those just true-siz'd instruments, of which the masters have a better command than the more unwieldly, inordinate siz'd ones are generally under. Straining me then close to his bosom, as he stood up fore-right against me and applying to the obvious niche its peculiar idol, he aimed at inserting it, which, as I forwardly favoured, he effected at once, by canting up my thighs over his naked hips, and made me receive every inch . . .

The whole thing is absolutely delightful, and if you like to fantasize about being penetrated by ridiculously large (and ridiculously colorful) penises, then this is the book for you.

The Classical Fantasy

Just to show that there needn't be anything disreputable about reading porn and looking at dirty pictures, let me tell you about Annie's fantasies. She's a tall willowy woman in her thirties who works as a graphic artist designing book covers, advertisements and so forth. I recently visited her in her apartment in Chicago where, over a bottle of Chianti, we got on to the subject of fantasy. "Well, what's your favorite?" I asked her.

"Oh, that's easy," she replied, and reached out to the bookcase and opened a large glossy edition of artwork. "I think some of the most erotic stories in the world are the Greek classics," she explained, flipping over the pages and showing me illustration after glorious illustration, many by the great Renaissance masters. "Most of my fantasies come from the Greek myths," she continued. "Marvelous stories, handsome gods—look at that torso—it's fantasy in all senses of the word: sexual as well as escapist. I must admit I do tend to envisage the gods themselves as any man I'm particularly interested in at that time. What I particularly like is that however lewd you make the fantasy, it never seems squalid. Also, you can read them on the train."

So, next time you want a helping hand when your man makes love to you, buy a book of the Greek myths and ponder Zeus's unusual seduction techniques.

After all, you can embellish with your own special details . . .

CHAPTER SIXTEEN

Know Your Orgasm

Whoever said orgasm wasn't important for a woman was undoubtedly a man.
——Woman quoted in *The Hite Report on Female Sexuality*

In this chapter I'm going to go into the nature of orgasm in greater depth. I must have looked up the word itself in over a thousand books. Enormous volumes professing to investigate sexual behavior often don't list it, rather as if the authors had barely heard of the subject, and suspect it might belong to another discipline—politics, perhaps, or some new particle found by the high-energy physicists.

Other books list it, but only one or two very brief entries. You can just see the writer fiddling with the word: "Orgasm? Again? Oh, dear!" And then, after a cup of coffee and a few worried paces about the room, he returns to his desk and crosses out the reference altogether. "Most likely it was a mistake."

Recently the situation has got a little better. Sexual research has become respectable and scientific; huge, confidential studies of the average person's sexuality have become popular—and since the average person in private is significantly more informative than the specialist in public, our understanding of the female orgasm has increased vastly. Feminism, aside from enforcing greater scientific objectivity, has helped to make sex *interesting,* and not just the subject of giggles and derision. Another advance is that animal behaviorists no longer focus entirely on the male of the species.

But although the complexity of the female orgasm has finally begun to excite widespread professional interest, our understanding of it is still slight. The female orgasm remains one of the most beguiling sexual mysteries of our time.

What Exactly Happens During Sex?

Many of us know what orgasm feels like, but you'd be surprised at just how much is going on inside our bodies. The sexual response cycle of the female (like the male) is commonly divided into four phases: excitement, plateau, orgasm, and resolution. (Other classifications are possible, but this one, from Masters and Johnson, is the most widely accepted.) I'll describe each phase briefly, partly because the way a given person responds during any one of these varies widely—there is no "correct" or "incorrect" way—and partly because the medical terminology is enough to make me feel quite queasy.

In the *excitement* phase, heart rate, blood pressure, and respiration all increase, and the muscles also become more tense. In certain parts of the body—those typically associated with sexual excitement—there is an increase of blood supply which may make those areas redden and grow warmer. It is this that is responsible for increase in breast size, nipple erection, and the so-called sexual flush that occurs in some women.

The genitals undergo major changes during this phase, although the vast majority of people do not notice most of them. The clitoris, vagina, and labia minora all increase in size due to more blood supply. The vagina also responds by producing lubrication, which allows easier penetration of the penis, and helps sperm survival by neutralizing the vagina's natural acidity.

The *plateau* phase is really a misnomer. It is not that everything levels off until orgasm, but that most of the responses begun in the excitement phase continue to change, though at a slower rate. Meanwhile, the clitoris is retracted under the clitoral hood. The phase does not last long—a few seconds, to several minutes at most—although an extended period can be very pleasurable and often followed by a relatively intense orgasm.

During the *orgasm* phase heart rate, blood pressure, and respiration all reach their peak and are accompanied by involuntary contractions of the outer third of the vagina, and often also of the uterus, rectal sphincter, and urethral sphincter. There are usually between three and fifteen contractions, occurring about every four-fifths of a second to begin with and then slowing down.

The most annoying aspect of orgasm itself is, of course, that it's over so quickly—a matter of seconds rather than minutes. Roberta gives an excellent description:

Just before I come, there's this slight pause as if I'm on the edge, just about to fall over but not quite making it. It's almost like the drawing in of breath before a sneeze—such a quiet thing to happen before so loud a noise. I know what I'm in for and I'm desperate for it to happen, and I know I can't stop it and that I have just a brief second to wait . . . and then I'm falling. It starts in my groin, a touch of pure, agonizing pleasure which suddenly pours forth and grips me for an instant, and then submerges me in a sea of release. I'm mixing my metaphors, but a decent orgasm makes it impossible to do anything else. It can be such an intense feeling. Before orgasm I was moaning and moving around because I wanted more sex, more this, more that. But during orgasm I'm on my

own; I'm groaning because of all that I'm letting go—all the sexual tension that I wanted to build up so much beforehand, all the tension in the world. . . . Occasionally it's a feeble affair. Still nice, of course, and not to be sniffed at, but without the explosion.

During orgasm, many women stiffen, become rigid and don't look at all as if they're enjoying themselves. There's an excellent murder mystery, *Rough Cider* by Peter Lovesey, which I thoroughly recommend, in which an important twist of the plot hinges on just this oddity. Other women make all sorts of evocative noises while they climax, as the following delightful episode from the life of the sixteenth-century adventurer Sir Walter Raleigh shows:

He loved a wench well; and one time getting up one of the mayds of honor against a tree in a wood ('twas his first lady) who seemed at first boarding to be something fearful of her Honour, and modest, she cryed Sweet Sir Walter, what do you me ask? Will you undoe me? Nay, Sir Walter! Sir Walter! At last, as the danger and the pleasure at the same time grew higher she cried in the extacey Swisser Swatter! Swisser Swatter! (John Aubrey, *Brief Lives*)

After orgasm (or orgasms), there is a slow, reverse-order return to normal, which is termed the *resolution* phase. The enlarged vagina and labia minora diminish, the clitoris reappears, lubrication ceases, heart and breathing rate decrease, and blood pressure lowers. There's usually a feeling of relaxation, calm, and emotional closeness.

Descriptions by women of female orgasm are very rare in literature because, over the centuries, erotica has been written almost entirely by men. The following piece comes from Mary McCarthy's *The Group:*

> **She struggled against the excitement his tickling thumb was producing in her own external part; but as she felt him watching her, her eyes closed and her thighs spread open. He disengaged her hand and she fell back on the bed, gasping. His thumb continued its play and she let herself yield to what it was doing, her whole attention concentrated on a tense pinpoint of sensation, which suddenly discharged itself in a nervous, fluttering spasm; her body arched and heaved, and then lay still.**

The intensity and sensation varies not only between one woman and the next, but between one orgasm and another. And, as I have already said, although many people go crazy in their descriptions of orgasm, it can just as easily be a pleasant but nothing-to-get-excited-about experience. In fact, it's one of my main complaints that sex manuals tend to glorify orgasm to a positively intimidating degree. As one married woman confided, "I get so worried that, much as I enjoy my climaxes, they never seem to be so deeply *significant* as some writers suggest."

Of course, a good orgasm is a profoundly satisfying experience, both physically and emotionally—especially if you're fond of your partner. But there are also scores of occasions for thousands of women when the earth doesn't move, it's over quickly, and all we want to do is get dressed and have breakfast. It's only by acknowledging the mundane side of orgasm that we can really appreciate the peaks.

Do Animals Have Orgasms?

Now, this *is* a fascinating subject.

To some extent, the problem of why women have orgasms (and why they have difficulty with them) is connected with the problem of the female orgasm in other species. If animals have them, that implies it's a much earlier evolutionary addition to female sexuality than if they don't. But it was only in the 1970s that nonhuman females began to attract much research. Before then it was wrongly assumed that males were the interesting sex, while females simply hung around passively waiting to have babies.

In looking at animals, the first question is what constitutes an orgasm? In males, at least, you'd think that was an easy matter. But no, because ejaculation and orgasm are not necessarily one and the same. It may be quite possible (who knows?) for a male monkey, dog, hyena, kangaroo, or whatever to ejaculate without experiencing any of the psychological sensations commonly associated with orgasm in human males.

How much harder, then, to decide about the female. After all, the bespectacled scientist can't *ask* a copulating female gorilla whether or not she's having an orgasm. The researcher who works outside the laboratory can only sit quietly in the bush with his binoculars and sandwiches watching and listening for sexual behavior to see if anything strikes him as familiar. The scientist in the laboratory is a little better equipped. He must attach wires to the female in appropriate places. Once she gets going with a male, he must register changes in blood pressure, heart, and breathing rate, in muscular tension and hormone levels. Now he must analyze them to see if they fit in with human behavior during orgasm. If most of the changes fit the human pattern, then the evidence for orgasm is pretty compelling.

For nonprimates, the evidence is inconclusive. Female mammals have a clitoris, which may be stimulated during copulation, but by any account female orgasm is rare, either because in many species orgasm simply isn't possible for the female, or (as the very existence of a clitoris strongly suggests) because the circumstances are rarely right. The interesting thing—especially for our purposes —is that most researchers seem to assume that orgasm is *a potential that all female mammals have.*

For nonhuman primates the situation is happier—because, gradually, apes and monkeys all over the world are being ruthlessly exposed in their moment of sexual ecstasy. In 1971 female rhesus monkeys were brought to orgasm *not* by their own mates, who (in common with too many of the male animal kingdom, alas!) suffered dreadful premature ejaculation, but by the researcher himself boldly stimulating them. (I hope they thanked him!) In 1979 a researcher reported actually witnessing an orgasm in a female gorilla—and, while we're on the subject of gorillas, back in the 1920s there was a romantic case of cross-species attraction. A female gorilla named Congo used to grasp men's hands and use them to masturbate herself. On one occasion, the famous animal psychologist Robert Yerkes narrowly escaped being raped by Congo.

In 1980 four Dutch scientists recorded uterine contractions and changes in heart rate and facial expression comparable to those in humans during orgasm in some female stump-tailed macaque monkeys—although the notable fact that immediately springs to my mind is that macaques are blissfully free from inhibitions (*four* Dutch scientists). But, in order to get stimulation to last sufficiently long (the male macaques also suffering premature ejaculation) the Dutchmen had to arrange an encounter *between two females*. Five years later, their finding was supported by studies of macaque monkeys in the wild. Just watch the pages of your favorite sex journal to find out who will be next.

Masturbation occurs frequently in nonhuman female animals, as most pet owners are aware. Cats and dogs in heat often rub their vulvas against objects—sometimes objects which you'd prefer they left alone. I remember being ravished by an eager female German shepherd when, aged about thirteen, I wandered into the local candy store to buy some chocolate. "Well, we *are* wearing our miniskirts today!" exclaimed the store owner, as if that somehow explained it. Since such behavior (the dog's, I mean) serves partly for stimulation and partly to leave a distinctive scent mark to attract males, it was rather fortunate I didn't meet a male shepherd on the way home.

But my favorite example has to be that captive female porcupines, who sometimes hold a stick in one forepaw, straddle it like a broomstick, and then walk around the cage, dragging it along the ground so that the bumps and vibrations can gently excite them.

Why Has the Female Orgasm Evolved?

It's easy, of course, to explain why the male orgasm has evolved. In bald evolutionary terms, it is to the advantage of the species (at least during times when there is not overpopulation) to encourage the male to deposit semen frequently and thus ensure reproduction. The very simplicity of this idea makes woman's capacity for orgasm difficult to explain. After all, according to the scenario, it's only necessary for the woman not to refuse, or be unable to refuse, intercourse. Physical weakness and/or a certain degree of enjoyment are all that's needed. Climax, says the pondering evolutionist, seems to be taking things a little too far.

Some researchers consider that the female orgasm helps to increase "pair-bonding" between husband and wife. Sexual gratification is supposed to make emotional attachment between partners stronger, and by encouraging a stable, happy family unit, the young have a better chance of survival. It's no surprise that this theory is held by researchers from widely different professional backgrounds —after all, it is the least adventurous and most socially respectable one that fits the bill. Hite does not support it.

Mary Jane Sherfey's theory is much more exciting, although (predictably) less widely held. In *The Nature and Evolution of Female Sexuality* she argues that orgasm—multiple orgasm even—was once the norm for women; so much so that men considered it needed suppressing:

Primitive woman's sexual drive was too strong, too susceptible to the fluctuating extremes of an impelling, aggressive eroticism to withstand the disciplined requirements of a settled life . . .

Because, biologically speaking, women are able to have unlimited numbers of orgasms one after the other, our distant ancestors were able to go from partner to partner enjoying themselves without limit—and where does that leave society? Far from encouraging pair-bonding, Sherfey conjectures that the female orgasm was ruthlessly suppressed because of its disruptive influence. Sexual repression of women therefore became a key characteristic of the development of civilization, and women's ability to have orgasms has suffered accordingly.

There is indeed historical evidence to show that in societies the world over women's sex drives have been considerably suppressed. Stone Age art indicates that 20,000 years ago there was no clear differentiation between the social power of women and men. Furthermore, cave paintings concentrate much more on the woman's sexual organs than on the man's, suggesting that the woman's sexual role was particularly appreciated.

But changes have taken place since then. About 10,000 years ago humans began to understand that sexual inter-course—and not simply lying in the moonlight, or appeas-ing the gods—was necessary for pregnancy. This, of course, raised the status of the penis—and our not-very-enlightened ancestors began to consider the woman as merely another type of fertile soil into which he planted his all-important seed.

Other theories state that female orgasm has a reproduc-tive purpose, helping to draw the sperm up towards the egg, while some researchers claim it has the opposite effect and actually blocks the sperm! And then, of course, there are those who believe it serves no particular function at all, but is very pleasant all the same.

Take your pick.

Male Versus Female Orgasm

Is there a difference between orgasm as experienced by men and orgasm as experienced by women? Hard to judge, of course, unless you've tried both, and sex-change patients are hardly typical examples. The authors of the *Arabian Nights* assumed the female's pleasure to be the greater, but the best one can say for certain is that verbal reports of orgasm by both men and women are very simi-lar indeed.

However, while most men report that one orgasm is pretty much like another, women tend to experience a great range of feeling, from the highly intense to the com-paratively mild. In my view, this all adds to the interest of women, but then I'm biased. Another difference is that while men generally find their first orgasm the most intense and any subsequent ones less so, with women it is the other way around. While on the subject I cannot resist quoting this perfectly leaden description of male orgasm from Ernest Hemingway's *For Whom the Bell Tolls:*

For him it was a dark passage which led to nowhere, then to nowhere, then again to nowhere, once again to nowhere, always and for ever to nowhere, heavy on the elbows in the earth to nowhere . . .

Aren't you glad you're a woman?

The interesting thing is that as we in the West become more sexually liberated (probably more so than ever before in history) and less tolerant of the traditional inequalities between the sexes, the difference between male and female desire and ability for orgasm is rapidly *decreasing.* Studies reveal that there is practically no difference between young men's and young women's desire for intercourse. If this surprises you, bear in mind that other factors can mask these essential similarities. For example, women are slower to warm up for sex (and, as some partners may have failed to notice, slower to cool down). And, because of their potential for pregnancy, women have far more at stake each time they have sex. It is very much in their own interests to select their partner with care.

In fact many researchers are quite convinced that women have *stronger*—though more readily suppressed—sex drives than men. Masturbation is commonly considered the best indication of sexual potential; and, as we have seen, women can easily masturbate to orgasm as quickly as men. Many can also have multiple orgasms, which is something very few males are capable of.

The Clitoral System and the Penis

We are accustomed to thinking of the male genitalia as very different from that of the female. I have made the point at various times in the book that this obvious difference contributes to many of our attitudes. Dr Sherfey, however, points out that although the genitalia of the two sexes may seem very different, there are in fact remarkable similarities.

She describes the clitoris as merely the small visible part of a hidden *clitoral system*. The penis can be compared to this system, both in terms of size and response to sexual stimulation. As she so nicely puts it:

We may say that the external genitalia of the female are homologous to the entire penis split open along its undersurface and the split-open scrotal sac.

And during sexual excitement (in Hite's words) "the only real difference between men's and women's erections is that men's are on the outside of their bodies, while women's are on the inside."

Both have analogous regions—the *crura* and the *corpora cavernosa*—which become filled with blood during sexual excitation and serve, in the case of the clitoral system, to contribute to the enlargement of the vagina and, in the case of the penis, to erection. Also, just as there are sets of muscles to help with the erection of the penis during the excitement phase, so there are homologous sets of muscles which retract the clitoris during the plateau phase. The rhythmic contractions of the vagina during orgasm are caused by muscles which have precise counterparts in the

245

man, causing contractions that force the ejaculation of semen. What's more, the contractions are at the same rate: i.e., every 0.8 seconds.

In terms of size, the penis and the clitoral system are about the same when excited. The clitoris itself, far from being the focus of sexual responsiveness as so many assume it to be, is just the tip of the iceberg—to use a most inappropriate metaphor.

The Vaginal and Clitoral Orgasm

The notion that women experience more than one type of orgasm began with Freud. His idea was that women who have not yet accepted their passive sexual role or learned to come to terms with penis envy, experience clitoral orgasm. He associated this type of (supposedly not very satisfying) orgasm with masturbation, which he considered to be stimulation of the female penis counterpart—i.e., the clitoris. Mature women, on the other hand, experience a vaginal orgasm due to vaginal stimulation during intercourse. Unlike clitoral orgasm this is supposed to be more satisfying because it occurs with women who have adapted comfortably to their sexually inferior status and receptive role!

It is an obnoxious theory, although for its time not unusually so. And, to be fair to Freud, though its reasoning is absurd, the idea is motivated by more than simple male chauvinism, which explains why the vaginal-clitoral myth continues to bumble along despite having been disproved and discredited.

Part of the trouble was that during Freud's time there was no material available on the sexual responses of the average woman—all studies, by the likes of Krafft-Ebing, Havelock Ellis, and Freud himself, being confined to cases of sexual oddity and perversity. It was only in 1953 that Alfred Kinsey—a soft-spoken, kindly academic who had a fondness for bow ties, and whose previous professional experience of females was confined to gall wasps—finally published the first sex survey of the average woman. Because it revealed so much—bad and unconventional—about sexuality, and because it raised sex to a scientific status, his results were attacked viciously by certain political elements; Kinsey died a broken man three years later. Small wonder that it wasn't until the mid-sixties that Masters and Johnson conclusively showed that the two types of orgasm are one and the same: sexual intercourse stimulates the clitoris indirectly by putting moving pressure on the clitoral hood.

Ignorance has done more than anything else to keep the vaginal-clitoral myth alive. Woman's sexual organs are complicated and difficult to understand. The remarkable discrepancy between the ease with which women can have orgasms during masturbation, and the difficulty so many seem to have during intercourse—although now known to be a result of either insufficient clitoral stimulation, or the need to learn sexual skills—might well lead less-critical scientists to suggest the existence of two types of orgasm. Even today it is promoted from time to time because general acceptance of sexual equality is still very young and tender, and among some members of the psychoanalytic world there continues a goodly amount of male chauvinist priggery.

But the hard fact is this: although most orgasms for women are *induced* by clitoral stimulation, they are always *expressed* by the vaginal muscles. The orgasms may vary in intensity and sensation according to whether there is intercourse or not, but this—in general—is a result of the different circumstances rather than a different type of orgasm.

Hite talks about a further type, the "emotional orgasm." This she defines—of necessity, rather loosely—as "a feeling of love and communication with another human being that reaches a peak, a great welling up of intensity of feeling" that may have sundry physical manifestations. I'm with her wholeheartedly when she advises that, as long as women are not pressured into using these as a substitute for real orgasms, they are just one more means of enjoyment.

Is There an Equivalent of Male Difficulty with Orgasm?

Yes, there is. (I'm not talking about impotence and failure to get an erection, which of course is very common, but simply failure to ejaculate.) But it's so rare that even those few researchers wanting to pursue it have had difficulty in finding individuals to study. One report (Mann) cites "religious orthodoxy, male fear of pregnancy, negative feelings toward or lack of interest in the partner and, in a few cases, evidence of homosexual orientation or maternal dominance." For those men who had once been able to ejaculate normally and had lost the ability, a stressful event could usually be traced to explain the problem: one failed after his wife was unfaithful, another after his wife's mother and sister moved into the house.

This same researcher noted another unusual factor: namely that several of these men masturbated in an odd manner that had very little similarity to coitus. But then if (as in one case) you're accustomed to getting your pleasure by striking the shaft of your penis forcefully with the heel of your hand, I suppose it's hardly surprising that a woman's body doesn't provide quite what you've been used to.

Occasionally men also fake orgasms, usually when they're simply afraid that they won't be able to ejaculate.

And, in this department, apparently, women are as easily misled as men.

The G-Spot

Having said all this, there is, famously, recent (inconclusive) evidence for a further type of orgasm resulting from stimulation of the so-called Grafenberg spot by deep penile thrusts during intercourse. This is not the vaginal orgasm of Freud, but some researchers believe it to differ from the clitoral orgasm.

The G-spot is a lump on the wall of the vagina about an inch or two inside the opening, toward the stomach. According to the theory, it is the female counterpart of the prostate. At first, stimulation of it causes a desire to urinate, but this is quickly replaced by sexual arousal and enlargement of the spot, which may lead to orgasm. In some women the orgasm is accompanied by the ejaculation of a fluid chemically very similar to semen.

But the theory has undergone a scientific battering since it was first publicized in the early 1980s. There are a number of alternative explanations for both female ejaculation, and for the fact that certain areas in the vagina feel better than others. And these are perfectly in accord with not having a G-spot at all.

Perhaps the most interesting aspect of G-spot discussions is that they give a good idea of the topsy-turvy, indecisive nature of academic sex literature. Different sorts of orgasm are all very interesting to read about, but it's much better to forget them when you get into bed. At the moment, they are little more than the suggestions of scientists at play.

Female Ejaculation

There is a great deal of debate still about so-called female ejaculation. Some say it doesn't exist; others argue over what exactly it is. From personal experience, I am convinced that it exists: a small amount of fluid given off at the moment of orgasm. Some men believe they can feel it being ejected, high up inside their partner.

I am equally convinced that it's not, as some researchers persist in arguing, urine, but something much more akin to the normal healthy vaginal lubrication. It's not only colorless and quite inoffensive, but many men find it extremely arousing. One other thing: it has been observed to occur mostly in women with strong pubococcygeus muscles. So, if you're really interested in it, turn to p. 85 and start exercising! Then you can pursue your own research on the subject.

Nocturnal Orgasms

We're all familiar with male nocturnal emissions, or "wet dreams" as little boys call them. Did you know that women, too, sometimes have orgasms while they are asleep? Just how often this happens is hard to gauge. Men know they have had a nocturnal orgasm even if they don't wake up during it, when they find the bed is wet. Because women leave no such telltale signs, female nocturnal orgasms seem comparatively rare. If, however, women are able to experience them without waking up, they could be quite common. As it is, most of the research has, by necessity, been on those instances when the woman awakes during the orgasm. A *Playboy* survey reported that approximately 40 percent of women admitted having had at least one—a figure less than half that of males.

What is especially common is for women to wake (often after a highly sexy dream) feeling maddeningly on the *point* of orgasm, only to find that they badly need to pee. I've lost count of how many times that's happened to me —usually just at the tantalizing moment in my dream when I have succeeded in bedding whoever it is who has inspired the dream. It's enough to try the patience of a saint!

I'd always assumed that nocturnal orgasms would be more prevalent among women with a repressive attitude to sex: if you don't allow yourself sex in the normal way, it has to come out somehow, sort of thing. I was surprised to read that in fact nocturnal orgasms are in general associated with women who hold liberal and positive attitudes towards sex. They are, however, predictably more common amongst those who have been without sex for a long while—in prison, divorced, etc. Interestingly, male nocturnal orgasms are most common during the late teens and early twenties, whereas women peak during their forties.

Do Aphrodisiacs Help with Orgasm?

Aphrodisiacs—potions that increase sexual desire and ability—are a lot of fun. Nothing else gives quite such a sense of how delightful, ingenious, and silly people can be about sex. But, sadly, they're rarely all they're cracked up to be. However, for the woman on this program, it's useful to know something about the subject, and also about possible *an*aphrodisiacs—those substances which might make orgasm more difficult.

It's no surprise to learn that most aphrodisiac experiments—both ancient and modern—have been centered on men and male sexuality. Very much less work has been done on substances with respect to female sexuality, and less still on women's ability to reach orgasm. After all, those men who were interested in female sexuality were usually interested just on getting the woman to want it more in the first place, rather than concerned with her satisfaction.

Among all the commonly used drugs and medicines, there is little evidence that they either increase or decrease women's ability to climax. Alcohol is surely the most familiar "aphrodisiac," although from the point of view of orgasm it is a mixed blessing. As Shakespeare puts it:

> MACDUFF: What three things does drink especially provoke?
>
> PORTER: Marry, sir, nose-painting, sleep and urine. Lechery, sir, it provokes and unprovokes; it provokes the desire, but it takes away the performance.

On the plus side, alcohol reduces inhibitions and "sex guilt"; it's also useful in slowing men down. But drink too much and the man is out of action altogether. And, in similar fashion, for women its desensitizing effects can make a difficult orgasm impossible. When I was first beginning my training, I found that I became quite skilled in judging how much I wanted to drink. Liquor kills the whole proceedings, but one to two glasses of wine helped me to overcome inhibitions without interfering with my responsiveness. If I drank much more, it meant no climax. Nowadays I find I can go to a party, get pretty merry and still reach orgasm, albeit more slowly.

Nicotine is best classed as an anaphrodisiac: not just because smokers reek, but because there is clinical evidence that smoking may be associated with impotence in some males, probably because nicotine reduces blood flow and thereby makes erection more difficult. As to the effects of smoking on female sexuality, there is—guess what?—virtually no information whatsoever. Why not try your own research? If you're thinking of giving up smoking, make a chart (similar to that in Chapter 5) of your own sexual responses both before and after stopping. It won't be precise enough to satisfy a scientist, but that doesn't mean it can't be valuable to you. And, if you plan to send your questionnaire responses in to me, why not add your nicotine findings as well? Bear in mind, however, that unpleasant symptoms associated with first giving up the habit will probably, in themselves, have an adverse effect on your desire for sex.

Oral contraceptives deserve a mention here. Despite the fact that the pill is thought by many people to have encouraged sexual promiscuity by removing fear of pregnancy, it does turn some women off sex. Its progesterone content can cause reduced clitoral sensitivity and may outweigh the effects of estrogen, which can help to increase libido for women with low sex drives. "It's certainly an effective contraceptive," moaned one man. "It's turned her off doing it at all." If you suspect the pill may be reducing your sex drive, try a different type before you give up altogether.

So-called "street drugs," such as marijuana, LSD, and cocaine have long been reputed to have a variety of dramatic effects on sexuality, and by implication, orgasm, but despite these extravagant claims the hard evidence in favour of their aphrodisiac qualities is pretty limited. In most cases, harmful side effects will immediately—or eventually—outweigh any positive aspects. There is no question that the opium-heroin-morphine group of drugs severely depresses sexual desire and responsiveness.

That leaves the more fanciful aphrodisiacs. Despite current medical skepticism, almost every culture in the world has, or has had, a lively aphrodisiac tradition, with every kind of concoction from oysters to crocodile teeth. Some, such as bull's testicles, are used because of their obvious association with sexuality, and I'm sure human testicles have been used at some time—although it's best not to think about that. In North Africa, the Siwanese men sometimes conceal some of their own semen in their partner's food. I once shared an apartment with an Oriental woman who whenever she had a new boyfriend began consuming large quantities of vanilla. When I asked the reason, she explained that vanilla pods resembled the female genitals, so that, according to the doctrine of signatures—the ancient belief that resemblance indicates similar powers— they would certainly increase her sexual arousal.

If your partner's lovemaking isn't all it might be, the *Kama Sutra* advises that he drink boiled clarified butter every morning during spring. If this doesn't work, he can try boiling a goat's testicle in sugared milk. And if, poor fellow, he still finds himself unable to satisfy you, he must resort to piercing his penis with a sharp instrument, increasing the size of the hole by inserting small pieces of cane and fruit stalks, and then washing the swollen member all over with licorice and honey.

Spanish fly is one of the classic aphrodisiacs, supposedly effective in vastly increasing female libido. In fact, Spanish fly is the poison cantharidin, and one–one thousandth of an ounce is a fatal dose. No wonder the Shakespearian euphemism for orgasm was "dying"! The reason it's become so famous as an aphrodisiac is that the cantharides irritate the genitourinary tract—in short it makes your vagina itch like mad so you need something up it to soothe the annoyance. A pharmacist named Arthur Ford accidentally killed the two women assistants whom he'd intended to seduce, and nearly did away with himself when he shared some coconut ice cream with them into which he'd pushed a huge amount of Spanish fly with a pair of scissors. The autopsy revealed that the victims' internal organs had been literally "burned away." Nowadays, cantharides is used mainly to remove warts.

Until recent centuries, the mythical mandrake was extremely popular as a sexual stimulant—notwithstanding the fact that it doesn't exist. It grows only at the foot of a gallows, glows in the dark and gives a lethal squeal when you pull it up. In order to avoid death on collection, a dog should be tied to the plant, and then called once the collector has retired to a safe distance. There are several real plants known as mandrake, and these are mentioned in the Song of Solomon as a cure for sterility, and in Genesis as the bribe with which Leah induces Jacob to sleep with her.

Ginseng is particularly popular in the East, and nowadays rather a fad in the West. Since the shape of the root can vaguely resemble the human form, according (once again) to the doctrine of signatures, ginseng should be beneficial to the whole body. And, indeed, if you pop into the local health-food shop, you'll find it recommended for just about everything. Analysis of the biochemical components of ginseng root has shown that it contains stimulants which are remarkably effective and low in toxicity, unlike coffee or tea. On the negative side, a recent survey suggested that it can cause diarrhea and skin eruptions—and you can't get more unromantic than that.

I'm sorry to be such a wet blanket, but the fact is it's easier to find anaphrosodisiacs than their happier counterpart, and if anybody tries to sell you an orgasmic concoction, denounce them to the Fair Trade Commission. Exercise and practice will work infinitely better and at a fraction of the cost. That's not to say, however, that your own imagination can't do service as the best aphrodisiac in the world. A year or two back, feeling my sex life had become distinctly drab, I consulted an ancient book of herbal remedies and devised my own love potion to end all love potions: plants picked by moonlight, stirred about with dew, and a few magic incantations muttered over them before I gobbled the lot. *Of course* I felt sexier that evening—wouldn't you?

CHAPTER SEVENTEEN

Conditions That Can Affect Your Ability to Reach Orgasm

We have seen how difficulty with orgasm can be overcome by training. However, there are some conditions—medical and otherwise—that can severely, or totally, impede your enjoyment of sex and reaching orgasm.

I have deliberately kept this chapter brief: its purpose is simply to alert you to possibilities. For a fuller discussion of medical conditions and how to treat them I strongly recommend Denise Winn's very helpful book *Below the Belt*. Some others, more broad-ranging, are suggested in the bibliography.

Vaginal Infections

As every woman knows, there is a whole host of conditions —some rare, some distressingly common—that affect female genital regions: monilia, gardnerella, herpes, trichomonas, chlamydia, gonorrhea, etc. Pain in the vagina, itching, discharge, or an unfamiliar smell are the most obvious symptoms, although not present in every case. If you have any one of these go to the doctor: most are treatable.

Monilia merits a special mention because it is one of the most common conditions preventing women from enjoying sex fully. It is a yeast which may already exist in your vagina without causing trouble. However, a change in the vaginal acid balance can cause it to run rampant and result in an infection: you'll know because, instead of the normal vaginal secretions, there will be a lumpy "cottage-cheese" type discharge, a bad smell, and sex will be sore. Indeed, many women know monilia is on the way simply because of a recognizable discomfort during sex. Monilia can be caused by many things—the pill, the IUD, even sex itself; it frequently appears after taking antibiotics.

At the first sign of symptoms, stop having sex and get treatment: it is fairly easily cured, although it has a maddening tendency to return. Because it can crop up so unexpectedly, I make sure I always have one or two extra months of medication handy, although, strictly speaking, you should see a doctor in case it's something else.

Cystitis

Cystitis is an infection of the bladder, one of the most miserable commonplace conditions women can get. It causes a burning pain in the bladder and a nasty feeling of constantly needing to pee. Sometimes there is fever as well, or an uncomfortable feeling in the groin. Most women suffer from cystitis at some time in their lives, some are repeatedly plagued with it. The trouble is that familiarity has made many women blasé. For many years I had attacks: horrible while they lasted, but as soon as the antibiotics began, I was okay. Of course, the antibiotics also brought monilia with them, but that was a blessing in comparison with cystitis. So I went along, not especially careful to take steps to prevent it. Until one day, after an attack I took my usual antibiotics—and the cystitis *still* wouldn't go away. Suddenly a comparatively minor complaint became something quite frightening that I could not shake off.

Angela Kilmartin's excellent books—now almost classics on the subject—helped me a lot and, eventually, I overcame cystitis. I don't mean to alarm you—just to say that this condition can be so horrible, and so damaging to a sexual relationship, that it's well worth taking deliberate precautions against ever getting it in the first place.

Always keep your genital area clean—and make sure your hands are clean when you touch yourself there. Wear cotton—not nylon—underwear. Use only fragrance-free soaps, deodorants, or talcs in your genital region, as all these can cause allergies. Perhaps the most important piece of advice is when you go to the toilet *always* wipe from front to back—never the other way around. Bacteria that are perfectly harmless in the intestine cause havoc in the bladder. Believe me, such precautions will stand your sex life in good stead.

Other Conditions

In general, sex should not be painful. If it is, there's probably something wrong. I've already mentioned the various infections. Very vigorous sex can make you sore inside, and you may have noticed that this often happens at the start of a new relationship, when you're so crazy about each other that you do it three or four times a day. Also, for women who have not had sex before, an unstretched hymen may be the cause. Being tense can also cause difficulties, by causing us not to relax the vaginal muscles properly.

Lack of sufficient lubrication speaks for itself. It can come about through tension, because your partner is using a condom, by your lack of estrogen, or simply because you're made that way: despite what the sex manuals say, not all aroused women get sufficiently wet. If it worries you, consult a doctor; but in most cases, it's simplest just to use saliva or lubricating jelly such as KY.

Vaginismus causes strong, involuntary tightening of the vaginal muscles which can make penetration extremely painful or impossible. Its origins are psychological, but not to be sniffed at because of that—the result is as physical as a pile of bricks. It might be because you have certain fears about sex, or because you feel angry towards your partner for some reason, or because you feel guilty about something. One woman suffered vaginismus because she knew her mother disapproved of her boyfriend, and was cured only when she became strong enough to break free of her mother's overpowering influence. Helen Singer Kaplan's *The New Sex Therapy: Active Treatment of Sexual Dysfunctions* discusses the subject at length and suggests a physical treatment which you can learn. You will probably also find that by working your way through the early steps of this program which do not involve penetration, the condition is greatly improved.

Pain deep in the pelvis might be due simply to your partner's penis being too large (see below), or for various treatable medical reasons about which you should consult your doctor.

There are also nonpainful, physical reasons that may hold back your progress with orgasm:

Slack vaginal muscles (as often results from childbirth) can limit your sensitivity for two reasons: one, by reducing the friction between the penis and the vagina; and two, because slack muscles mean a less vigorous blood flow. By exercising your vaginal muscles and keeping them strong and fit, you greatly increase the flow of blood, while at the same time probably improving both the ease and the intensity of your orgasm. These Kegel exercises are discussed in Chapter 5.

Intercourse during pregnancy is almost always harmless, but there are a few unusual circumstances in which penetration and/or orgasm can cause problems, particularly if you've had miscarriages before. Talk to your doctor if you feel worried, because your sexual reservations may well be unjustified and can interrupt your progress to orgasm for no good reason.

The Missionary Position (woman lying on her back, man on top) can be difficult or uncomfortable in late pregnancy. Although this is helped by putting pillows under your back, it's probably more advisable to use other positions.

Factors Affecting Your Partner Which Affect You

Premature ejaculation is discussed in more detail in Chapter 10. This troublesome condition can be treated by well-established and successful methods. I recommend Helen Singer Kaplan's book, *The New Sex Therapy*.

A large penis may sometimes be *too* large. By hitting the cervix, it causes pain deep down, particularly in certain positions: man entering the woman from behind, or woman lying on her back with her legs drawn up. Indeed, in some positions, even an ordinary-size penis can be uncomfortable—if your coil is badly fitted, or if you have constipation, for example. Putting a pillow between the two of you can help. Also make sure you are fully aroused before penetration, because arousal causes the cervix to move back.

The French (of course) devised a special protection against an outsize penis—something called a *bourrelet,* which was a small, rounded pad of silk, stuffed with cotton, with a hole in the middle corresponding to the size of the circumference of the penis. So if this is your problem, perhaps you could make your own. . . .

CHAPTER EIGHTEEN

A Chapter for Men

There is no such thing as an uninvolved partner in a marriage where sexual dysfunction exists.
——Masters and Johnson, *Human Sexual Inadequacy*

The Hite Report on Male Sexuality reveals that men's greatest complaint against women is that they don't want sex often enough:

> **Too many women find sex disagreeable, painful, messy, even disgusting and resort to pretexts to avoid it.**

> **I would like to have a wife that was *interested* in sex, more often, more variety, more times.**

> **I could be supremely happy with her if she were excited about me.**

> **I would change sex primarily by increasing my wife's urge, or by decreasing my own. That's the biggest problem.**

> **More. I just want *more*.**

If this is true in your case, there is one overwhelmingly simple remedy: *make sex for your partner more enjoyable.*

Now imagine the following scene. It is evening. You and she have been to dinner, then to the theater. You have sat opposite each other for two hours, watching each other, anticipating the moment when you will make love together. You go home; you undress, turn out the light. You begin to make love. Just as you are getting really worked up, your partner climaxes, pulls away from you, rolls over happily and goes to sleep. When you show distress, she actually has the gall to suggest that it's your fault!

That is what sex is like for many many women.

The circumstances may be very different, but the fact remains that thousands upon thousands of women do not get as much out of sex as their partners do. Which, considering the vast female *potential* for orgasm, is tragic. For both sexes.

The Hite Report on Female Sexuality reveals the astonishing fact that approximately 70 percent of sexually active women have trouble with orgasm. Either they have *never* climaxed, or they can do so only now and again, or with effort.

It is sometimes difficult for men to realize just what sexual frustration means for a woman. The fact that a sexually aroused man who has not climaxed has a large and very prominent erection staring his partner in the face leaves her in no doubt of his state. But sexually aroused women have nothing obvious to *remind* men that they may be feeling terrible inside—frustrated, angry, disappointed.

The fact that for a variety of reasons most women don't like to be insistent about their sexual needs only compounds the situation.

It is not true that women as a category have lower sex drives than men, or that women don't want orgasms as much as men, or that women are less sensual than men. Believe me, women can have sexual needs just as powerful as men's, even if they are shy about insisting on them. One bad experience can leave a woman feeling that sex is not all it's cracked up to be. Quite often years of putting her partner first, sexually, leaves a woman believing that she doesn't have much of a sex drive herself—or, the self-deprecating comment I've heard so often, "not one that really matters." The fact that these women have not had the *opportunity* to enjoy a satisfying sex life is quite a different matter. Seeing your partner satisfied night after night, when you are left to look after yourself, creates not only sexual tension but emotional discord: after all, it is supposed to be a *partnership*.

Most generalizations about the sexes are crude and unhelpful. But it *is* true to say that, sexually, women tend to defer to men, to give their partner's sexual needs more importance than their own. (For a more detailed discussion of this, turn to Chapter 4, "Women Take Control.") There are many reasons for this, but at the heart of them all are centuries of conditioning.

Whereas, on the whole, men are able unselfconsciously to make the most of sex for themselves, it is very hard for them to realize that women often find it difficult to do so. I've lost count of how many times I've heard a male friend say to me, "She only has to ask. But she doesn't seem to mind if I go right ahead and enjoy myself." If you add women's reticence about being assertive in the bedroom to the fact that, physiologically speaking, women need more careful and patient sexual attention, it's not surprising that so many individuals are dissatisfied with their partner's lovemaking. Of course I am not suggesting that this is necessarily so with you. But I do know the problem is much more widespread than our "liberated" era would suggest.

A large part of this inability to appreciate a woman's sexual needs and frustrations is due to the fact that the male and the female orgasms are not simply two versions of the same thing. They evolved at different times, and they involve different factors. Unlike the male orgasm, the female orgasm is extremely subtle and sensitive. In the right circumstances, with a partner who understands and satisfies her needs, a woman can realize a huge sexual potential that under less favorable conditions might never have got the chance to show itself. In fact, scientists and sex researchers have found that, if anything, women have *higher* sex drives than men. Biologically speaking, women can climax again and again, even while the man lies exhausted on the bed. Their second and third orgasms are usually more intense than their first. The reason they don't enjoy sex as often as men is because sex hasn't been *made* as enjoyable for them. I should, however, add that I am speaking of women as a category. Individual women vary in their sexual needs just as much as individual men.

It's Not Simply Her Concern, It's Yours, Too

It is certainly not my intention to cast unnecessary doubts on your own relationship. After all, 30 percent of women are apparently quite satisfied with their sex lives. I want to suggest some means whereby, if you are concerned that your partner is not getting as much satisfaction as you are, or even that you would like to be able to give her *more* orgasms than she is already having, you can help. Your relationship will benefit, not only in the bedroom, but in all sorts of nonsexual ways as well.

Women's difficulty with orgasm is not simply due to men's inadequate understanding of their needs. It sometimes happens that everything is absolutely as it should be, and the lover is doing a wonderful job, yet still no orgasm. Perhaps she is feeling tense about contraception, perhaps a hundred different things. But inadequate understanding is certainly a very important factor, and if men really knew how to make love to a woman, women's difficulty with orgasm would be vastly diminished. This says nothing about men being less sexually adept than women, it is simply a consequence of the fact that women's sexuality and orgasms are more complicated. Not better, or worse— different. Just as women need to *learn* how to make the most of their sexuality, men need to *learn* how to become successful lovers. In certain cultures this is recognized. Men and women are *taught* how to make sex satisfactory for both partners; and in those cultures *all the women have orgasms all the time*.

It takes some courage for a man to pick up a book like this. Yet this chapter is relevant to *all* men, whatever the status of your current partner in regard to orgasm. If she is having trouble with orgasms, then it is obviously important for you. If you would like to make love with her more often, then understanding the subtlety of her needs is the clue to achieving it.

I think if men knew just how rare and desirable a considerate and attentive lover is they would fall over themselves to learn how to be one.

What Can I Do to Help?

Ideally, you should read the rest of the book. Chapters 2, 3 and 4 are the most important. These will explain in greater detail that while men's orgasms are comparatively straightforward affairs, women's are complex. "A damned nuisance," we call them when we're feeling pissed off; "delicate and exquisite" when things go well. As you read the steps of the plan, attempt to understand why they progress as they do, and what they say about a woman's needs. Don't feel shy about this. Men and women psychologists and researchers alike still regard female sexuality and the female orgasm with awe: they are baffling subjects.

You will also learn that for all the sex on TV, in the

films, magazines, and on the bookshelves, there is still a great deal of ignorance. Age-old sex myths still persist. Almost everyone I've ever come across, male and female, believes in a number of complete sexual falsehoods that sex researchers have been trying to dispel for decades. Did you know, for example, that many men still fear masturbation—not, as in the olden days, because they worry they will go mad or blind, but an updated version of that superstition that they will fall ill through losing too much protein and body fluids? Did you know that most women don't find a large penis any more satisfying than a small one? Did you know that the clitoris should hardly ever be stimulated directly? Do you have any idea how many women feel forced to fake their orgasms out of desperation and guilt?

This ignorance is nothing to be ashamed of—communication between men and women about their intimate needs and feelings is notoriously difficult, and our society is still one that tends to giggle about sex rather than discuss it—but it is something to be corrected as soon as possible.

If you're interested in finding out more, read *The Hite Report on Female Sexuality,* a survey of the sexual attitudes of 3,500 American women of all ages and backgrounds. It's a very good way to put yourself in the picture about women's attitudes on sex.

Asking Your Partner

Books can tell you only so much. As I have tried to make clear in this one, the one thing that *is* certain about women's sexual behavior is its diversity. Ultimately, the only way of finding out your lover's individual needs is to ask her. I cannot overemphasize how important this is.

"I can't ask," protested one man when I gave him this advice. "She'd think I was a wimp. I mean, men are supposed to *know* about these things."

This seems to me one of the tragic misunderstandings between the sexes. Believe me, it is men and not women who cling to this idea of being "macho" above everything else. No woman worth her salt will be put off by a man because he takes the trouble to ask her what she likes, rather than painfully plunging ahead.

Think of it the other way around. I remember when I first tried to give a boyfriend manual sex—absolute disaster! I'd seen pictures of penises in the books (pored over them, in fact) and they looked simple enough. But I'd never considered the difficulties of lubrication and pressure until the time when I was suddenly faced with one in the flesh, and I was too embarrassed to ask what I should do with it. So I simply took a deep breath, clasped the presented object tightly, and began rubbing away hell-for-leather until his agonized cries stopped me. At a teenage party, my friend Anne bravely plunged her hand down the pants of a boyfriend she was petting with in a dark corner—only to be hideously embarrassed when her rings got caught in his pubic hair!

If asking outright really is beyond you, do as recommended in Chapter 12 and "ask" with your hands. That is, explore her gently, tentatively, and listen and watch her response. Just because a sex manual suggests something does *not* mean your partner will automatically enjoy it. Some women, for example, love having their nipples sucked; others hate it.

Techniques for enjoyment may take time to perfect. But remember that there is nothing more off-putting to a woman than a man who assumes he knows exactly what she wants—puts his own "technique" into effect—and succeeds only in making himself foolish. And there is nothing more *enjoyable* than a man who takes care to find out what she—personally—wants, and how best to give it to her.

Telling Your Partner

If you have a permanent partner who has (or whom you suspect to have) difficulty with orgasm, be cautious about mentioning your involvement in any "help" program.

One of the biggest mistakes sex therapists, counselors, and sex manuals make is assuming that just because a couple are a couple that they need to "tackle it together." Certainly you are both *involved*. You may well want to tackle it together. But that is not the same as saying that you should necessarily work at it in unison. Of course there are couples that will prefer to do this and to follow this plan together. But I devised the plan especially for women who wanted to be completely independent.

There is a very good reason for this: by announcing your participation, you may make her feel that the pressure on her to have an orgasm has increased; and it is precisely this sort of pressure that can make it hard for her to have an orgasm in the first place.

If your partner does want to enlist your help, then that should be her prerogative. Don't feel resentful if she doesn't. This has nothing to do with lack of love or failure of sympathy between you. Sometimes the opposite in fact —the very closeness of the relationship can, paradoxically, make her feel shy. Far better to make it easier for her by quietly training yourself to become as satisfactory a lover as possible, and letting her get on with her training program in her own way.

The Essential Qualities of a Good Lover

Before you start spluttering about my incredible nerve in trying to teach you your job, stop and—once again—think of it the other way around. Would you object to a woman having done a little reading first, to try to find out the best way to please you in bed? And remember, most women would have much less difficulty with orgasm if their lovers knew their business. Read about those marvelous Mangaian boys in Chapter 2 and you'll see what I mean. That's not to say that all you have to do is learn a few skills, read up some Oriental texts on how to delay ejaculation and—bingo!—problem over. Eavesdrop on any gathering of women who have got on to the subject of sex, and you'll soon realize that there are all sorts of qualities that most of us prize in a lover. Of course there are exceptions, but the following suggestions I think most women would agree are a good starting point.

1. *Understand what sexual influences—superficial or profound—are at work:* her worries about contraception, fears about not looking attractive enough, guilt about wanting sex desperately but being unable to find it satisfying.

You may not like the feel of rubber and decide to forgo the condom just this once when you make love, but you could be spoiling *her* chance of orgasm because she will be worrying about getting pregnant. *You* may prefer to have the light on during sex, which results in *her* not being able to relax because she feels "too fat," or her breasts are "too small." The fact that *you* don't think she has these faults is not always enough to set her mind at rest. Black stockings and a garter belt may look sexy, but they can be damned uncomfortable to wear. When you make love, think carefully about this sort of thing—give her the opportunity to feel *really* relaxed.

2. *Encourage equality:* the second biggest complaint among Hite's men was that women didn't take the initiative. This is the result of another great misunderstanding between the sexes, because many women resent having to play submissive, yet feel they need to because that's a woman's role and to do otherwise would seem "cheap" or "unfeminine." Recent studies have shown that women find erotic stories in which women take the initiative significantly more arousing than those in which men do. And part of the reason why there seems to be some connection between education and ability to orgasm is because better-educated women tend to be more assertive about their sexual requirements. Having an element of control in the lovemaking does wonders for a woman's enjoyment. *Allow and encourage* your partner to take the initiative. Many women want to but don't dare because they are afraid of putting men off, or of being labelled "crude," "pushy," "slutty." Indicate that you enjoy it when she takes control or initiates sex.

3. *Learn to control your own orgasm:* what is premature ejaculation? Quite likely you thought of it as a medical condition with which some unfortunate men are afflicted, which makes them ejaculate immediately they enter a woman— sometimes even before. The definition given by Masters and Johnson, in their pioneering work on sexual difficulties, might surprise you:

[The authors consider] a man a premature ejaculator if he cannot control his ejaculatory process for a sufficient length of time during intravaginal containment to satisfy his partner in at least 50 percent of their coital connections.

In short, "premature ejaculation" refers not just to the speed with which a man climaxes, but also to the satisfaction he affords his partner. A mature lover is able to continue intercourse long enough so that *both* partners have a chance to be contented.

Of course, the Masters and Johnson definition is a little too simple. Some men suffer badly from what we traditionally think of as the medical condition of premature ejaculation—to the extent of climaxing within a few seconds, *despite* their best efforts during intercourse to prevent it. With proper training and sympathy, this problem can be corrected.

But for many men the ability to last long enough to give maximum pleasure is either a skill which they could acquire with a bit of effort, or a capacity which they don't bother to use, preferring instead to climax as soon as they feel the urge. Premature ejaculation is then no longer a medical condition, it is simply idle and selfish.

The simplest and most common way to delay ejaculation is to spend more time in foreplay arousing and relaxing your partner. In fact, this is so much the usual way that it has led to the common misconception that women in general *prefer* extended foreplay as opposed to extended intercourse. But this is untrue—the fact is that extended foreplay is for many women the easiest way to get the proper amount of attention.

It is much better if you can develop techniques to delay your ejaculation *during* intercourse. There are several ways of going about this. First, you can slow everything down. Women tend to approach their climax more gradually than men: the speed of your movements matters less than their constancy, rhythm and duration. Twenty thrusts at a sprint will usually have less effect than ten minutes of slow buildup. If you find yourself growing too heated, then stop or withdraw: men cool off far more quickly than women, and when you begin intercourse again your partner will have kept much more of her original level of arousal than you have. Anyway, in the meantime you might try gently using your hand or mouth.

Robert developed a useful method that helped both him and Miriam:

> **Instead of moving your penis in and out, you can keep it almost stationary inside the vagina and gently move your hips. This way you continue to excite your partner's clitoral region by the motion, without exciting yourself at the same rate.**

One trick to delay ejaculation recommended by the Orientals of old (who devoted a lot of time to sexual skills) is this: if you feel yourself to be on the point of ejaculation, relax all the muscles in your body, especially your buttocks. The novelist Henry Miller recommended filling your head with mechanical thoughts (try multiplication tables) to prevent orgasm, while one ancient Chinese philosopher found that an infallible method was to imagine himself balancing precariously on the branch of a tree!

There are various books (see the bibliography) which have been written to help men overcome the problem of premature ejaculation. And finally, a useful tip. If you are planning to make love later in the evening and worry you will come too quickly, masturbate an hour or two beforehand.

4. *Never rush your partner:* if a woman finds it difficult to have an orgasm, then it doesn't make it any easier if the man is coaxing her on like a racehorse. Gail explains:

> **Do you know what the single biggest bar to orgasm is for me? Worrying that I'm taking too long. Normally I have no trouble climaxing—I just need a little time. But if I start to worry that I'm taking too long, then I'm caught, because if I worry then**

it takes me longer which makes me worry more, etc. Often the whole thing is ruined and I have to give up in frustration. Then I get really angry.

In regard to women who are slow, or have difficulty with orgasm, it is very difficult for a man to strike a balance between going on long enough to allow her to climax, and knowing when she'd prefer to give up. After all, going on too long can be painful and dispiriting. All you can do is be as sensitive as possible to her mood in general.

5. *Never think that all sex must end in orgasm:* this is a very common mistake. Women in particular are sensitive to the fact that sex is *not* simply about orgasm—each minute of it should be a pleasure in itself. Chapter 8 deals with this in more detail.

A really good lover should encourage sexual situations with his partner which *don't* end in orgasm for either of you. Caress and fondle all you like, have intercourse, even; but let it be recognized by both of you that neither intends to have an orgasm. If you can set up these situations and make them a regular, familiar occurence, this will probably do more to help your partner than anything else.

The idea is to draw attention away from the subject of orgasm, to make it something about which you can both feel relaxed, not to insist on it being the focus of your activity. If you announce that you're going to make her come, or make a great show of waiting for her to come, then you'll simply make both of you feel uptight, and consequently it will be much much more difficult for her. Only bad lovers think that satisfactory sex is simply a matter of sufficient thrusting and climax; a good lover makes his partner relax and enjoy each moment as it comes, rather than making her fret over whether or not she'll have an orgasm.

6. *Experiment gently with manual and oral techniques:* both manual and oral sex are a great deal harder for men to do to women, than for women to do to men. A woman's sexual area is no simple matter: as a *female* friend of mine says earlier on in the book. "I'm damned glad I don't have to make love to another woman. I wouldn't have the first clue about how to arouse her, or where to caress!" Chapters 12 and 13 will make clear that it's not simply a matter of finding the clitoris and rubbing away merrily. The clitoris is a much more sensitive organ than the penis, and too much concentration on it can be extremely painful. You must learn to excite it indirectly, by rubbing or massaging the region around it, and over it when it is not exposed. Once again, no two women are alike, and you should be aware that what one woman may find pleasant another might not like at all. But if you do learn the skill of giving good manual and oral sex, you will be a great prize.

So, if you don't quite know how to give your lover manual sex, oral sex, anything—*ask*. Even the most sexually sophisticated man will have to ask (either directly or by knowing how to read the signs his lover is giving him) what a woman wants. Asking will not only make you more accomplished and her more satisfied, it will also help to build up a supportive atmosphere that will greatly help her if she has difficulty, and improve the quality of your sex life in general.

7. *Don't be demanding:* it is a standard female complaint that men who demand sex, or expect it as their due, turn them off and are offensive.

If you want to make your partner feel her best and think of you as a really enticing prospect, don't be pushy. Don't go shoving her hand into your pants—I can tell you from personal experience that that's a real turn-off! And if you want oral sex, *don't* demand it, or start pushing her head down into the right region—there's a world of difference between demanding or strongly hinting for a blow job and making it clear that you love it when she offers. Sexual demands are threatening and they build up resentment, particularly if your partner has difficulty with satisfying her own sexual needs. As Robin puts it:

> **I love performing oral sex on my boyfriend. Give me half a chance and I'm down sniffing between his thighs like a dog. But it turns me off completely when he demands it. My arousal drops to zero, *and* I feel annoyed and tense.**

And, conversely, just because *you* would ask for something if you really wanted it, don't assume that your partner would, too. Women are encouraged to be unselfish in bed to the point of forgoing their own pleasures. She may not *please* you in bed, but it's unlikely to be because she's *selfish*.

In this respect it always pays to take that extra bit of trouble sexually with her. In enjoying your partner's unselfishness, you may seem to be doing okay—the "if she's prepared to do it, why shouldn't I take advantage of it?" sort of attitude. In fact it's quite likely that if you met her halfway *both* your sex lives would be enhanced. You might at least give it a try.

8. *Positions:* one of the most pernicious sex myths is that the more exotic the position, the "hotter" the sex will be. Unless your woman is very experienced in orgasm it's unlikely that she will find those positions fulfilling. Read the section entitled "Which Position?" in Chapter 10 and familiarize yourself with some of the advantages and drawbacks that women are conscious of. If you want to help her towards more orgasms, let *her* choose the position. When she is more adept, she'll probably be quite happy to try—and really appreciate—something more adventurous.

9. *Faking:* if you suspect that your partner is faking orgasm, don't get angry. Firstly, you may well be wrong. The way a woman displays her orgasm varies from individual to individual, from day to day, from circumstance to circumstance. Unless you've got a flashlight and some measuring devices with you, there's no way you can tell for certain whether her orgasm is genuine or not.

However hurt and distressed you may feel, you can be quite certain that she feels even worse. And if you are right, remember: no woman in the world wants to have to fake, and *of course* we'd all much rather be quite open. Read Chapter 14 and you'll see why we do it nonetheless. Confronting her will not help either of you; it will simply make matters more tense. Think of it as a challenge: you will try to work her out of faking naturally. After all, it would be more rewarding if she stopped of her own accord, because sex had become sufficiently arousing to have a genuine orgasm, rather than because you prevented her, making her difficulty public each time you have sex.

Bear in mind the above advice, and you'll be well on the way to an improved relationship. Good luck!

CHAPTER NINETEEN

Conclusion

The evening after I'd finished writing this book, there was a very loud pounding on the front door. The crowds already begging to get a copy? I wondered. Publishers clawing at my mailbox to secure the world rights? I double-checked myself in the mirror and then hurried to let them in. There, dressed in the most outrageous mauve and silver dress I'd ever seen, with a bottle of champagne in one hand and something vaguely resembling a poodle in the other, was Dorothy. Remember Dorothy, the girl who had been president of the Love Club at school?

"I heard down the grapevine that you were writing a sex book," she exclaimed with a broad but disbelieving smile. "Just thought I'd crop up and tell you a little bit about the subject."

Before I could sweep the manuscript out of sight, her keen eyes had spotted it. She picked it up languidly, read the title, and immediately burst out: "You might have told me! I wouldn't have got through nearly so many husbands if you'd written this a bit sooner!" Dorothy was the last person in the world from whom I expected to get such an admission.

This book has amazed me. When I began writing it I was apprehensive. I knew the plan worked, I had access to a first-class university library in which to do all my re-

search, the subject was fascinating and desperately important to millions of women and men; but orgasm was orgasm, for Christ's sake. What would the neighbors say
when they found out they were living next to a woman
who spent her spare time investigating female orgasms?
And what, oh what, would my mother think? I had visions
of the rest of my life spent in a greasy raincoat, dodging
down back alleys trying to avoid the vice squad.

But to my surprise, as soon as the subject was broached
and it became obvious my interests were genuine and
sympathetic, people I wouldn't previously have mentioned the word "sex" to, let alone "orgasm," suddenly
opened up. "It's so relieving to talk about it honestly. I
love my husband. I love having sex with him, but I hate
the way women's orgasm, my orgasm, one of the results of
my love, is taboo and somehow thought to be faintly disgusting." Over and over again I met with this response.

What the women and men I talked to particularly liked
about the book, why they enjoyed being involved with it,
was that it didn't idealize sex. As one woman whom I'd
thought very prudish remarked, "Sex can be good and
bad. It can be funny or downright uncomfortable. That's
what makes real sex, the way it actually happens, so interesting. But idealized sex—the sort you read about in
gushy books with soft-focus photos and flowers on the
cover—is something apart from the human race. It's almost indecent. It's like you're furtively peeping at a world
where everybody's either a model or an earth mother."

When I sent the manuscript to friends for comments, I
got letters back from the whole family, some even from
the neighbors. One, a woman of eighty, exclaimed, "I wish
there'd been books like this when we were young!" And
after she'd read it, rushed it to her fifty-three year old
daughter, who had in turn given it to her grand-daughter,
who is keeping a copy in store for her two year old great
grand-daughter for when she reaches her seventeenth
birthday!

One Friday evening, after much hesitation, and a couple of gin and tonics, I finally, finally plucked up the courage to send a copy off to my mother. She wouldn't get it till Monday, and I spent the weekend in mortal terror. But on Sunday night my nerves gave way and I reached for the telephone.

"Mom," I explained neatly, "by accident I mixed up two parcels I was sending last week, could you return the one I sent to you . . ."

"You must be joking," she retorted. "It's the best thing you've ever done in your life." The post office, in an unexpected burst of efficiency, had delivered it on Saturday morning.

There were some who objected. A couple of people thought that women's orgasms shouldn't be talked about in public. I cannot understand this point of view. Any child who walks into a newsstand can look at porn magazines, and read about sexual violence, rapes, and mutilations of women in the papers. TV frequently airs films in which men abuse women. We can't escape the violent, perverted aspects of sex. Isn't it a good idea that we concentrate on the pleasurable side—the private, safe side that harms nobody? I was once asked how old did I think a girl had to be before she should be allowed to read my book. "As young as she starts thinking about having sex," was my reply. Any parent will tell you how young that is.

Writing this book has been an enormous liberation. When I look back now at all the years I put up with mediocre sex, I can hardly believe it. Until I was in my thirties I thought orgasm during sex was about as likely as travelling to the moon. But even after I'd devised the plan and begun research for the book, I still couldn't quite escape my upbringing, which said that sex—and, by implication, orgasm—was more important for men than for women. It was this book that finally got me to see what nonsense that is.

It's a view still constantly endorsed from all sides,

though increasingly less so than when I was growing up. Just recently in a radio show I found myself sitting opposite a schoolboyish presenter—a short, fat, singularly unprepossessing character—who immediately we were on air started boasting about the power of testosterone, as if that were the only hormone responsible for sex drives. I quietly pointed out that once the man's first orgasm is over he's usually pooped, while their non-testosterized partner could go on non-stop for the rest of the night. "But that's not the point," he protested. "It's that men need to do it, whereas women don't." To which I could reply only: "That says far more about your selfishness than your sex drive." At this he grew noisy, and boasted that he'd once done it thirty-three times in one night. I could hardly stop myself from laughing. And then I suddenly thought, Christ! Maybe it's true. Poor woman!

But it's not only a male attitude. Many women have grown up to accept their secondary position, and in doing so perpetuate it for their daughters. Others support the injustice for the best of reasons, claiming that for a woman orgasm is unnecessary. They hope by this limp announcement to make those of us with difficulty suddenly forget all about it and not mind in the least. Women's magazines are constantly running features on how to satisfy your man, almost never on how to satisfy yourself. It was only once I'd begun talking to women and men honestly and openly about the subject, and had to force myself to look at and challenge all my own prejudices about women and sex, that I fully realised my right to expect and have an orgasm during sex, whenever I wanted one.

Writing this book is my testimony to that belief in my sexual equality. I wrote it not only for the millions of women and men who care and are concerned, but also as a right of passage for myself.

Bibliography

In a few cases I have added a short comment about the book or article which I hope you may find helpful. In most cases I have given the publisher and the edition used, except for those books that are widely available in various editions, in which case I have usually given just the date of the first or most important edition.

Abel, Ernest L., *Drugs and Sex: A Bibliography*, Greenwood Press, 1983.

Allardice, Pamela, *Aphrodisiacs and Love Magic*, Prism Press, 1989.

Anonymous, *L'Escholle des Filles*. My quote comes from the unattributed translation in Parker's *Anthology of Erotic Prose*.

Anonymous, *Les Tableaux Vivants*, English translation, 1888 (quoted in Atkins.)

Apollinaire, Guillaume, *The Exploits of Don Juan*, A. Lykiard (trans.), Star Books, 1986.

Atkins, J., *Sex in Literature*, Vols 1-4, Caldar and Boyars, 1970. An invaluable, broad-ranging survey, written with intelligence and humor.

Aubrey, John, *Brief Lives*, O.L. Dick (ed.), 1949.

Beltrami, E., A. Dupras & R. Tremblay, "The Effect of Sexual Fantasy Frequencies on the Outcome of Short-term Treatment Program for Sexual Inadequacy in Heterosexual Couples" in *Progress in Sexology*, R. Gemme & C.C. Wheeler (eds.), Plenum Press, 1977.

Bond, S.B., & D.L. Mosher, "Guided Imagery of Rape: Fantasy, Reality, and the Willing Victim Myth" in *Journal of Sex Research* Vol. 22, No. 4, May 1986.

Boston Women's Health Collective, *Our Bodies, Ourselves*, A. Phillips & J. Rakusen (British eds.), Penguin Books, 1979. An excellent book: strong, intelligent and informative.

Cleland, John, *Memoirs of A Woman of Pleasure*, 1748–9. Popularly known as *Fanny Hill*.

Cole, M., "Normal and dysfunctional behavior: frequencies," in M. Cole & W. Dryden, *Sex Therapy in Britain*, Open University Press, 1988.

Crépault, C., G. Abraham, R. Porto & M. Couture, "Erotic Imagery in

Women" in *Progress in Sexology*, R. Gemme & C.C. Wheeler (eds.), Plenum Press, 1977.

Douglas, N., *The Norman Douglas Limerick Book*, Anthony Blond, 1969.

Dworkin, A., Pornography: *Men Possessing Women*, The Women's Press, 1981. Essential reading for anyone interested in the politics of the subject. It's powerful, provocative and bold. For a criticism of Dworkin, try Alison Assiter's *Pornography, Feminism and the Individual*, Pluto Press, 1989.

Davidson, J.K., & L.E. Hoffman, "Sexual Fantasies and Sexual Satisfaction: An Empirical Analysis of Erotic Thought" in *Journal of Sex Rsearch* Vol. 22, No. 2, May 1986.

Fisher, Seymour, *The Female Orgasm*, Basic Books, 1973. A huge, relentless survey of all the literature on the subject. Only for the dedicated.

Friday, Nancy, *Men In Love: Their Secret Fantasies*, Dell, 1983. It was my feeling, after reading this, that they were best kept secret.

Garcia, L.T., et al., "Sex Difference in Sexual Arousal to Different Erotic Stories" in *Journal of Sex Research* Vol. 20, No. 4, November 1984.

Greer, Germaine, *The Change: Women, Aging and the Menopause*, Knopf 1992. Characteristically opinionated. I found it inspiring.

Harrell, T.H., & R.D. Stolp, "Effects of Erotic Guided Imagery on Female Sexual Arousal and Emotional Response" in *Journal of Sex Research* Vol. 21, No. 3, August 1985.

Harris, Frank, *My Life and Loves*, Grove Press, 1971.

Heiman, J.R., & J. LoPiccolo, *Becoming Orgasmic*, Piatkus, 1988. A competitor! Informative and doubtless well meaning, but its rambling, humorless tone did not inspire me. Why must sex manuals be so *precious?* It is also the source of the ignominious illustration discussed in Chapter 5.

Hello!, January 4, 1992.

Hemingway, Ernest, *For Whom the Bell Tolls*, Macmillan & Company, 1977.

Hite, Shere, *The Hite Report on Female Sexuality*, Dell, 1987. A fascinating book that I have often referred to.

The Hite Report on Male Sexuality, Ballantine Books, 1987. A much longer and less sharp book than the original *Hite Report*, but interesting if you've got the time and stomach for it.

Ibara, S., *Life of an Amorous Woman*, I Morris (trans.), Chapman and Hall, 1963.

Jong, Erica, *Fear of Flying*, New American Library/Dutton, 1974.

Kaplan, Helen Singer, *The New Sex Therapy: Active Treatment of Sexual Dysfunction*. New York: Brunner-Mazel, 1974. Something of a classic.

Kilmartin, Angela, *Cystitis: A Complete Self-Help Guide*. New York: Warner Books, 1988. Invaluable even for women who have never had cystitis. I highly recommend all Kilmartin's books.

Kinsey, Alfred C., Wendell B. Pomeroy, C.E. Martin & P.H. Gebhard, *Sexual Behavior in the Human Female*, Philadelphia: W.B. Saunders, 1953.

Kitzinger, Sheila, *Women's Experience of Sex*, New York: Viking/Penguin Books, 1985.

Krafft-Ebing, R.V., *Psychopathia Sexualis*. First published in 1886, the seventh edition was translated into English in 1892 and continued to influence for a long time. My translation is from the grandly described "only authorized English adaptation" of the twelfth edition, Physicians and Surgeons Book Company, 1931.

Lazarsfeld, S. *Woman's Experience of the Male,* London, 1940.

Leiblum, Sandra R., & Raymond C. Rosen (eds.), *Principles and Practice of Sex Therapy.* Guilford Press, 1989.

Lovesey, Peter, *Rough Cider,* New York: Warner Books, 1988.

Magoun, H.W., "John B. Watson and the Study of Human Sexual Behavior" in *Journal of Sex Research* Vol. 17, No. 4, November 1981.

Maier, Richard A., *Human Sexuality in Perspective,* Nelson Hall, 1984. A good broad-minded textbook for university students.

Markowitz, H., & W. Brender, "Patterns of Sexual Responsiveness During the Menstrual Cycle" in *Progress in Sexology,* R. Gemme & C.C. Wheeler (eds.) Plenum Press, 1977.

Marshall, D.S., & R.C. Suggs (eds.), *Human Sexual Behavior: Variations in the Ethnographic Spectrum,* Spectrum, 1971.

Masters, William H., & Virginia E.Johnson, *Human Sexual Inadequacy.* Boston: Little, Brown and Company, 1966.

McCarthy, Mary, *The Group,* New York: Harcourt Brace Jovanovich, 1991.

Moore, George, *Memoirs of My Dead Life,* London, 1906.

Ovid, *The Art of Love,* J.H. Mozley (trans.), Loeb Classical Library, 1929.

Percy Folio MS (c. 1620–1650). The extract is taken from a verse entitled "Off a Puritanine," quoted in Atkins.

Réage, Pauline, *The Story of O.* New York: Ballantine Books, 1981.

Reuben, D., *Everything You Always Wanted to Know About Sex . . . ,* W.H. Allen, 1970. Whatever it is, you'd be better off asking someone else.

Roding, Frances, *Some Sort of Spell,* Harlequin, 1988.

Sherfey, Mary Jane, *The Nature and Evolution of Female Sexuality.* New York: Random House, 1972.

Sparks, J., *The Sexual Connection,* Sphere Books, 1979.

Stevens, Serita D. & Anne Klarner, *Deadly Doses: A Writer's Guide to Poisons,* Cincinnati: Writer's Digest, 1990. A fascinating book, filled with all manner of toxic gruesomeness.

Stimpson, Catherine R. & Ethel S. Person, *Women: Sex and Sexuality.* Chicago: University of Chicago Press, 1980. This collection contains a long list of literary books about sex. Also a whole chapter on women writers.

Symons, David, *The Evolution of Human Sexuality,* Oxford University Press, 1979.

Sue, David, "Erotic Fantasies of College Students During Coitus" in *Journal of Sex Research* Vol. 15, No. 4, November 1979.

Taberner, P.V., *Aphrodisiacs—The Science and the Myth,* Croom Helm, 1985.

Vatsyayana, *Kama Sutra,* Richard F. Burton & F.F. Arbuthnot (trans.), New York: Viking/Penguin, 1991.

Vizinczey, Stephen, *In Praise of Older Women.* Chicago: University of Chicago Press, 1990.

Winn, D., *Below the Belt,* Macdonald Optima, 1987. Very good guide to genitourinary infections for women. It is direct, clear, informative and with plenty of straightforward advice.

SUGGESTED READING FOR FANTASY

The trouble with many explicit erotic books is that they are written by men, and often don't ring true on the subject of women and women's desires. Whether or not these limitations bother you you'll have to decide for yourself. I've tried to give a short selection that caters to most literary tastes.

Barbach, Lonnie—has written a number of books about women and sex and edited *Erotic Interludes* and *Pleasures,* collections of erotic stories by women.

Bible. "The Song of Songs" is a marvelous biblical erotic book. Many consider it the finest in the English language. Some still insist it merely expresses the love between the Church and the Lord, but it is obviously not so innocent.

Cavalier Poets—the Earl of Rochester in particular.

Cleland, John, *Memoirs of a Woman of Pleasure,* also known as *Fanny Hill.* The subject of a famous obscenity trial. One of my favorites.

Colette—the Claudine stories. Also *Cheri* and *La Fin de Cheri,* about a woman's affair with a younger man.

Defoe, Daniel, *Moll Flanders* and *Roxana.* Stories of mildly libidinous women, but I've always found them pleasantly suggestive.

Friday, Nancy, *My Secret Garden,* Quartet Books, 1979—a record of women's fantasies. Not all of them the most subtle stuff you'll read, but very encouraging and her discussions are frank, intelligent and refreshing. If you're interested, she's also done a book entitled *Men In Love: Their Secret Fantasies*, Dell, 1983.

Harris, Frank, *My Life and Loves.* The greatest of the male self-applaudatory fantasies, but I sometimes find something in it if I'm in the right mood.

Hollander, X., *Emmanuelle* and others in a similar vein.

Jong, Erica, *Fear of Flying.* Very funny novel about a bored married woman's search for sexual liberation.

Lawrence, D.H., *Lady Chatterley's Lover*—because it's generally thought to be great literature, people tend to think it full of insight into female sexuality. I've never agreed.

Harlequin romances, I've always had a soft spot for. They're getting more explicit these days, and the sex and courtship can be quite exciting. The heroines nowadays tend to be an odd mixture of fifties housewife and eighties go-getter.

Miller, Henry, *Tropic of Capricorn.* If you like lots of thrusting and male penile prowess, then this one is for you. Self-indulgent rot if you ask me.

Nin, Anaïs, *Little Birds.*

Ovid, *Metamorphosis* and *The Art of Love.*

Parker, D., *An Anthology of Erotic Prose,* Constable, 1981. Very useful for giving you a wide range of familiar and unfamiliar authors—and giving you an idea of whose books are worth following up.

Vidal, Gore, *Myra Beckinridge.* A strong, "significant" book, but I never really felt that I understood the significance, or particularly wanted to.

Vizinczey, Stephen, *In Praise of Older Women.* A sensitive, humorous and very well written book about a young man's exploits after the war.

Zola, Emile, *Nana.* The story of a French courtesan whose corruption of men's morals is irresistible, and who resorts to women whenever she finds men too unpalatable to endure.